本书获得北京大学上山出版基金资助,特此致谢!

青年学者文库

德语指示词研究
基于哥伦比亚学派框架的再思考

The German Demonstratives
A Study in the Columbia School
Linguistics Framework

林琳 著

北京大学出版社
PEKING UNIVERSITY PRESS

图书在版编目(CIP)数据

德语指示词研究：基于哥伦比亚学派框架的再思考/林琳著. —北京：北京大学出版社，2018.3

(青年学者文库)

ISBN 978-7-301-29283-9

Ⅰ.①德… Ⅱ.①林… Ⅲ.①德语—词语—研究 Ⅳ.①H333

中国版本图书馆CIP数据核字(2018)第034868号

书　　名	德语指示词研究——基于哥伦比亚学派框架的再思考 DEYU ZHISHICI YANJIU——JIYU GELUNBIYA XUEPAI KUANGJIA DE ZAI SIKAO
著作责任者	林　琳　著
责任编辑	朱房煦
标准书号	ISBN 978-7-301-29283-9
出版发行	北京大学出版社
地　　址	北京市海淀区成府路205号　100871
网　　址	http://www.pup.cn　新浪微博：@北京大学出版社
电子信箱	zhufangxu@yeah.net
电　　话	邮购部 62752015　发行部 62750672　编辑部 62754382
印　刷　者	北京京华虎彩印刷有限公司
经　销　者	新华书店
	650毫米×980毫米　16开本　19印张　310千字 2018年3月第1版　2018年3月第1次印刷
定　　价	56.00元

未经许可，不得以任何方式复制或抄袭本书之部分或全部内容。

版权所有，侵权必究

举报电话：010-62752024　电子信箱：fd@pup.pku.edu.cn

图书如有印装质量问题，请与出版部联系，电话：010-62756370

To my mom Haiqin Wang (1960—2017)

Abbreviations

The abbreviations follow Li and Thompson (1981, p. xxiii) and Wu (2004), with slight adaptions.

ABBREVIATION	TERM
ADP	adverbial particle (function word)
[ACC]	accusative
ART	article
BA	preposed object maker (*ba*)
CL	classifier
COMP	comparative
CRS	currently relevant state (*le*)
CSC	complex stative construction (*de*)
[DAT]	dative
DC	directional complement
DM	demonstrative
DUR	durative aspect marker (*zhe*, *zai*)
EXP	experiential aspect marker (*guo*)
EXT	existential (*you*)
[FEM]	feminine noun
fut	future tense
GEN	genitive (*de*)
IJ	interjection
inf	verb infinitive
[MASC]	masculine noun

MM	modifier marker (*de*)
[NEUT]	neuter noun
NOM	nominalizer (*de*)
[NOM]	nominative
NP	noun phrase
PC	potential complement
PFV	perfective aspect (*-le*)
pl	verb plural
PL	plural (*-men*, *-xie*)
PM	plural marker
POS	modal verb indicating possibility (*hui*)
pp	past participle
pres	present tense
sg	verb singular
SG	singular
subj	subjunctive
QN	quantifier
QS	question marker
RC	resultative complement
RF	reduce forcefulness (*a/ya*)
VC	verb complement
1sg	first person singular
2sg	second person singular
3sg	third person singular
1pl	first person plural
2pl	second person plural
3pl	third person plural

Preface

This volume explores, analyzes, and compares the usage of German and Chinese demonstratives. Discourse and textual uses of the forms will be considered as well as their locative and temporal uses. I observe that in both languages the demonstratives can be used to refer to referents. However, they depart from the common sense that proximal demonstratives refer to entities or places close to the speaker and non-proximal demonstratives to entities or places far from the speaker. With the result of analyzing a language sample consisting of a German text and a Chinese text, I argue that both German and Chinese proximal demonstratives can signal the meaning of HIGH DEIXIS in a semantic system of DEIXIS in the Columbia School of Linguistics framework, whereas their non-proximal demonstratives the meaning of LOW DEIXIS. In addition, the Chinese demonstratives can be used under more circumstances than the German demonstratives due to the lack of articles in Chinese. I also argue that Cognitive Linguistics analysis will better help a language learner, whereas Columbia School Linguistics may be of greater assistance if the learner has advanced to a level where he/she needs to know more about the most intrinsic differences between words with similar meanings and usages.

Chapter 1 postulates the problems that exist in the German and Chinese demonstrative systems (despite their radical typological differences), and contains earlier works of linguists who extended the study to many other Indo-European languages (as for Latin, see Diver, 2012; for French, Reid, 1977; for Dutch, Kirsner 1979; etc.). In terms of theory, they reflect what is known as Columbia School linguistics, which was founded by William Diver at Columbia University in the 1960s (see Diver, 1969) and then flourished by his graduate students in the second half of the 20th century. Among them was my *Doktorvater* 'Ph.D. advisor' Professor Robert S. Kirsner. His study of phenomena in the grammar and lexicon of Dutch and his sister language Afrikaans lacks the presence of Generative Grammar (see Chomsky, 1957, 1965) and presents deficiencies of this generative analysis on the Dutch article system and Dutch "flavoring particles" (Kirsner, 2014, p. 1).

In Chapter 2 I discuss the nature of demonstratives. This is not limited to German nor Chinese. Demonstratives, similar to articles, pick out referents from other similar or identical entities and, in addition to that, provide information on how distant the referent is located from the speaker. Proximal demonstratives generally refer to entities close to the speaker, while distal demonstratives to ones far from the speaker. It is worth noting that proximal and distal demonstratives may refer to entities at the same place. If so, other factors should be taken into consideration, such as psychological distance (i.e. whether the entity is favored by the speaker).

Columbia School analyses take place in Chapter 3 and Chapter 4. German as an inflecting language with an article system, bears the notion that there are three interlocking systems of semantic oppositions that determine an entity's differentiation: the system of NUMBER, the system of DIFFERENTIATION, and the system of DEIXIS. In the system of NUMBER, whether a noun is singular (signaling ONE) is taken into account; in the system of DIFFERENTIATION, whether the noun is preceded by a definite article, an indefinite article or not preceded; and in the system of DEIXIS, whether there is a proximal or a distal demonstrative is present. In contrast, Chinese does not change word forms according to their different grammar roles (i. e. is isolating) and nor does it have articles. In this case, only the system of DEIXIS plays a role. Note that whether the noun is generic, definite or indefinite is not part of the study. Particularly, in a system of DEIXIS, as the referent is already definite, demonstratives do not describe where the referent is but rather urge the hearer to "seek out and attend to the referent" (Kirsner, 2014, p. 1). Also, it should be kept in mind that it is the article not the demonstrative that makes a referent (in)definite and stand out from other entities.

Chapter 5 consists a comparative study of demonstratives in both languages with the assistance of parallel texts. It also contains a summary and conclusions drawn from the studies in this volume. It is shown that German and Chinese demonstratives, though differing from each other morphologically and syntactically, still share many similarities linguistically and extra-linguistically.

Columbia School analysis is a top-down approach and provides relatively sparse meaning to the forms in question with qualitative and quantitative evidence. Cognitive Grammar performs bottom-up researches and shows how messages are processed in reality. It is beneficial to apply both approaches to the same question and gain a more insightful starting point and a full-fledged conclusion. On one hand, Columbia School analysis does not provide explicit meaning for language forms, while Cognitive Grammar is more specific and clear with how messages are processed and under which conditions one form can be utilized; on the other hand, Cognitive Grammar is not able to help advanced language learners with understanding the more intrinsic differences between words or usages (e. g. synonyms etc.), it is then better to turn to Columbia School analysis, which provides a form with its sparse meaning from a native speaker's perspective (Diver, 1969, 1995; Garcia, 1975; Langacker, 1987; Smith, 1987).

CONTENTS

Chapter 1　Introduction　　　　　　　　　　　　　　001

　1.1　Introductory Remarks　　　　　　　　　　　　001

　1.2　The Problem　　　　　　　　　　　　　　　　003

　1.3　Literature Review　　　　　　　　　　　　　　008

　1.4　Research Methodology　　　　　　　　　　　　027

Chapter 2　Demonstratives　　　　　　　　　　　　　033

　2.1　The Nature of Demonstratives　　　　　　　　　033

　2.2　The Scope of the Study　　　　　　　　　　　　043

　2.3　Typological Features of the Chinese and
　　　　German Languages　　　　　　　　　　　　　046

Chapter 3　The German Demonstratives　　　　　　　093

　3.1　The System of NUMBER　　　　　　　　　　　097

　3.2　The System of DIFFERENTIATION　　　　　　115

　3.3　The System of DEIXIS　　　　　　　　　　　　142

Chapter 4　The Chinese Demonstratives · 167

　　4.1　A Language Without an Article System · 167

　　4.2　The Problem · 174

　　4.3　The Hypothesis · 177

　　4.4　Qualitative Validation · 178

　　4.5　Quantitative Validation · 205

　　4.6　Alternative Studies · 215

　　4.7　Conclusion · 222

Chapter 5　German and Chinese Demonstratives in Discourse · 223

　　5.1　The Data · 224

　　5.2　Overview · 228

　　5.3　Similarities in the Use of German and Chinese Demonstratives · 231

　　5.4　Differences Between the Use of the German and Chinese Demonstratives · 248

　　5.5　Conclusion · 271

　　5.6　Discussion · 272

References · 275

Acknowledgements · 289

Chapter 1　Introduction

1.1　Introductory Remarks

This study will explore, analyze, and compare the usage of German and Chinese demonstratives. Discourse and textual uses of the forms will be considered as well as their locative and temporal uses. In both languages, the demonstratives form a closed system and may therefore be considered "grammar" rather than lexicon (Diver, 1995). But do the individual demonstratives in Chinese have the same uses as the German demonstratives? If so, can one say that there is a one-to-one match between the members of the two systems and, at a more abstract level, that the corresponding members signal similar meanings within their own systems? Or are there differences in the number and kind of uses in the two languages? If there *are* differences, are these best attributed to a difference in semantics (a difference in meaning) or a difference in what the Columbia Schools would call strategies of exploitation (i.e. the speaker forms the speech differently according to the aim of the communication, the hearer's background information, and/or the environment of the communication etc.) (Garcia, 1975)? Moreover, if there are differences, how much may this be considered the domain of pragmatics, in addition to the vast differences between the cultures of Chinese speakers and German speakers?

One difference, for example, in the use of demonstratives between the two languages is worth noting. With respect to German, where demonstratives could be analyzed in traditional locative terms, with *dieser* signaling proximate and *jener* signaling distal, we must note that pedagogical and even reference grammars almost totally omit *jener*, since it is rare in the modern spoken language. The deictic use of articles, i.e. *der*, *die* and *das*, is the replacement for *jener*, while a combination of articles and locational adverbs, i.e. *dort*, *da* etc., is used to refer to distance in time and space. The Chinese demonstratives *zhe* 'this' and *na* 'that,' in turn, have been analyzed only in terms of the relative proximity of the referent. In both cases, the non-locative uses of the demonstratives have been more or less ignored. One purpose of this book is to discover precisely what these discourse uses are, and how similar and how different they are.

The theoretical and methodological approach to be used in this book is that of the Columbia School. Although less well-known than other approaches (such as, in formal linguistics, generative grammar; and in discourse-functional linguistics, cognitive grammar), the Columbia School has the advantages of first, having devoted considerable attention to the discourse functions of demonstratives, pronouns, verb tense systems and negation; and second, of having proposed interesting and radically non-traditional semantic analyses of these elements. It also has been shown that Columbia School analyses may be "translated" into Cognitive Grammar analyses by considering what the Columbia School has viewed as "strategies of exploitation" to be independent and conventionalized uses of a polysemous item (Kirsner, 1993; Langacker, 1987, 1995).

This study attempts to show that there are many similarities in the use of the German and Chinese demonstratives in real space and in the deictic hierarchy in the Columbia School framework. At the same time, cultural differences account for differences between the German and Chinese demonstratives both in their syntactic structures and in the messages signaled to the hearer. They affect the ways in which facts are perceived and ideas are expressed in language use.

1.2 The Problem

Demonstratives, for example 'this' and 'that' in English, are supposed to signal the meaning NEAR and FAR, both in time and space. Accordingly, when looking for the German words for 'this' and 'that,' one will find words *dieser* and *jener* in grammar books respectively. However, current German textbooks (e.g. *Vorsprung*; *Stationen*; *Deutsch*; *Na Klar*!) avoid mentioning *jener*, because it is rarely used in spoken language, sounds archaic, and is used only under special conditions. A combination of article (i.e. *der*, *die* or *das*), and/or demonstrative adverb (i.e. *hier*, *da* and *dort* etc.), is often used instead.[①] For example:

1.1) der   Mann   dort
     ART   man   there
     'that man'

1.2) die   Tafel   da
     ART   blackboard   there
     'that blackboard'

[①] This structure, however, is limited to concrete nouns in the spoken language. An abstract noun, such as *Begriff* "concept" or *Idee* "idea," does not qualify for this structure in light of the fact that abstract nouns do not exist physically and thus cannot be perceived as either near or far from the speaker.

1.3) das   Buch   hier
     ART   book   here
     'this book'

Hopkins and Jones (1972) summarize the following categories where *jener* could be used before a noun phrase: 1) followed by a relative clause; 2) known or previously mentioned; 3) followed by time expressions; 4) the noun phrase is further modified by adjectives; 5) meaning "that over there"; 6) fixed phrases and 7) not classified. This summary does not give a clear picture of the use of *jener*. In the case of a language learner, it is not realistic to consider all the categories before deciding to use *jener* in the communication. Also, when one only keeps in mind that *jener* means something FAR, one is not sure when *jener* can be applied to refer to a particular referent. Hopkins and Jones (1972) provide the following examples:[①]

1.4a)   Vom   Westen   sah   man   eine   Kirche.
        from   west   see.3sg.past   one   ART   church
1.4b)   Jene   Kirche   stand   auf   einer   Anhöhe.
        DM (that)   church   stand.3sg.past   on   ART   hill
1.4b') Diese   Kirche   stand   auf   einer   Anhöhe.
        DM (this)   church   stand.3sg.past   on   ART   hill
1.4b'') Die   Kirche   stand   auf   einer   Anhöhe.
        ART   church   stand.3sg.past   on   ART   hill

But not:

---

① In both the German and the Chinese examples which follow, we will first give the forms of the language under study in the utterance or sentence in question. Under that, we will provide a word-for-word (or morpheme-for-morpheme) gloss. In the case of German, this amount of information will usually be enough for the reader. In the case of Chinese, in contrast, it will sometimes be necessary to add an additional idiomatic English translation. In the final version of the book, the Chinese examples will also be given in the Chinese character-based writing system; but for now, to keep things simple, we will present them only in the Pinyin Romanization.

We should also note that the grammaticality judgments were obtained by asking four native German speakers (UCLA teaching assistants) to rate the examples. The author of this book the source of the grammaticality judgments for Chinese.

1.5a) Es   war   ein   hübsches   Dorf.
       it   be.3sg.past   ART   pretty   village
1.5b) *Jene   Kirche   stand   auf   einer   Anhöhe. ①
       DM (that) church   stand.3sg.past   on   ART   hill
1.5b') Diese   Kirche   stand   auf   einer   Anhöhe.
       DM (this) church   stand.3sg.past   on   ART   hill
1.5b") Die   Kirche   stand   auf   einer   Anhöhe.
        ART   church   stand.3sg.past   on   ART   hill

(as cited in Vater, 1963)

Imagine that the sentences in both examples are describing a picture. The describer first gives an introduction of the picture. In the first example, the describer introduces the picture from the west side where there was a church on a hill. In the second example, he/she begins the introduction with a story-telling style and suddenly mentions a church on a hill. *Diese* 'this' can be used in both examples, conveying the meaning that the church which *diese* is modifying is not the one which has already been mentioned (as in Example 1.4), or is the one the describer is pointing to (as in Example 1.5). In either example, the referent is disconnected from the previous information (i.e. that it is the one on the west side or that it is in a pretty town). Also, the definite article *die* may precede the noun *Kirche* 'church' in both examples, but in the second example, *jene* may not be used to mention something FAR in terms of distance. However, a person can argue that this is because the church within the second example is a first-time mention. Then, the question is: what is appropriate to use when we want to refer to something far in distance if *jener* is not always the choice? More specifically, what exactly does *jener* mean?

---

① While a distinction between * and ? can be made, for this thesis, I only requested that my informants make the distinction between "natural" and "unnatural."

Consider the following examples:

1.6a) Essen Sie   nicht diesen sondern diesen!
       eat   you.formal not   THIS   but   THIS!

1.6b) *Essen Sie   nicht jenen   sondern jenen!
       eat   you.formal not   THAT   but   THAT!

Both sentences instruct which entity in sight (for example, an apple) should be eaten. However, the second sentence is not customary and will confuse the hearer, because the hearer is unable to distinguish which apple the speaker refers to; even if the speaker is stressing the second *jenen* in the second sentence, the hearer cannot find out which apple is 'that' apple and which one is the other 'that' apple, unless the speaker is pointing to the apple to which he is referring. In this case, however, the speaker would favor *diesen*, the proximate-signalling demonstrative, rather than *jenen*. Consider that, in the first sentence, there may be one apple which is relatively nearer and another which is relatively farther from the speaker. In this instance, how is the speaker able to avoid ambiguity by nature, without differentiating two referents in distance? Moreover, why can *jener* not be used in such cases? In simple words, why is there a paradoxical phenomenon here: *diesen* and *diesen* is not a problem, but *jenen* and *jenen* is a problem?

We have posted paradoxes in German in the above passages. In Chinese, however, the demonstratives have different problems from the German demonstratives. According to Wang (1954), the Chinese demonstratives refer to things different in space.

$$\text{Demonstratives:} \begin{cases} \text{NEAR} \begin{cases} \text{SINGULAR: } zhe, zhege \text{ 'this'} \\ \text{PLURAL: } zhexie \text{ 'these'} \end{cases} \\ \text{FAR} \begin{cases} \text{SINGULAR: } na, nage \text{ 'that'} \\ \text{PLURAL: } naxie \text{ 'those'} \end{cases} \end{cases}$$

Figure 1.1

But this does not apply to all situations, such as in the following scene from Qian's 1954 novel *Weicheng* '*Fortress Besieged.*' There are several people sitting at the dinner table. In this scene, both Chao Hsin-mei and Fang Hung-chien were invited to a dinner by Miss Su. Chao Hsin-mei had known Miss Su since their childhood and had loved her. However, Miss Su and Hung-chien were college classmates and had met each other by chance on a ship from France back to China. Miss Su was determined to have Hung-chien as her boyfriend, but the girl that Hung-chien was in love with was Hsiao-fu, Miss Su's cousin. Miss Su wanted to show Hung-chien that she had other men courting her and maybe through this she could change Hung-chien's mind. Hung-chien was not aware of Miss Su's intentions, while Hsin-mei saw Hung-chien as his number one rival and tried his best to blame him in front of Miss Su. Here, Qian employs different demonstratives to refer to Hung-chien and Hsin-mei:

1.7)	NA	Chao	Hsin-mei	benlai	jiu	shenqihuoxian,
	DM (that)	Chao	Hsin-mei	originally	already	arrogant
	ting	su	xiaojie	shuo		
	hear	Su	Miss	say		
	Hung-chien	que	shi	gen	ta	tongchuan	huiguo	de,
	Hung-chien	really	be	with	she	same boat	return	NOM
	tade	biaoqing	jiu	fangfu				
	his	face	just	seem				
	Hung-chien	hua	wei	xidan	de	kongqi,	
	Hung-chien	change	become	thin	MM	air	
	yanjing	li	mei	you	ZHE	ge	ren①.
	eye	in	not	have	DM (this)	CL	person

(Qian, 1954, p. 50)

---

① The words are underlined in order to show that they are the referents of the Chinese demonstratives.

'Chao Hsin-mei looked smug to begin with, and after hearing Miss Su confirm that Hung-chien indeed came home with her on the same ship, he acted as if Hung-chien had turned into thin air and ignored Hung-chien completely.' (Qian, 1979, p. 54)①

Here *na* 'that' refers to Chao Hsin-mei and *zhe* 'this' refers to Fang Hung-chien, but both are at the same table eating. It is thus not reasonable to state that Chao Hsin-mei is farther and Fang Hung-chien is closer. The question is, then: what does *zhe* and *na* exactly mean in Chinese? This question will be answered in Chapter 4.

1.3 Literature Review

1.3.1 On language origin and the Columbia School theory basics

It is not surprising to think that at the very beginning of the human beings, there is no language, either in the form of speaking or in the form of writing, since language is not needed under any circumstances, if human beings live separately and only take care of themselves. It was not until later in the human evolution that language arose. There were several hypotheses on when, why and how human beings started to have and use language, but in any case, they were urged to use language to communicate. Taking all circumstances into consideration, we can conclude that they all fall in the following three categories: the hunting theory, the hunted theory, and the grooming theory.

For example, in the hunting theory, human beings needed to hunt for food to survive, but there were animals that were too large for a man to trap or kill by himself, lacking the convenience of science and

---

① The official translation of Qian (1954).

technology. Even a modern human is not capable of conquering a beast of prey on his own. Therefore, human beings needed to collaborate and work together to tame the prey, carry it back to the cave where they lived, and share it along with other members of the group. Therefore, it is understandable that human beings were in the need of sharing information, figuring out the steps and giving orders: they needed to know where the preys were, how to get them and what to do if there were an emergency or incident. At this time, pure changing of the length of the sounds or using gestures was not enough to provide precise information on things that were abstract or not present, such as the size of the prey and the plan on how to trap it, not to mention potential ideas or plans of action. Then, it was time to have language and use it.

Another theory on the origin of language is the hunted theory. According to this theory, human beings are considered the prey of beasts, either tigers, lions or any other carnivores. In order to survive and reproduce, they had to find a safe place to live in and be able to fight against the carnivores attacking them. Again, a single or a couple of ancient human beings was not able to accomplish the task. Then, a crowd was to be formed to look for safe and fruitful places and to be organized in order to fight in dangerous situations and defend themselves. In order to show the route to a newly found place, one needed to tell other members in the group how far it was, in which direction they should go and how long it might take to get there. These pieces of information are hard to show only with facial movements or gestures, because they are very complicated. It was even harder to cooperate in a defense against a beast. Pointing to a beast may mean "throw stones to it" or "light up with a torch" or "there is a beast over there, watch out." But there was limited chance to figure out the appropriate meaning right at the time seeing the finger that was pointing to the beast. If the person receiving orders needed plenty of time to be sure what the person making gestures was talking about, there was great chance that he might have already been devoured by the beast. This is very inefficient communication.

  A third theory is called the grooming theory. The theory is about the needs of social-networking. Being an animal or human being, one cannot live disconnected from the outside world. In ancient times, human beings did not have the technology to be able to fight against the beast alone. Either in size, speed or strength, ancient human beings were disadvantaged compared to larger-sized carnivores. There is no doubt that human beings would have died away if they did not unite and defend themselves together. When gathering together, they had to be aware whether the other people joining their society would be beneficial to the society, or harmful to it. Therefore, communication was an indispensable part of the admission process. In addition to the needs of survival, according to Maslow's hierarchy of needs theory (see Maslow, 1943), human beings have social needs, such as love, affection, care, belongingness and friendship. It is hard to build up any kind of relationships without communicating with each other and being familiar with each other's preferences and dislikes. Admittedly, human beings were able to dance, make gestures and some noises to express themselves, but how much information were they able to share with others and to which extent were they able to make themselves understood? Take bees for example, they have all kinds of dances to show where the flowers are and how far away they are and how difficult it is to get there. They can dance in a circle to show the direction of the flower, and they can also dance slowly to indicate how long it takes to get to the flowers. But they are not able to let other bees know about their feelings: are they in love? Or are they experiencing heartbreaking moments? One may argue that bees do not have the needs to be emotionally attached to each other, but it is not deniable that human beings need more than the dance or intervals of the dance steps to show their most "intrinsic thoughts" (Heim, 2011), the abstract feelings that cannot be measured nor displayed merely by time, number or space. When human beings were forced to let others know how they felt about each other and tried to form cliques among them, they had to use language, which is capable of making clear things beyond time and space. This is known as displacement, a design feature of language (Hockett, 1960).

For any reason why human beings began to use language to communicate, they had specific meanings that were to be conveyed by either words, phrases or sentences. It is understandable that at the very beginning of language, there were only sounds but no written languages, and human beings were not able to tell word boundaries, and of course, morphemes. The sound waves (Diver, 1995) the human beings, a.k.a. the speakers, produced were the only things other human beings, a.k.a. the hearers, could receive to collect the information they were supposed to get. It is logical to make the statement that meanings are associated with sounds produced by the speakers. To be able to correctly get the information signaled by the sounds, the hearers have to have the sounds as assets or inventory, i.e. they have to be exposed to the sounds before puberty and be able to decode the sounds respectively. Among the thirteen design features (Hockett, 1960), language has the characteristics of "creativity," which means human beings are able to make unlimited meanings from limited sounds and comprehend sound combinations to which they have never been exposed before.

It is experimented by the scientists that any new born is able to pick up any language if exposed to it after birth and kept in the language environment until puberty. There is no wonder that a Chinese baby can speak English perfectly, if the baby is adopted right after birth and transported to the US to stay with his/her American stepparents thereafter. Plenty of facts have proved that human beings have difficulties in acquiring language if they are kept away from the human society until puberty, for example, a child who has lived isolated from human contact from a very young age where he has little or no experience of human care, behavior, or, most importantly in this case, human language. Like a child that was brought up by the wolves can most likely communicate with wolves, but he is unable to understand human beings or make himself understood by them. It is not surprising, because human sounds are new and foreign to the wolf kid and are therefore not in his inventory, and thus do not make any sense to him.

If human beings use language to communicate with each other, can anyone talk to anyone? Many people may have the experience of successfully communicating with foreigners without knowing each other's language, such as my mom who came to the US in 2009 for my master's graduation ceremony without any English education but managed to switch seats with an American gentleman in the plane without any help. She was very proud of her ability of merely using Chinese to communicate with him by pointing at their seats respectively. It is true that people sometimes do not have to know each other's language in a conversation. But once again, how well are they able to share information with each other? Or, to which extent can they express themselves? We have to admit that in this case, the conversation cannot get further than that of animal talks: they are not able to exchange information that contains abstract thoughts, displacement or history and so forth. The reason is obvious: different languages may have different sounds. Even if two languages have similar or the same sound systems, meanings associated with the sounds are not the same. When communicating, the hearer is not able to decode the sounds correctly. Similarly, a Chinese native speaker is unable to talk to an English native speaker, if none of each has ever known the other's language. It is easy to think that the sound "tree" does not mean tree to the Chinese, because the sound "tree" is not associated with the meaning, which is: a plant with a brown chuck and green leaves. Similarly, an American cannot understand the Chinese word *shu* 'tree' without any knowledge of the Chinese language.

We should not be disappointed with the fact that there are hundreds of languages spoken in the world. Like what is conveyed by the Babel story (Genesis, XI, pp. 1—9): the God creates various languages for the salvation of human beings, not for the chastisement, because human beings are saved from the tyranny of a single "totalitarian" language and ideology. This at least points out two clear facts: first, there are various languages and they are different from each other; second, one should approach to the ideology the language represents when studying a language. Ideology can be simplified to the form of culture, to some extent. An example is that there is a saying in the German language that he is not yet as tall as three pieces of cheese 'er ist noch nicht drei Käse hoch,' but in Chinese, since there was no cheese until it was imported from the West, the saying is he is not yet as tall as three pieces of tofu 'ta hai mei san kuai'r doufu gao. ' Meanwhile, this example adds more evidence to Wholf's hypothesis of linguistic relativity, in which he states that a language is defined/shaped by its culture and gives the example of the Eskimo language, which has more than 70 ways to name snow flakes.

Though Whorf's hypothesis of linguistic relativity (and its strong version: linguistic determinism) is not supported by a great number of linguists, there is still some evidence that a language may be influenced by the culture it is spoken in. For example, there are three genders (here: grammatical gender) in the German noun system: male, female and neuter. When a German says that he talked to his neighbor yesterday night, he unconsciously releases the information of the neighbor's gender to the hearer, c. f. *Ich habe gestern abend mit meinem Nachbarn gesprochen* 'I talked to my male neighbor yesterday night' and *Ich habe gestern abend mit meiner Nachbarin gesprochen* 'I talked to my female neighbor yesterday night.' But it will not be the case when it is translated in the Chinese or English language, c. f. in Chinese *wo zuotian wanshang gen wode linju shuohua le* 'I talked to my neighbor yesterday night.' And in either translation, the gender of the neighbor is not mentioned by the speaker nor marked by the language. It does not mean that Germans pay more attention to the gender of human beings, because they assign genders to existing or none-existing subjects too: a table is male, a blackboard is female, a book is neuter, and an idea is female, too. They are just more used to having either natural gender or assigned gender for everything in the world. They do not have to take more time to think about what is male and who is female—there is no evidence showing that Germans speak slower than any other non-gendered language speakers in general. Nor is there evidence that Germans learn the gender of each subject just as they learn how to spell and read (see Pinker, 1994). All the facts prove that the gender is genetically programmed in the German language. There is no need to ask why there is gender in the language or when the gender dates back to. Similar to language arbitrariness, where no one would ask why the sound of "tree" means the plant that has brown trunk and green leaves, the gender system is in the German language at the very beginning of it. The genders of some nouns have changed over time or differ themselves from region to region (such as Butter 'butter' can be female or male, or even neuter in some southern areas of Germany), but it is not a problem for native speakers: one doesn't need to know how to speak a language in the Middle Ages, and native speakers are perfect at the current sound and meaning system.

Native speakers, defined as people with a specific mother tongue, are able to perfectly use their native language to express their most intrinsic feelings and abstract thoughts. The native language, or mother tongue, is programmed in the genes of its native speakers (see Chomsky, 1969). That means, native speakers may unconsciously reveal their innermost thoughts by their language choices: either by word order, word choice or grammar choice and so forth. For example, in German, one may either use the active voice or the passive voice to signal the meaning "there are people working here." If the passive voice is used, *Hier wird gearbeitet*, it signals the meaning that the speaker is not one among the people working here. To the contrary, if the active voice is utilized, *Viele arbeiten hier*, then, it does not exclude the speaker from the people working here.

A language learner is not expected to use the target language as perfectly as its native speakers do for two reasons. First, because the sound-meaning association is not programmed in language learners' genes, it is impossible for them to study all the sound-meaning associations of the target language; there are too many. Not to mention that lexicon is an open system, i.e. there are new words joining the lexicon with time, and there are old words that become obsolete over time. Native speakers may have encountered situations, in which they have misunderstanding with non-native speakers due to their imperfection of the language. Also, because of the insufficient skill in formulating thought in the non-native language, non-native speakers may have fuzzy formulations, which may be understood as fuzzy thoughts (Heim, 2011). In either conversations or literatures of non-native speakers, there may be miscommunication or misunderstanding arising from the imperfect expressions or descriptions. Therefore, I will limit my study to conversations and literatures by native speakers.

According to Stevens (unpublished manuscript; see Hockett, 1960), language is a system of signs designed for the purpose of communication. In a communication, there need to be a speaker, a hearer, and the information to be shared. In order to successfully deliver the information, the speaker has communicative goals, i.e. what the speaker needs to deliver to the hearer, and communicative strategies, i.e. how the information should be delivered to the hearer (see Kirsner, 2014). As soon as the speaker knows what to deliver, he/she, in the mental process, will encode thoughts and information into language, which includes structure and word, or grammar and lexicon. The speaker makes specific choices of structures and words in order to make the hearer comprehend the utterance and recognize what is supposed to be received in the conversation. Here the speaker needs to consider how to make the utterance comprehensible especially to the hearer. In order to achieve the goal, the speaker needs to take the hearer's background knowledge into consideration and then leads his/

her mental process to the joint attention. In Chafe's famous pear story (Chafe, 1979, p. 160), he mentions that if a story is watched by people from different cultures, their centers of focus are different. A person from a culture, where there is no pear planted or imported, pays more attention to the pear and uses more effort in how to verbalize the fruit, which he/she has never seen before. But, to the contrast, a Californian does not have any problems identifying pear in the video clip and thus pays less attention to the pear than the person, who does not know pear.

In the process of communication, the speaker evaluates the feedback from the hearer in the interaction, and adds more hints or gestures if needed. In Levy (1979, p. 187), a girl is asked what classes she is taking and how her schedule looks like. Levy postulates four steps in which the girl mentally processes as the speaker in the communication with feedback from the hearer. First, she mentally lists the points that need to be included in her utterance, i.e. the information she delivers. Second, the girl thinks about how to describe the course she takes and give further specification. Third, the girl realizes that there may be a potential ambiguity in her utterance and tries to reduce it by establishing a subsidiary goal and satisfying it. Fourth, the girl provides further elaboration to minimize the potential ambiguity at best. In this experiment, the girl clearly has the communicative goal in her mind, which is to make the hearer familiar with her academic schedule, and changes communicative strategy according to her mastery of the information and the feedback from the hearer.

In Li and Thompson (1979, pp. 311—312), they admit that structure and word choice is vital, but there is more beyond the words:

> Since the inception of linguistics as an empirical science, a justifiably

primary concern of grammarians has been the discovery of structural regularities in language. There is no doubt that statements of such regularities are vital to our understanding of the nature of language. It is equally true, of course, that not all aspects of sentence formation can be described by rules stated in terms of grammatical or even semantic properties. Rather, there are a number of facts about sentences that can only be understood in terms of speakers' and hearers' abilities to make inferences beyond what sentences actually say. Further more, certain rules that are pragmatically based are conditioned by the perception of the speaker at the time of the utterance. The speaker's perception of the world and his interpretation of the pragmatic factors may change from instance to instance, making such rules difficult to formulate.

There is no doubt that the speaker has to take the hearer's background into consideration. Howling at the moon may still work after a long time to a certain degree, but it is not an efficient and successful communication, because first, the communicative goal is not completely achieved, and second, taking the same time and effort, the speaker should have a huge chance to provide the hearer with all the details the speaker wants the hearer to be familiar with and make the hearer completely comprehend the utterance. For example, if a country girl, say Mary, from Alabama talks to a local Los Angeles city girl, say Connie, and supposes that Connie understands that people in Alabama air dry laundry on a rack in the open air, and uses this fact as an analogy, Connie would have difficulty in understanding what Mary actually means, since there is barely anyone air drying laundry in Los Angeles: people would use a dryer to dry it, because the rent is high and no one has a yard to air dry laundry.

Similar to what has been discussed before, in Wholf's theory of linguistic determinism, a culture may have influence on how people perceive the world and how people use language to express themselves, in the case that it is possible that the German unconscientiously notice the gender of people in sight, which is most probably not in the focus of Chinese people. Besides, culture also has influence on to which part of the speech one pays more attention to. A traditional Chinese is educated not to exaggerate individual achievements and thus is interested in the praise of individual performance, which is most likely in Western people's main focus. Therefore, the speaker should take the cultural background into consideration and changes communicative strategy according to the hearer.

In addition to culture, Hopper (1979, pp. 214—215) discovers that it is the sequentiality that tells foreground sentences (the "main line" events) from the background sentences (the "shunted" events):

> The foregrounded events succeed one another in the narrative in the same order as their succession in the real world; it is in other words an iconic order. The backgrounded events, on the other hand, are not in sequence to the foregrounded events, but are concurrent with them. Because of this feature of simultaneity, backgrounded events usually amplify or comment on the events of the main narrative... Strictly speaking, only foregrounded clauses are actually NARRATED. Backgrounded clauses do not themselves narrate, but instead they support, amplify, or COMMENT ON the narration.

If a hearer is unable to differentiate important information (here: foregrounded events), from peripheral information (here: backgrounded events), he/she may be confused as to which information is worth giving more effort to go into details and which information can be left out. If a student misses the part in a book, which he needs to study for the final, but studies the parts that are not quite related to the test, he/she may fail the course. In a worse and more serious case, a military officer's failure to attack the right city may be detrimental to a battle. In all, if the hearer is not able to get the most important part of the conversation, the communication is bearing a failure. Ochs (1979, p. 51) quotes earlier literatures that an infant at his "one word stage" in the language development at first "deletes certain highly predictable information in the utterance, which will be expressed by itself at a later stage" (Bates, 1976; Greenfield and Smith, 1976). This too adds more evidence that human beings unconscientiously tend to put unpredictable information to the focus of the utterance.

In addition to structural signs that show different levels of importance in meaning, word choice may also result in change in meaning. Taking "it" and "that" for example. Both can be used to refer to something or someone mentioned before. Say, you meet your neighbor in front of your house. And your neighbor tells you that his son is admitted to the best school in the States. You say "I know it," for example, and mean "let's talk about it; I have more about it to share with you."[①] In opposition, you say "I know that," and you mean "that's the end of this topic, I do not want to talk about it." This is confirmed by Linde (1979, pp. 347—349). In her study, she finds out that the speaker chooses "that" to move from the event, to which "that" makes reference to, to the next event. Besides, she (1979, pp. 344—348) also points out that "that" is used to accomplish the task to refer to a preceding statement taken as a statement, while "it" is used to refer to a statement that is discussed and emphatically affirmed. In addition, "that" also involves contrasting with a previous evaluation and typically refers to an item that is "not within the node of focus." This, however, contrasts with the characteristics of the German definite articles *der*,

---

① This survey was done in December 2012 among English native speakers (faculty and staff) at the lycée français in Los Angeles.

die and *das* (and their inflected forms) and personal pronouns, which will be further discussed in Chapter 3.

1.3.2 On demonstratives

Diessel (1999) postulates that there are three features demonstratives should possess. First, demonstratives are deictic and have specific syntactic functions. Second, they serve pragmatic functions. And third, they have semantic features. This study will be limited to the semantic aspect.

Previous studies also show that the meaning of demonstratives comprises or contains two components or features: deictic and qualitative (Lyons, 1977; Fillmore, 1982). Deictically, demonstratives can indicate a stationary referent as well as a moving referent. Qualitatively, they may indicate speaker's attitude towards the referent or the quantity of the referent (i.e. whether the referent is a single entity or a set of identical entities) (Diessel, 1999).

Most reference grammars focus only on the deictic feature of demonstratives. For these traditional grammars (*Xiandai Hanyu Cidian*, 2004; *Duden*, 2002), *deixis* means to point to the referent without marking the degree of attention the speaker urges the hearer to put onto the referent. In contrast, in the Columbia School linguistic theory, there is a hierarchy of the differing levels of attention given when different demonstratives are used (Garcia, 1975). Within the school's linguistic theory, the demonstratives are recognized as instructive and urge the hearer to pay attention to the referent (Kirsner, 1993). If the demonstrative means HIGH DEIXIS, it will make the hearer pay more attention to the referent. And if the demonstrative has the meaning of LOW DEIXIS, it will tell the speaker to pay less attention to the referent. Finally, in Cognitive Grammar, demonstratives "represent a conventionalized, grammaticalized means of connecting nominal referents to the subjects of conception" and, therefore, function to provide a platform which is shared by the speaker and the hearer (Langacker, 1997). Similar to the cognitive view, Diessel (1999, 2006) argues that demonstratives do not necessarily show relative location, but rather direct the speaker's and hearer's joint attention.

The term which will be the center of the study is *deixis*, which is used in different ways by different people. It is a device through which every language incorporates contextual information (Weissenborn & Klein, 1982). Since *deixis* is the place where language and reality meet, deictic meaning shifts according to the contextual information, such as where, when, by whom, etc. Denny (1978) calls it a "relativity of lexical semantics" that refer to a "particular man-environment relations found for particular human groups" (p. 72). Some other factors such as relative distance and visibility can affect the meaning as well.

There are many studies on the German demonstratives in light of their deictic force. Ehrlich (1982) examines German demonstrative adverbs, and states that there is an opposition between *hier* 'here' and *da* 'there' as well as *hier* and *dort* 'there,' clearly differentiating the speaker's place, reference place, and denotation place. Hartmann (1982) has written about the differences between Rhineland German and standard German. He shows that there are two definite articles in the Rhineland German with two functionally distinct paradigms; one is deictic, and the other is non-deictic. He points out further that the non-deictic mode indicates that the noun-phrase is common or known information to both the speaker and the hearer. Pasierbsky (1982) studies the development of person deixis in Chinese and posits that the original personal pronoun system has been taken over by a more socially oriented system with an account of speech participants.

As noted above, the term *deixis*, when used in Columbia School analyses to describe the dedicated, invariant meaning indicated by a specific signal (morphology, word order, etc.), has had a different, more technical interpretation than is given in general linguistic literature. Rather than being a description of where the referent is with respect to speech act participants, it is an instruction to the hearer to seek out and attend to the referent, and may exist in different degrees. There are analogs to this in other areas of grammar. Reid (1977) examines two tenses in French and finds out that *passê simple* means HIGH FOCUS, whereas *imparfait* means LOW FOCUS. Here the meaning FOCUS is an earlier term for DEIXIS in the Columbia School. It should be noted, however, that there has been a recent tendency among some Columbia School linguists to dispense with DEIXIS as a meaning or component of a meaning. Working on Serbo-Croatian and Spanish pronouns, Gorup (2002) and Garcia (2009) have analyzed the deictic effect attributed to these elements as a pragmatic consequence of the amount of information (nature and number of different dedicated meanings which they do signal).

Several analyses of demonstratives in various languages have been made within the Columbia School framework covering such languages as Afrikaans, Dutch, and Swahili, but little has been done on the German and Chinese demonstratives, especially beyond the syntactic level. Kirsner (1979, 1993) was the first one who studied Dutch demonstratives *deze* 'this' and *die* 'that' in the Columbia School framework. His hypothesis is that by using *deze* (with the allomorph *dit*), the speaker necessarily urges the hearer to exert more attention to the referent, and the opposite by using *die* (with its allomorph *dat*). Thus, the employment of demonstratives is rather a consideration of interaction.

Following Garcia (1975), Kirsner (1979) defined *deixis* as "the force with which the hearer is instructed to find the referent" (p. 359). He further postulates three aspects of deixis: first, "... deixis, urging the hearer to find the referent, communicate[s] that the referent's identity cannot yet be taken for granted"; second, "... [deixis] provides a 'tighter link' with its first mention... insisting that the hearer search for the world, alerts him to it more, induces him to pay more attention"; and third, "the command to search for the referent favors the inference that effort is required to find it and, hence, that a specific referent exists—that is, that it is a localizable entity rather than a disembodied general concept" (Kirsner, 1979, pp. 358—359). He anticipates that *deze* 'this' "will be used when the hearer's task is more difficult (i.e., when it is harder to select the referent in question)" and "will suggest more forcefully than *die* that a specific referent exists" (Kirsner, 1979, p. 369).

Moreover, Kirsner (1979) gives three strategies that are consistent with the definition of deixis: first, "NOTEWORTHINESS. The speaker will direct attention strongest to entities that he, the speaker, is most interested in talking about"; second, "GIVENNESS. The speaker will direct the hearer's attention strongest to entities that are not given, 'in the hearer's consciousness' (Chafe, 1976)"; and third, "FOREGROUNDING. The speaker will use more than one means of drawing the appropriate amount of attention to the noun's referent, so that strong urging of the hearer to find it will be coupled with devices for foregrounding the noun in question and weak urging will be coupled with devices for backgrounding" (p. 360).

Now Kirsner (1993), comparing a Cognitive Grammar and Columbia

School analysis of the Dutch demonstratives, shows that it *is* possible to derive deictic-like effects from purely locative meanings, such as NEAR and NON-NEAR. For example, by claiming that a referent is near the speaker with *deze*, one can suggest to the hearer that the object is more vivid, seen in more detail, and is more zeroed in upon and perceived more precisely in the way that near objects are when compared with far objects, which in turn entices the hearer to pay more attention to *deze*'s referent. ① Thus, his original (1979) Columbia School analysis could be replaced by one less radical, not postulating purely instructional meanings such as HIGH DEIXIS and LOW DEIXIS, making it actually unnecessary to postulate meanings such as HIGH DEIXIS and LOW DEIXIS. However, Kirsner (2011) argues that Afrikaans differs from Dutch in having an unmarked demonstrative *dié* contrasting with proximate *hierdie* and distal *daardie* and the definite article *die*. Since one cannot derive the deictic effect of unmarked *dié* from a locative meaning (since it specifies neither near nor far), it forces the analyst to postulate DEIXIS as a meaning in the Afrikaans demonstrative system. We should also note that Diessel (1999, 2006) includes the German demonstrative *dies* 'this' in his examples to support his argument that demonstratives do not always show relative location.

In addition to Diessel's analysis on *dies*, Hopkins and Jones (1972) review German grammar books and summarize that *jener* 'that' is mostly omitted for the sake of reducing learners' confusion, because

---

① The following examples and explanations belong to Robert Kirsner: Compare the English expression *Look closely*, in which claiming the relevance to the communication of nearness tells the hearer to *concentrate his or her attention on the intended referent*. Furthermore, there is no converse term. (While two members of a large family can be either *closely related* or *distantly related*, there is no command * *Look distantly*.) That communicating precision of location, in turn, suggests nearness and hence that the two concepts are related is shown by the sentences *The pole is near you*, *The pole is far from you*, *The pole is right near you* versus * *The pole is right far from you*.

jener is rarely used. They summarize conditions where *jener*, instead of article plus locative, is used. For example, the referent is mentioned before or *jener* is followed by relative clauses or adjectives. They also point out that *jener*, which is commonly thought to be the translation for 'that,' is not a demonstrative or deictic pronoun.

In the case of Chinese demonstratives, as stated in the traditional grammar book *Xiandai Hanyu Babai Ci* (Lü et al.; 1981), *zhe* refers to people or things that are close to the speaker, whereas *na* refers to people or things that are close to the hearer. Tao (1999) comments on this idea, saying that "this may be true for isolated sentences, but is not always true with discourse data" (p. 72).

Since Teng's (1981) idea of freeing the referent from a spatial distant view and expanding the data to speech act, the referred distance has been expanded to a contextual or psychological level (Lü, 1985; Tao, 1999; Fang, 2002; Biq, 2007; Yang, 2007; Xu, 2008), where demonstratives are not limited to spatial distance, but rather to metaphorical distance, such as the speaker's positive or negative attitude towards the referent. Biq (2007) argues that demonstratives are going through stages of lexicalization in spoken Mandarin in Taiwan. She specifically mentions the distal demonstrative *na*, along with its associated phrase *nazhong* 'that kind,' which has the meaning of "approximation, vague identification and speaker's uncertainty" (p. 130), while Fang (2002) describes that the proximal demonstrative *zhe* is in the process of lexicalization. Xu (2008) considers the distal demonstrative *na* as a discourse marker in spoken Chinese. He scrutinized 8.22 hours of spoken Chinese data and proposes that *na* enables the intersubjectification of both participants of the discourse and thereby induces discursive and social interaction. Tao (1999) puts forth more factors which will influence the use of demonstratives. Factors such as the shift of discourse structures, discourse properties of focused referent, the building of the text, the speaker's assumption of the hearer, and the speaker's attitude towards the referent.

Other usages of the Chinese demonstratives are studied in Hayashi and Yoon's cross-linguistic research on the use of demonstratives in discourse (2006). They see demonstratives as "filler words" when the speaker fails to find the appropriate word immediately in an on-going discourse (pp. 485—486). In their paper, they mention three types of functions: the placeholder use, the avoidance use, and the interjective hesitator use. This discourse phenomenon exists mostly in East Asian languages such as Chinese, Japanese, and Korean, but it can also be found in Finnish. The existence shows that the use of demonstratives as "filler words" is extremely culture-related and thus, to some extent, is limited to being applied within East Asian languages in general.

1.4 Research Methodology

1.4.1 Theoretical framework

The theoretical framework that will be mainly utilized in this study is the Columbia School Linguistic theory, which holds the idea of one-form, one-meaning (Diver, 1969, 1995). Distinct from traditional grammar, the Columbia School theory (a framework within functional linguistics, which is opposed to formal linguistics), is sign-based and postulates that there are different meanings if the messages are different (Huffman, 1997, 2006; Reid, 2006). In the Columbia School framework, the main purpose of language is to communicate and there are extra-linguistic (i.e. psychological, strategic etc.) factors. That these factors may affect linguistic forms and should be taken into consideration is a tenet of Columbia School and not necessarily other linguistic schools. Take ego-centricity, for example, which means human beings generally consider their own experiences the most interesting ones (James, 1950; Kirsner, 1979). As people strive to be the center of attention, the words urge the hearer to put more attention on the speaker. Also, human beings tend to give more information when speaking about things in which they are interested (Reid, 1977; Diver, 1969, 1995).

1.4.2　Research methodology

Instead of language structure, this study emphasizes language use (i.e. how speakers/writers exploit the resources of their language). Hence, it is reasonable to study language use in real-world texts (i.e. in corpora), rather than in artificially created sentences (non-natural sentences) for qualitative and quantitative study. Therefore, corpus linguistics will play a significant role in this study. That is to say, this is a study of real texts, as opposed to Chomsky's splitting of performance from competence (Biber, Conrad, & Reppen, 2002; Chomsky, 1965). The goal of using corpora is to obtain the probability of certain language use in specific situations, in order to give a more explicit meaning of the demonstratives in both languages.

There are written languages and spoken languages. Spoken language, the informal-unplanned discourse in communicative situations, bears the following characteristics, which written language, a.k.a. literatures, does not have (Givón, 1979): first, COMMUNICATIVE STRESS: in a conversation, the speaker may be under communicative stress, where the speaker does not have time to plan before talking, and thus may not have the best communicative strategy and express him-/herself perfectly; second, TIME PRESSURE: in case of emergency, the speaker may not be able to take the best word choice under time pressure; third, DEGREE OF PLANNING: in a real-time conversation, a speaker does not have time to plan the utterance to a higher degree as a writer does (and of course, a writer can also go back and polish his/her writing before final submission); fourth, FACE-TO-FACE MONITORING: in a conversation, the speaker and the hearer have eye contact and gestures can be involved, which make the information sharing less dependent on the words; fifth, SHARED GENERAL PRAGMATIC BACKGROUND: in a conversation, there are several factors that are obvious and do not need to be signaled by utterance, such as topic familiarity, mood, context and so forth (p. 105).

Based on the aforementioned characteristics, only written data will be analyzed in this study. There are two reasons why spoken data are not examined. First, unlike written data, spoken data does not provide background information of the speaker and the hearer. The relationship between the speaker and the hearer is not clear. We do not know their communication strategies and goals. In short, the lack of contextual information makes it difficult to account for extra-linguistic factors. Second, although speakers do not have the privilege of planning and editing their words during the discourse, they can use their intonation, gestures, and complexions to express themselves. Therefore, it is very likely, that not all the information is contained in the language. Consequently, there is a less precise description in the spoken data, which will inevitably affect the result of this study.

Due to the aims of this study, there are three main considerations when selecting the data sample. First, there should be two major texts.

One should be in German and the other, in Chinese. It is necessary that both texts possess adequate instances of deictic and qualitative features of demonstratives in the target language. Second, both texts should involve discourse, culture, and social settings. Since language is for the purpose of communication, language content should not be taken away from reality; thus there is no ideal speaker or hearer, and there are special language uses, which may only be applied under this circumstance. In other words, language in both texts has to sound natural to native speakers and hence possesses a high degree of "communicative fidelity," "a one-to-one correlation" between the sign and the message (Givón, 1979, p. 108). Third, for the sake of a comparative study, it would be preferable to have parallel samples from both target languages with an official translation in the other language (Chafe & Danielewicz, 1987; Christensen, 1994, 2000; Li & Thompson, 1987).

Qualitative and quantitative studies will be conducted on both texts. Qualitative studies are supposed to explore the nature of demonstratives in the target languages. Note that, even in reproducing Chafe's pear stories (1980), a movie in which a set of consequent and simultaneous things happen while a farmer is harvesting pears, which contains strikingly small cultural differences among east and western countries, German speakers tend to use only one sentence to summarize the story. On the other hand, Chinese speakers tend to include moral judgments in the narration. Therefore, it is important to take cultural factors into consideration, because culture influences speakers' attitude towards facts and thus affect their word choice. Hence, in this book, for each example, the context will be given first and then the sentences will be analyzed based on the culture. In addition, the goal of the communication will be considered in order to uncover the meaning conveyed by the message. Moreover, examples will be compared to their counterpart sentences, which do not have a special communicative goal and are plain declarative sentences.

Quantitative analysis is necessary to this study as well. We would expect that human beings are rational and would make decisions based on their best interests. But in reality, we should not suppose that human beings are all ideally rational and well-behaved; first, human beings may not behave in the most rational or ideal manner; and second, human beings may be affected by various factors, either physical or emotional, and might not behave in the way they claim they would. Therefore, in this study, we need to "supplement subjective with objective data, specifically statistical observations" (Kirsner, 1979, p. 361; cf. Contini-Morava, 1976). Therefore, in the quantitative part, this study will not declare which demonstrative will be used under which circumstance, without exception, but rather will identify general tendencies. A prediction is not expected regarding which one is used more commonly in real language, since language itself is creative and thus impossible to predict.

It is, however, not favorable to use translations (i.e. parallel texts, in cross-linguistic studies). Generally, using translation is recognized as biased, because translations from the original language into the target language cannot avoid being influenced by the translator's understanding. A translator must either be a native speaker of the original language or of the target language, as it is not possible to be a native speaker of two languages. Even if the translator is truly bilingual, the more frequently used language will override the one used less often and so the less-used language will be below the level of a native speaker. If a translator's understanding is inevitably added to the translation, the original meaning may be misunderstood or not be signaled in the translation.

However, using parallel samples (here the word parallel should be taken in the sense that the genre of text would be the same in the two languages, such as a German novel and a Chinese novel or a German essay on evolution and a Chinese essay on evolution) is a good way of having control of the usage of demonstratives in both the German and Chinese discourse. By the definition we have just given, parallel texts will likely contain the same or similar propositional contents. This enables a comparison of how demonstratives in the target languages operate within similar or the same propositional contents. In this way, differences between the target languages can be easily located and extra-linguistic factors largely controlled (Wu, 2004, pp. 25—26).

Chapter 2   Demonstratives

2.1   The Nature of Demonstratives

The term "demonstrative" is considered a semantic category rather than a word class. It is defined as a deictic word that indicates which entity the speaker refers to and thus demonstrativeness is intrinsic to its linguistic meaning. It encodes a sense of pointing, which involves a speaker, an entity pointed to, and a hearer. The pointing process starts from the speaker, or the speaker's ego, goes through the speaker's perception of the referent (and the way in which the speaker orients the hearer's attention to the referent), and ends with the hearer's recognition of the referent.

With the application of the demonstrative, the speaker fulfills a communicative goal through the following several steps: he/she relates the referent to himself/herself, shows their relationship and distance, and urges the hearer to follow the meaning conveyed by the signal to investigate the relative position from the speaker, in order to locate the referent. In the following pages, I will analyze each component of the referring event.

The speaker is the starting point and the final deciding agent. He also fills a role that is important to the referring action, because it is the speaker who picks out an entity from other entities to refer to and whose point of view decides the specific method of the referring. The reason why the speaker selects an entity and the way in which the speaker perceives the referent are both subjective. There is no objective standard to follow for choosing an entity. Nor is there an absolute rule to describe the conditions whereby referents should be defined as either physically or emotionally close to or far from the speaker.

It is hard to set boundaries regarding the vicinity of the object to the other actors. One's vicinity can be out of another's sight and reach. We cannot judge that one individual's perception is correct and the other one's is wrong, since it is impossible to stand in someone else's position and to know exactly what he is thinking or wishes to convey. It depends on the speaker's ego, which is the speaker's self. Education, background, likes and dislikes, and everything that defines the speaker make up the ego. The speaker, as the source of the pointing action, points in the direction of the referent, and perceives the physical or emotional distance relatively, based on the speaker's position at the moment of the utterance. Therefore, the demonstratives equip the speaker with an orienting power that embeds a deictic guide in the utterance that is perceived by the hearer. They are encoded with the speaker's point of view and are thus relative and dependent on the speaker's perception of the distance. The main issue is that the objectivity of the speaker is encoded in the demonstrative based on the relative contexts of the speaker and the referent at the time of communication. The concept that the speaker is an indispensable part of the pointing activity is supported by the egocentric and orientational features of the demonstratives.

The pointing process, graphically, is "the arm and finger gesture of a man" that directs the attention to a place or an entity (Bühler, 1990,

p. 93) and represents the speaker's egocentricity, which implies the speaker's position at the moment of the utterance, which "serves as the deictic center" (Wu, 2004, p. 33). The pointing is generated from the deictic center, or the speaker's ego, and signals demonstrativeness, which can be regarded as a deictic force, which the speaker uses to urge the hearer's attention to the referent. The difficulty of the pointing activity is related to the relative distance from the speaker's ego to the referent.

There are two steps involved in the pointing: first, locating where the deictic center and the referent are; and second, referring the referent from the deictic center. Here there is a dual sense of subjectivity entailed in both steps. On one end, locating the referent cannot be separated from the context the speaker is in and it changes along with the moving of the deictic center. On the other end, referring from the deictic center depends on the speaker's perception of distance to the referent and how the speaker prefers to direct the hearer's attention. As discussed earlier, the pointing process involves the speaker's intentionality and also needs to take the speaker's individuality into account.

The demonstratives usually take place in the process of pointing, have the entailment of the deictic reference-signaling power, and serve as the determiner that aids in providing more clues to locate and identify the referent with which the speaker is concerned. In both steps of the activity of pointing, the demonstratives not only are able to locate and refer to the referents, but can also track the referent from the speaker's position at the moment of the utterance (Nunberg, 1993). If the speaker changes location, the change of demonstratives which refer to the same referent will also track the relative distance between the speaker and the referent.

The opposition between the proximity-signaling and non-proximity-signaling demonstratives entails what is called *contrastiveness*; there is no proximity if it is not contrasted against non-proximity. The reason for this is that either physical distance or emotional distance is relative and there is no clear boundary that separates proximity from non-proximity.

The referent, or the potential target of the pointing process, can either be a place or an entity. It may be found in the vicinity or non-proximity of the speaker's position. It is the final destination of the demonstration. The pointing process can be regarded as successful only if the referent is recognized or identified by the hearer. This means, the referent, either a place or an entity, cannot be indefinite (Lyons, 1977). If the referent were indefinite, there could not be any demonstrativeness in which definiteness is presupposed; there would not be any intention, since an intention can only be directed to a definite destination.

As stated in Lyons (1991), "there is an ontological distinction to be drawn between entities and places," because "places (as distinct from spaces) are ontologically secondary, being identifiable as such by virtue of the entities that are located in or near them" (p. 142). This shows the distinction between the place-referring and entity-referring demonstratives, given that the entity-referring demonstratives "encode relation to both entity and location in a broad sense from the speaker's point of view" (Wu, 2004, p. 31). For example, the English entity-referring demonstrative *this* signals the meaning that the referent is in vicinity of the speaker, a.k.a. *here*, which is the English place-referring demonstrative. An NP made of an entity-referring demonstrative, for example "this" and "book," can be glossed as "the book here," or "the book which is relatively close to the speaker" (Brown, 1995).

Moreover, Kirsner (1993) claims that "the 'imperative-like character' of the English demonstratives apply equally well to the Dutch ones (p. 94; Wierzbicka, 1980, p. 37 fn. 20). The "imperative-like character" of the demonstratives is not limited to the locative information of the referent, but rather a "directive force" which makes the locative information "more immediate" than in "putative paraphrases" (Kirsner, 1993, p. 94). In order to find out whether the same holds true in German, I carried out a survey among six native speakers of German at UCLA. I presented the following sentences to them, and asked them which one they would use if they want to sell *this car* in question.

2.1a) Dieses   Auto   ist   schneller als   jenes   Auto.
      DM (this) car   be.3sg   faster   than DM (that)   car
      'This car is faster than that car.'

2.1b) Das   Auto   hier   ist   schneller als   das   Auto.
      ART   car   here   be.3sg   faster   than ART   car
      'The car here is faster than the car there' or 'This car is faster than that car.'

My informants state that they all would use the first sentence, because they feel that the second sentence sounds strange. It is because not only the repetition of "das Auto" is confusing, but also sentence 2.1b sounds as if it were a pure description rather than a promotion or a piece of exciting news. If we replace *das Auto* with *das andere* 'the other one,' informants claim that sentence 2.1b is still not a promotion.

In German and Chinese, there are proximity-signaling and non-proximity-signaling demonstratives to refer to both place and entity. Thus, each of the three languages has four different demonstratives for the combinations: a proximity-signaling and entity-referring demonstrative, a proximity-signaling and place-referring demonstrative, a non-proximity-signaling and entity-referring demonstrative, and a non-proximity-signaling and place-referring demonstrative. The table below is a summary of the demonstratives in the three languages (cf. Wu, 2004, p. 31):

Target	PROXIMITY			NON-PROXIMITY		
	English	German	Chinese	English	German	Chinese
PLACE	*here*	*hier*	*zher/zheli*	*there*	*da/dort*	*nar/nali*
ENTITY	*this, these*	*dies-*	*zhe, zhexie*	*that, those*	*jen-*	*na, naxie*

Table 2.1

As shown in the table above, the Chinese demonstratives, either place-referring or entity-referring, start with the same syllables or, more clearly, with the same characters: all proximity-signaling demonstratives start with *zhe* 'this' and all non-proximity-signaling ones start with *na* 'that.' As such, the Chinese place-referring demonstratives can be seen as a combination of *zhe* 'this' or *na* 'that' and a possible word with the meaning "place": either *er* 'place' or *li* 'place'; and the entity-referring ones are either *zhe* 'this' or *na* 'that' by themselves, or a combination of *zhe* 'this' or *na* 'that' and a classifier or measure word, such as *xie* 'some' signaling plurality in the table (with its English cognate 'these' and 'those').

The pointing action will not be considered successful until the hearer is able to obtain correct information from the conversation or the demonstrative used in the utterance, and locate the referent that is pointed to. To be able to follow the speaker's orientation, the hearer needs to share a joint platform with the speaker, for the reason that the demonstrative used by the speaker signals the relative distance between the speaker and the referent at the moment of the utterance. Therefore, the distances, as well as the demonstratives, are temporal and only valid for a limited time until the speaker's position changes. In this sense, proximity-signaling demonstratives signal temporal proximity and non-proximity-signaling demonstratives signal temporal non-proximity. As for emotional distance, it can be interpreted as the speaker's attitude towards the referent (cf. Lyons, 1977, pp. 100, 647). If the referent is emotionally close to the speaker, it indicates the speaker's intimacy to the referent. If the referent is emotionally detached from the speaker, it shows that the referent is definitely not to the speaker's liking. Adamson (1994a, 1994b, 1995b) also points out that in English narratives, a substance that is temporally or spatially remote but is preceded by a proximity-signaling demonstrative that has the empathy of the speaker.

The hearer, in addition to having to decode the meaning conveyed by the demonstrative, has to locate and identify the referent in the speaker's concern (cf. Janssen, 1995a, 1995b, 1996). Note here that a referent associated with a non-proximity-signaling demonstrative does not necessarily mean that the referent is out of the speaker's sight. Nor does it mean that the referent is within reach of the speaker's vision if the referent is referred to by the speaker with a proximity-signaling demonstrative. Again, the relative distance is not objective but subjective, perceived by the speaker, and thus should not be judged by the reach of one's vision. Also, adding emotional distance into consideration, the proximity-signaling-demonstratives denote a more immediate focus on and a stronger interest in the referent; whereas a non-proximity-signaling demonstrative indicates that the speaker is less interested in or indifferent to the referent.

It may be more difficult for the hearer to locate a referent associated with a non-proximity-signaling demonstrative, because a referent is easier to physically identify if it is closer to the speaker. There is an asymmetry as a referent within the reach of the speaker's vision can be either referred to with a proximity-signaling demonstrative or a non-proximity-signaling demonstrative, but a referent beyond the speaker's sight is most likely referred to with a non-proximity-signaling demonstrative. Despite this asymmetry, a referent associated with a proximity-signaling demonstrative is more accurate and explicit than a referent associated with a non-proximity-signaling demonstrative. For example, in English:

2.2a) Don't take this! Take **this**!

2.2b) * Don't take that! Take **that**![①]

The second sentence in the example sounds ambiguous in the sense that the hearer is not necessarily able to figure out which object is supposed to be taken. In the first sentence, both referents are referred to with 'this' and are in the boundaries of the speaker's immediate focus and better knowledge; they are easier for the hearer to locate and identify. In contrast, in the second sentence, both referents are referred with 'that' and are both outside the boundaries of specificity. As discussed earlier, a referent has to be definite to be identified. Neither referents in sentence 2.2b are familiar to the speaker, nor are either of a higher specificity, which would serve as "a facilitating factor in locating the referent," both references in sentence 2.2b would require other information or other actions, such as pointing to the referent or providing more detailed information, to enable the hearer to locate them and then fulfill the communicative goal of the conversation (Wu, 2004, p. 42).

---

① Both bolded words are stressed in the actual communication.

What can also be derived from the example is that the opposition of the proximity-signaling and non-proximity-signaling demonstratives is not exclusive, but inclusive.① Admittedly, stating that an entity or a place is not in the proximity naturally entails non-proximity in the entity or in the place. But by stating that an entity or a place is not 'there' does not mean that it is 'here,' given that non-proximal demonstratives do not carry the strong sense of contrast that proximal demonstratives do (Lyons, 1977; Brown, 1995).

To make it easier, an entity or a place that is not in the vicinity of the speaker is not close to the speaker, but an entity or a place that is not in the non-proximity of the speaker does not necessarily indicate that it is near the speaker. 'Here' is practically limited because it is tied to a speaker. On the other hand, the concept of 'there' must be infinite.

Some languages, such as Korean and Armenian, make a three-way distinction among demonstratives, which serves as evidence of the notion that the concept of *there* can be finite. A demonstrative, in such languages, can either signal *proximal* (referent close to the speaker), *medial* (referent close to hearer), or *distal* (referent not in proximity of either). In these languages, it is clear that an entity or a place that is considered *proximal* is neither *medial* nor *distal*. However, an entity or a place that is considered either not *medial* or not *distal* does not necessarily mean it is *proximal*, but may be *distal* (not *proximal*) or *medial* (not *proximal*). To illustrate the inclusive opposition, another example can be provided here:

2.3a) The bag is not there, but **there**!

2.3b) * The bag is not here, but **here**!②

---

① For opposition of exclusion and opposition of inclusion see Diver, 1995.
② The bolded words are stressed.

Sentence 2.3b does not communicate its meaning well unless the speaker points to the bag since 'here' refers to a finite space whereas 'there' refers to infinite space. Therefore, negating an entity that is 'here' automatically bears the fact that the entity is 'there.' On the other hand, negating an entity that is 'there' does not necessarily mean that it is 'here.'

Just as it is the speaker who decides the boundaries of the vicinity, whether an entity or a place is close to the speaker, depends on how the speaker perceives the spatial or temporal or emotional distance; or, how the speaker naturally or intentionally conceptualizes the referent: the speaker's point of view, or the deictic center, a.k.a. the speaker's ego. And Wu (2004) maintains that

> [T]he egocentric point of view involved renders the relationship between the perceiver and the entity perceived and conceptualizes it into one between the observer and the observed. (p. 41)

This provides evidence for the above argument that the relative distance does not depend on the actual distance between the speaker and the referent, but rather depends on how the speaker perceives and conceptualizes it.

It seems that "one cannot perceive the 'real world as it is'"; rather, people perceive the real world as they want to perceive it and as they are conditioned to perceive it (Jackendoff, 1983, p. 26; cf. Garcia, 2009). Of course, one would not "see a horse out of a deer" (cf. Sima, 91BC). But it is undeniable that one may perceive a diamond out of a square. One may argue that this perception may be because one has not encountered a square before and a diamond matches more closely to the prototypical representation of the shape from one's prior experience. However, it still provides evidence that different people may have various perceptions of the same entity.

Similarly, human cognition plays an essential role in the assessment of distance between one and the entity or place involved and is mostly contributed by the mind (cf. Langacker, 1987, 1995). In some situations, one may ignore some characteristics of a referent, but in other situations, one pays more attention to other features of a referent (cf. Talmy, 1983). And because of ego-centricity, when people measure the distance between themselves and the entity, there is an "egocentric viewing arrangement," in which "the natural interest that most people have in themselves" and "the relations they bear to entities around them" are accommodated in building the meaning that will be reflected in the semantics of the utterance, i.e. the use of demonstratives (Langacker, 1985, p. 12). Hence, demonstratives encode the spatial conceptualization of the speaker, and "represent that part of language which maps onto the innate properties of human cognition" (Wu, 2004, p. 41). And, demonstratives are part of the "rather deeply seated, innate properties of the human organism and the perceptual apparatus, properties which determine the way in which the world is conceived, adapted, and worked on" (Bierwisch, 1967, p. 3).

2.2　The Scope of the Study

Both Chinese and German demonstratives encode a two-way contrast in the sense of either physical or emotional distance from the speaker: proximate and non-proximate. They can refer to either an entity or a place and give information about the relative distance between it and the speaker, so that the hearer is able to both differentiate and locate it. Based on the goal and framework of this study—to research demonstratives beyond their spatial semantic functions—only entity-referring demonstratives will be included here, while place-referring demonstratives will not be included, as they are limited to space and would be misleading in the later quantitative study.

2.2.1 Contemporary German demonstratives

Contemporary German demonstratives are more complicated than both Chinese and English demonstratives. The German cognates for 'this' and 'that' referring to entities are *dies-* and *jen-* respectively. Though both German and English are Germanic languages, German tends to inflect more than English does. As such, there are several possible forms for *dies-* and *jen-* when inflected based on the gender, number and case of the noun being modified (see the table below):

DM	Possible Forms
dies-	*dies, diese, dieser, diesen, dieses, diesem*
jen-	*jene, jener, jenen, jenes, jenem*

Table 2.2

These two "authentic" demonstrative forms are considered "obsolete" when referring to an entity that only has a relative physical distance to the speaker. Alternatively, a combination of a definite article and a locative are used to replace the "obsolete" ones. Similarly, the German articles have multiple possible forms due to inflection. The following table provides all possible forms of the German definite articles *der*, *die* and *das*.

ART	Possible Forms
der	*der, des, dem, den, die*
die	*die, der, den*
das	*das, des, dem, die*

Table 2. 3

The possible locatives include *hier* 'here,' *da* 'there,' *dort* 'there,' and *dort/da drüben* 'over there.' Therefore, a possible combination (format: article noun locative) would be: *der Mann hier* 'the man here' literally, or a better translation, 'this man.' This form is used predominantly when signaling NEAR or FAR in physical distance, which also explains why the "obsolete" forms are still in use: *dies-* and *jen-* must precede the noun when a demonstrative needs to signal more than NEAR or FAR in space (see Chapter 3).

As they will be mentioned in the Chinese demonstrative section (see next section), the place-referring demonstratives are *hier* 'here,' *dort* 'there' and *da* 'there.'

2.2.2 Contemporary Chinese demonstratives

Contemporary Chinese demonstratives have prototype demonstratives, *zhe* 'this' and *na* 'that,' along with their plural allomorphs *zhexie* 'these' and *naxie* 'those' (Wang, 1987, p. 34). The former (*zhe* 'this' and *zhexie* 'these') are used to point to a person or object that is closer to the speaker, whereas the latter (*na* 'that' and *naxie* 'those') are used to point to a person or object that is far from the speaker (*Xiandai Hanyu Cidian* [The Contemporary Chinese Dictionary], 2012).

Wang (1987) further provides four additional subtypes of Chinese demonstratives. The first subtype is place- or location-referring, which consists of *zheli/zher* 'here' and *nali/nar* 'there.' The second subtype is time-referring, such as *zhehuir* 'at this moment' and *nahuir* 'back then.' The third subtype is manner-referring, for example *zheyang/zheme* 'such, so' and *nayang/name* 'like that.' And the last subtype is degree-referring, like *zhedeng* 'at this degree' and *nadeng* 'at that degree.'

Both prototypes and subtypes of Chinese demonstratives are essential parts of the Chinese demonstratives system, which will be examined further in Chapter 4.

It is notable that in Chinese, the place-referring demonstratives *zheli/zher* 'here' and *nali/nar* 'there' are a subtype of *zhe* 'here' and *na* 'there.' Unlike Chinese, German and English have their unique place-referring demonstratives: 'here' and 'there,' and *hier* (here) and *da* (there), respectively. The Chinese place-referring demonstratives are comparable to the English and German place-referring demonstratives in meaning, but depart from them morphologically, in that they are compounds of the prototypes and words for 'place,' literally meaning 'this place' and 'that place,' respectively (cf. 2.1; Liu et al., 1983; Lü, 1985; Wu, 1991).

2.3 Typological Features of the Chinese and German Languages

The two languages under examination differ greatly from each other. Namely, German is a Germanic language, grammatically and lexically closer to English. In contrast, Chinese grammar has not yet been fully explored. Therefore, in this section, more weight will be given to the description of Chinese, while German will be described briefly, only if there is a notable typological difference between the German and English languages (cf. Quirk et al., 1985).

It bears mentioning that the most prominent feature of the Chinese language is the fact that it is an isolating language, unlike German and English. This means that there are no morphological inflections in the language to distinguish words from different word classes. Typically, in Chinese, there is no correspondence between word class and grammatical role, which is the main feature of inflectional languages like English and agglutinative languages like Swahili. For example, Lu (2003) states that a verb in Chinese can, in addition to being the predicate of the sentence, also play the role of the subject, object, or attribute, without any morphological changes. Take the verb *xingfu* 'to be happy' for instance. It occupies different word classes with their corresponding grammatical roles in the following sentences. However, the verb *xingfu* itself does not change at all.

2.4a)　wo　　hen　　xingfu.
　　　　I　　very　be happy
　　　　'I am very happy.'

2.4b)　xingfu　　　zui　　zhongyao.
　　　　being happy　most　be important
　　　　'Happiness is the most important (thing).'

2.4c)　ta　　buzai　　　yongyou　　xingfu.
　　　　he　no longer　have　　　　happiness
　　　　'He is no longer happy.'

2.4d)　meimei　　　　　xingfu　de　　kan　dianshi.
　　　　younger sister　happy　ADP　see　TV
　　　　'The younger sister watches TV happily.'

In addition, there is no verb conjugation, i.e. no subject-verb agreement in Chinese: the verb stays unchanged, no matter if the subject is singular or plural. For example:

2.5a) wo   zaoshang   ba   dian   qichuang.
      I   morning   eight o'clock get up

'I get up at eight in the morning.'

2.5b) wo   he   mama   zaoshang ba   dian   qichuang.
      I   and   mother   morning   eight o'clock get up

'My mother and I get up at eight in the morning.'

As shown in the above examples, the verb qichuang indicates the action of a single person in 2.5a, while designating to the action of two people in 2.5b. We can conclude that there is no subject-verb correspondence in the Chinese grammar system.

Also, Chinese does not share the English and German tense system. If one wants to give information about where he/she was last month, where he/she is this month, and where he/she will be next month, there is no change in the verb form to indicate that the tenses are different in the three clauses. See the following example:

2.6a) wo   shang ge   yue   zai   dongjing,
      I   last   CL   month be at Tokyo

      zhe   ge   yue   zai   beijing,
      this   CL   month be at Beijing

      xia   ge   yue   zai   nanjing.
      next   CL   month be at Nanjing

'I was in Tokyo last month, am in Beijing this month and will be in Nanjing next month.'

The German translation of this sentence is not very different from the English version grammatically:

2.6b) Ich   war   letzten   Monat   in   Tokyo,
       I   be.1sg. past   last   month   in   Tokyo
                   bin   diesen   Monat   in   Beijing,
                   be.1sg. pres   DM (this)   month   in   Beijing
       und   werde   nächsten   Monat   in   Nanjing.
       and   be.1sg. fut   next   month   in   Nanjing

'I was in Tokyo last month, am in Beijing this month, and will be in Nanjing next month.'

In addition, there is no distinction between finite and non-finite verbs in Chinese, which means that, for instance, there can be subject-predicate phrases. English and German differ in that these two languages only allow for subject-predicate sentences and do not allow for subject-predicate phrases. For example:

2.7) haizi   kuaile   chengzhang   shi   mei   ge   mama   de   xinyuan.
      child   happy   grow up   be   each   CL   mother   MM   wish

'It is every mother's wish that her children can grow up happily.'

It is not difficult to see that *haizi kuaile chengzhang* 'children happily grow up' is a subject-predicate phrase that functions as the subject of the sentence, which does not exist in English (see the English translation above). If a word-for-word and grammatical translation is needed, it should be: "That the children grow up happily is every mother's wish." Similarly, a subordinate clause is needed when translated into German: "*Dass die Kinder glücklich aufwachsen können, ist ein Wunsch jeder Mutter.*"

What can be concluded from the aforementioned points is that in Chinese, grammatical roles or word classes cannot be illustrated by morphological changes within the words, but rather must be indicated by word order or the use of function words or *xuci* 'empty words,' i.e. words lacking concrete meaning or reference to concrete nature (cf. Li &

Lu, 1980; Wang, 1987; Lü, 1990; Lyons, 1995). *Xuci* can "exhibit relatively different degrees of affinity with the full or the function nature" and thus can manifest the part of the sentence to which the targeted word is assigned, and is "crucial for grammatical analysis and cross-linguistic comparison" (Wu, 2004, p. 7).

The Chinese writing system is another obvious feature that immediately distinguishes Chinese from German and English. Unlike German and English, Chinese has its own writing system in addition to its sound system, i.e. one does not necessarily know the sounds when reading the characters, whereas in both English and German, one reads words and knows their sounds. This can be attributed to the limited number of possible sounds in the Chinese sound system, although tones expand the sound variations greatly. This difference can also be attributed to the fact that most Chinese words are monosyllabic, which eliminates the possibility of having long words with limited sounds (a feature of the Japanese language, for instance). In order to be able to produce infinite meanings out of very limited sounds and sound combinations, there are several characters associated with a possible sound (a possible syllable in a sense-making tone) which signal various meanings. It has been shown that ninety percent of all Chinese characters are composed of a radical, signaling the category of the meaning, and a simple and existing character, which signals the inflection of the "combination" (Chao, 1968, pp. 102—105). Given that there are 70,000 frequently used characters in Chinese, it is obvious that some characters are the same in sound but different in meaning because of the different radicals they have. Sometimes the meaning cannot be ascertained solely through the sound signals and needs to be further shown by the character with which it is associated. Therefore, one would hear plenty of such conversations in China:

2.8a)　A: ni　　　jiao　　　　shenme　mingzi?
　　　　　　you　be called　what　　　name
　　　　'A: What is your name?'
　　　　B: Lili.
　　　　　Lili.
　　　　'B: Lili.'
　　　　A: Na　　ge　　li?
　　　　　which　CL　li
　　　　'A: Which li is that?'
　　　　B: meili　　　de　　li　he　　moli　　　de　　li.
　　　　　beautiful　GEN　li　and　jasmine　GEN　li
　　　　'B: The first li means beauty and the second means jasmine.'

To the contrary, the following conversation is impossible (grammatically correct, but with tiny possibility to exist in real life):

2.8b)　A: What is your name?
　　　　B: Lily.
　　　　? A: Which Lily? /How do you spell it?

This example comes across as unnatural and superfluous because one does not need to know the spelling in order to figure out the meaning in a face-to-face conversation. In addition, even if the spelling of the word is not what is typically used, the meaning does not change accordingly. The word L-I-L-I does not depart too far from the word L-I-L-Y and does not have a meaning other than lily, otherwise speaker B would have already mentioned it in the reply and given the meaning of the unusually used lily-sounding word. In contrast, in the Chinese example, *li* has too many characters with different meanings and thus needs to be specified.

In the following sections, I will only examine the features of Chinese that are relevant to this study. German is typologically close to

English and will not be specifically analyzed here. If any typological feature needs to be explained, it will be briefly discussed in Chapter 3.

In light of the fact that if one compares two languages, one automatically admits "the assumptions about language universals" (Comrie, 1989, p. 35; cf. Chomsky, 1964). Chinese and German differ greatly as Chinese is an isolating language and German is an inflecting language. English, a language that is not as isolating as Chinese and not as inflecting as German, can function as the connecting medium, or the "language universals" for the two languages under examination. In this way, we can minimize the factors of features that are dominant in one language but sporadic in the other and illustrate that the differences are a matter of typological emphasis.

2.3.1 Typological features of the Chinese language

2.3.1.1 Lack of an article system

There are no articles in the Chinese language. In contrast, English and German include both indefinite articles and definite articles: in English, the indefinite article is "a" (and its allomorph "an") and the definite article "the"; in German, "*ein*" 'a' (and its inflected variations) and "*der*," "*die*," and "*das*" 'the' (and their inflected variations) respectively. In languages that use articles, each common noun is most likely preceded by an article: either a definite article, if the noun is already introduced or unique, or an indefinite article, if the noun is a first-mention, an unspecified entity from a category, or something that is not especially identified. There are also exceptions where an article is likely absent. For example, if a noun is in its plural form, preceding it with the indefinite article "a" or "an," signaling ONE item of the category, would provide information that is conflicting with the existing plural form, which signals the meaning of MORE THAN ONE (cf. Kirsner, 1972, 1993, 2011). Also, if a noun is a mass noun, or an uncountable noun, such as "water" or "mud," using an indefinite article to modify the noun would also be confusing to the hearer too: if something is unable to be counted, it is impossible to point to one unit of it. In such cases, "some" is usually used in lieu of an indefinite article.

As a result of the absent article system, the Chinese demonstratives *zhe* 'this' and *na* 'that' partly take over its function. In general, demonstratives not only differentiate an entity from other objects, but also locate the entity by providing its relative distance from the speaker (see Chapter 1, 3, and 4 for a more detailed discussion). Therefore, Chinese demonstratives, by their nature, can be used to function as definite articles. For example:

2.9) wo xihuan <u>NA</u> ge zai kafeiguan gongzuo de nühai.
   I like DM (that) CL at coffee shop work MM girl
   'I like the girl who works at a coffee shop. '

This sentence indicates that the girl who is working at the coffee shop has been mentioned before, and the speaker now refers to her in such a way as to make her stand out from other girls: the speaker does not like other girls, but rather only the girl working at a coffee shop. In Chinese, the noun "girl" is preceded by the demonstrative *na* 'that. '

If a common noun is the only one in its category, it is preceded by the definite article "the" in English, but does not follow any article in Chinese. For example:

2.10) taiyang gei dadi dai lai wennuan.
    sun to earth bring DC warmth
    'The sun brings warmth to the earth. '

Both the sun and the earth are unique to nature and are very easy to locate without further information. In English, both are preceded by the definite article "the," signaling DIFFERENTIATION REQUIRED (cf. Chapter 3, Kirsner, 1972, 1979, 2011). In Chinese, however, there is no article or *xuci* 'empty words' used to show the grammatical meaning of nouns.

Now that I have discussed both situations in which a definite article is used, I will move to situations in which an indefinite article is used and how it functions in Chinese.

If an entity is a first mention in conversation, an indefinite article is used to signal DIFFERENTIATION NOT REQUIRED (cf. Kirsner, 1972). For example:

2.11a)　tu　　　　shang　you　　yi　　ge　　fangzi.
　　　　picture　on　　　EXT　one　CL　house
　　　　'In the picture, there is a house.'

In the above example, the first mentioned house is following the indefinite article "a" in English, but is modified by a combination of number, *one* and classifier, *ge* 'item.' Generally, such combinations would not be used if the quantity *one* does not need to be specified. Compare the following two sentences:

2.11b)　tu　　　　shang　you　　fangzi　ma?
　　　　picture　on　　　EXT　house　QS
　　　　'In the picture, is there a house?'

2.11b')　tu　　　　shang　you　　yi　　ge　　fangzi　ma?
　　　　 picture　on　　　EXT　one　CL　house　QS
　　　　 'In the picture, is there A house?'

The difference in meaning between example 2.11b and 2.11b' is clear: the former is questioning the very existence of any house in the picture, whereas the latter is questioning the quantity of houses. There is no doubt that the house exists, but rather uncertainty about how many houses there are.

Let us return to example 2.9, where the noun "girl" is definite but the noun "coffee shop" is not definite and is preceded by the indefinite article "a." Obviously, a girl cannot split herself into two or more pieces and work at several locations at the same time; therefore, there is no need for the speaker to emphasize the quantity of the work place. The coffee shop, however, does not stand out from other coffee shops. It is not wrong to suppose that the speaker knows where the girl he likes works, but the coffee shop is neither identified nor specified, because it does not need to be specified, or specification is irrelevant to the topic of conversation.

A final situation where an indefinite article is used is a general mention, i.e. any item of the category. In this case, any item from the category can be applied to the position or has all the required features. Consider the following example:

2.12) ni   you   gege   ma?
      you   have   older brother   QS
      'Do you have an older brother?'

Again, in the Chinese translation, there is nothing preceding the noun "older brother." The speaker does not know whether the hearer has any older brothers. Anyone who is an older brother has the unique feature of an older brother, which is defined as an older male sibling. Therefore, the quantity of the noun is not part of the speaker's focus and meaning, and thus a combination of number and classifier is not employed in the Chinese translation.

When a noun is in its plural form, either a definite article will be employed, or there will be no article at all; as previously discussed, indefinite articles signal ONE and will be in conflict with the meaning that the plural form signals: MORE THAN ONE. For instance:

2.13a) pingguo mai diannao. diannao dou zai zhuozi shang.
　　　 Apple　sell computer computer all be at table on
　　　 'Apple sells computers. The computers are all on the table.'

In this example, the plural noun "computers" is first unpreceded and then preceded by the definite article "the" in the second sentence. This is because "computers" is a first time mention in the first sentence and the "computers" are not specific, nor do they need to specification. In the second sentence, the word "computers" has already been introduced and it is obvious which "computers" the speaker is referencing. Hence, the definite article "the" is utilized in the second sentence. In both sentences, however, there is a clear difference in applying articles in English. Moreover, neither articles nor *xuci* 'empty words' are used in either Chinese sentences.

If the introduced article is specified and followed by further information, i.e. the noun is further modified by a relative clause especially "the," the definite article in English is employed. But unlike the above example, a demonstrative is needed in Chinese:

2.13b) wo　xihuan　pingguo　mai　de　naxie　diannao.
　　　 I　like　apple　sell　MM　THOSE　computer
　　　 'I like the computers that are sold by Apple.'

And compare:

2.13b') wo　xihuan　pingguo　mai　de　diannao.
　　　　I　like　apple　sell　MM　computer
　　　　'I like computers sold by Apple.'

Example 2.13b expresses the meaning that the speaker likes SOME of the computers that are sold by Apple, while example 2.13b' clearly shows that the speaker has a preference for all computers sold by Apple. The "computers" in the latter example is a general mention, whereas it is a specific amount of computers with specific features in the former example: the amount is big enough to be pointed out. In Chinese, then, a demonstrative is needed to locate the noun in focus.

Similarly, an uncountable noun can be either preceded by the definite article "the," or unpreceded, if not specified. See below:

2.14a) wo   xihuan   he   shui.
         I   like   drink   water
         'I like to drink water.'

2.14b) ni   meitian   he   de   shui   bu   ke   xunhuanshiyong.
         you   everyday   drink   MM   water   not   can   recyclable
         'The water you drink every day is not recyclable.'

The "water" in the first example is any water from the category, a drinkable fluid from the earth, while in the second example the water is specific, because the water from the category cannot be counted. As indicated by the sentence, the "water" is just a tiny part of the complete water category: it refers to the water you drink every day.

2.3.1.2 Classifiers

According to Wu (2004), in Western languages, it is the article system that normally carries referentiality and definiteness. However, this is absent in Chinese. Therefore, bare nouns can be either referential or non-referential, definite or indefinite, if there is no article modifying them. In addition to demonstratives, which will be in the main discussion of this study and signal DIFFERENTIATION MADE AND LOCATED (Kirsner, 1972, 1979, 2011), a classifier is "perhaps the closest to the English definite article in that it is a mark of referentiality" (Wu, 2004, p. 15). Classifiers must co-occur with the nouns that they modify, with the exceptions of cases where the number is one and the noun is modified by a demonstrative; or where the noun is not preceded by any words to form the NP and means any of the category (see the previous section). This phenomenon, however, is not common in English (cf. Lehrer, 1986)

A classifier is a word that provides information on a noun's categorical or itemized status. As described in Li & Thompson (1981), a Chinese classifier phrase is constituted by a classifier and a quantifier (QN) and/or a demonstrative (DM), unless the quantity is one and the quantifier can be left out. A classifier normally takes place before a noun in an NP, as demonstrated below:

2.15a) san   kuai   qian
        QN (three) CL   money
        'three bucks' (QN+CL+N)

2.15b) na   ge   ren
        DM (that)   CL   person
        'that person' (DM+CL+N)

2.15c) zhe   si   ge   panzi
        DM (this)   QN (four)   CL   plate
        'these four plates' (DM+QN+CL+N)

2.15d) zhe   shu   nar   dou   you.
        DM (this)   book   where   all   EXT
        'You can find this book anywhere.' (DM+N)

2.15e) women   xian   he   bei   cha   zai   xuexi.
        we   first   drink   CL (cup)   tea   then   study
        'We first have a cup of tea and then study.' (CL+N)

Given that a classifier phrase usually co-exists with a noun, it can also be used by itself to stand for an NP, i.e. the noun is left out in such NPs. This is called an independent classifier phrase and can convey referentiality and definiteness (cf. Lyons, 1977; Lu, 1988; Wu, 2004). It can only be used to refer to entities, either definite ones or indefinite ones, and only if the referent can be inferred from the context and can be easily located by the hearer. For example:

2.16) zai   wode   houyuan
      at   my   backyard
      keyi   kanjian   qiang   wai   you   liang   zhu Shu
      can   see   wall   outside of   EXT   QN (two)   CL Tree
      yi   zhu   shi   zaoshu
      QN (one)   CL   be   date tree
      haiyou   yi   zhu   ye   shi   zaoshu
      also   QN (one)   CL   too   be   date tree
                                                              (Lu, 1956, p. 5)

'Behind the wall of my backyard, you can see two trees. One is a date tree. The other is also a date tree too.' (Lu, 1956, p. 6)

In the example, both classifier phrases *yi zhu* 'one' semantically bears the meaning of the noun *shu* 'tree.' They play the role of English pronouns and give more information about the type of the noun, which is a tree. Since it can be inferred from the previous clause that the trees which the classifier phrases refer to are the ones outside the backyard wall, it is obvious that the classifier phrases here "substitute and index the NP" (Wu, 2004, p. 14) whose categorical information is revealed by them.

In another example, we can see how a classifier phrase consisting of a demonstrative, a quantifier, and/or a classifier is used to refer to the noun in the previous sentence:

2.17) wo   chi   zhe   guanzi   shi   diyici.
      I   eat   DM (this)   restaurant   be   first time
      na   bu   wen   shenme   cai   zui   pei   weikou.
      figure out   not   for sure   which   dish   most   match   appetite
      duo   dian   liang   yang,
      more   to order QN (two)   CL (kind)
      changshi   de   fanwei   guang   xie,
      taste   MM   range   broad   more
      zhe   yang   bu   haochi,

DM (this)	CL (kind)	not	be delicious	
hai	you	<u>na</u>	<u>yi</u>	<u>yang</u>,
still	EXT	DM (that)	QN (one)	CL (kind)
bu	zhi	e	le	ni.
not	lead to	starve	AP	you

(Qian, 1954, pp. 64—65)

'This is the first time I've been to this restaurant, and I am not sure which dish I like best. If I order a few extra, then I'll have a wider choice. If this one isn't any good, then there's that one. I won't starve you this way.'

(Qian, 1979, p. 68)

Based on the context, it is not difficult to infer that the classifier phrase *zhe yang* 'this kind' refers to one dish on the table and *na yi yang* 'that kind' refers to another dish on the table. Both easily locate the referent for the speaker and the hearer during the conversation. The demonstratives *zhe* and *na* provide information on distance from the speaker to the referent, while the quantifier and/or the classifier elaborate how the referent is itemized. Therefore, the indexical and referential function of the classifier phrases is explicit.

In conclusion, in Chinese, an NP with a classifier phrase is undeniably referential (cf. Li & Thompson, 1981). Moreover, an independent classifier phrase can belong to the reference-tracking system, as well (cf. Chen, 1986). It, along with demonstratives, forms an important part of the referential category.

2.3.1.3 Zero anaphora

There are three referential categories in Chinese: the nominal category, the pronominal category, and the zero anaphora category (Chen, 1986). As discussed above, an NP with a classifier phrase belongs to the nominal category, and an independent classifier phrase belongs to the pronominal category. According to Chen (1986), the nominal category is the least frequently used category to refer to an entity in Chinese discourse, while the zero anaphora category is the most frequently used. In contrast, there are barely any zero anaphora phenomena in English. The English reference-tracking system consists mainly of two categories: the nominal and the pronominal. The pronominal category is predominant in English discourse (Clancy, 1980; cf. Bolinger, 1987).

The zero anaphora phenomenon in Chinese discourse has been studied extensively (Chao, 1968; Li & Thompson, 1979, 1981; Lü, 1980; Chen, 1986). There are two facts that need to be mentioned here: first, the zero anaphora phenomenon mostly appears in the subject position in a sentence and rarely in an object position (Chen, 1986); second, zero anaphora follows a clause that the referent has clearly elucidated and that is not beyond the scope of reference. In other words, as Li & Thompson assert (1981), the clause should be the start of a "topic chain," "where a referent is referred to in the first clause, and then there follow several more clauses talking about the same referent" (p. 659).

The zero anaphora phenomenon may be attributed to the fact that in the ancient Chinese there were no third person singular pronouns with which to start a sentence. If the subject position has to be filled in, an NP will be taken into consideration (Wu, 2004; Lü, 1980). Moreover, the female and inanimate pronoun did not exist until it was introduced by Bannong Liu (1920) in his poem, "*Jiao wo ruhe bu xiang ta*" 'How can I not miss her.' Given that a nominal category of reference is very rarely used, and that a third person singular pronoun did not exist for a long period of time, it is therefore understandable that the zero anaphora category of reference plays a major role in the subject position.

2.18)
Hongjian	you	dianr	zhanqian	dushuren	de	biaojin,
Hongjian	have	a bit	prewar	scholar	MM	principle

Øjide	na	xing	zhang	de		
remember	DM (that)	last name	Zhang	NOM		

zai	meiguoren	yanghang	li	zuo	maimai,	
at	American	company	in	do	business	

Øbu	yuan	gen	zhe	zhong	suwu	wanglai,
not	be willing to	with	DM (this)	CL (kind)	vulgarian	deal with

Ødan	zhuannian	yi	xiang,			
but	reflect at	once	think			

Øziji	cong	chuyang	dao	xianzai,		
self	since	go abroad	until	now		

hai	bushi	yong	shikuai	de	qian?	
yet	not	use	philistine	MM	money	

(Qian, 1954, p. 37)

'Hung-chien, who held to some of the principles typical of the prewar Scholar's class, remembering that this Mr. Chang was a comprador in an American firm, wanted nothing to do with such a vulgarian. But then he reflected, hadn't he himself, from the time he went abroad until now, been using a philistine's money?' (Qian, 1979, p. 41)

In the example, the places marked by a Ø symbol denote where the third person singular male pronoun should be placed in English to refer to Hung-chien, the subject of the sentence and the agent of the sequence of actions. Admittedly, not each Ø is translated into "he." But, it is clear that there is a limit as to how many relative and attributive sentences are allowed as subordinate clauses in English, otherwise a "he" would not appear in the English translation in the sentence starting with *dan* 'but.' In addition, according to Wu (1994, 2004) and Liu (1994), Chinese, unlike English, does not rely on conjunctions such as "if," "and," "but," and "when," to illustrate the relationship between clauses; rather it supposes that the relationship between clauses can be inferred from the context. In contrast, English relies on linguistic devices for textual cohesion (Halliday & Hasan, 1976). Linguistic devices include conjunctions, which are often used to mark subordination. Consider the following example where an English sentence is translated into Chinese.

2.19) I like apples, but I don't like bananas.
  'wo xihuan pingguo, bu xihuan xiangjiao.'
  I like apple not like banana

This example illustrates the way that the English use of conjunctions far exceeds the usage of conjunctions in Chinese. When a conjunction is needed to show the relationship among clauses, it is unavoidable that a subject, or most likely a pronoun (see previous section for verification), has to follow the conjunction, in order to make the sentence grammatical and indexically possible. Therefore, we can infer from this discussion that in a topic chain Chinese departs from English in the sense that "the co-referential entities to the topic often occur in zero form, whereas in English they normally are coded in pronouns" (Wu, 2004, pp. 11—12).

Example 2.19 and its translation also demonstrate a difference between Chinese and English: in Chinese, "referents low in inherent or plot saliency, i.e. high continuity of the referents concerned usually receive ZA [zero anaphora] encoding if their identity can be easily established through linguistic and extralinguistic information available in the discourse" (Chen, 1986, p. 194). However, in English, subject constructions are "typically used when the topic maintained is the SAME, that is, when it is reasonably easy to identify, and topic constructions are typically used when the discourse topic is CHANGED, that is, when it is harder to identify" (Givón, 1979, p. 85).

2.3.1.4 Topic-prominent

Chinese is a language that is still under exploration. In a Chinese textbook, it is not unusual to find Chinese described as a SVO (Subject-Verb-Object) language, where the subject of a sentence should precede the verb, while the object of the sentence should not. This statement is generally true, with several exceptions. One of these exceptions is the BA structure, where BA is a linguistic device used to foreground the object, thus urging the hearer to pay more attention to the foregrounded object and focus on the final state of it, as it is either changed or dislocated (cf. Jing-Schmidt, 2005).

One exception that is related to this study is that of the topic sentence. In a topic sentence, the subject can follow the object, if the object functions as the topic of the sentence. A topic sentence starts with a topic, or the object, and continues with a comment on the topic. For example:

2.20) A: ni   mai   feijipiao   le   ma?
           you   buy   air ticket   PFV   QS
       B: feijipiao   wo   yijing   mai   le.
           air ticket I   already   buy   PFV

'A: Did you buy your air ticket?

B: I already bought it.'

However, if "air ticket" does not serve as the topic in the conversation, i.e. it will not be further discussed in a following conversation, it will not be foregrounded as the topic, but left out. See example:

2.20') B: mai   le.
            buy   PFV

'B: I already bought.'

Here, both the subject and the object are left out, since they can be inferred from the context. In the previous example, the object "air ticket" will be further discussed, or more detailed information will be provided. But in this example, talking about an air ticket will stop when the sentence ends, and the conversation on buying an air ticket will not be continued.

It is not difficult to come to the point that Chinese and English are syntactically at variance. In Chinese, a syntactically absolute correct grammatical frame seems to be lacking. Other factors, such as semantic and pragmatic factors, seem to play an important role in determining the word order (Li & Thompson, 1976, 1981). LaPolla (1990, p. 2) further points out that it is the pragmatic relations (a.k.a. information structure) that mainly determine word order. In all, Givón proposes (1979, 1983) in Chinese, syntax is not autonomous, but rather dependent on the explanatory parameters. This, however, cannot be accommodated by the English grammar with equal adequacy, because word order and sentential relationships mainly rely on syntactic structure, which can be reflected in rules such as subject-verb agreement or contracted verb forms (Comrie, 1985).

Li & Thompson (1976) propose that "some languages can be more insightfully described by taking the concept of topic to be basic" (p. 460). As predominant as topic-comment sentence structure in Chinese is, Chinese is a topic-prominent language, whereas English, as syntactic as it is, is a subject-prominent language, where an actor-action relation is presented. An actor-action relation, however, does not form the main part of the Chinese language, because the subject matter being discussed fills the subject position, not the agent of the action. In addition, it is the job of the speaker to comment on the topic that fills in the predicate position, not the verb that presents the action of the subject (Chao, 1968).

Therefore, in Chinese, the speaker's view determines the word order of a sentence. When setting up a topic, the speaker actually sets an individual frame of reference within the subsequent reach in discourse (Chafe, 1976), which reflects the speaker's communicative strategy (Li & Thompson, 1976). In a conversation, in order to achieve communicative goals, the speaker needs to predict the hearer's knowledge and evaluates it with the hearer's interaction and feedback. When discussing a topic, the speaker needs to ensure that the hearer is on track and does not get lost. Hence, by using topic-comment structure, the speaker packages his/her thoughts in a linear chain, with the topic/focus at the beginning of the topic chain. In such cases, both the speaker and the hearer will benefit from topic-comment structure, in the sense that the speaker no longer needs to modify his/her communicative strategy to the hearer's interaction, and the hearer automatically knows that what follows deals with a certain topic and, thus, has little chance of getting lost during the speech. In any case, it is the speaker determines topics (cf. Brown & Yule, 1983; Zubin & Li, 1986).

2.3.2 Typological features of the German language

Both German and English are Germanic languages. They are similar to each other in the sense of grammar and lexicon. Historically, they used to be daughter languages of the Indo-European protolanguage, but then departed from each other around the time of the Middle Ages. Old English, brought to England by the Anglo-Saxons in the 5th century, is a West Germanic language and was at one point as inflecting as Old High German, having inflections based on the three categories: gender, number and case. Old English, just like Old High German, has many words stemming from the Latin language, because Latin used to be the *lingua franca* of the Christian church and European intellectual life. Though Old English was not influenced by Old Norse due to the invasion of the Vikings in the 8th and 9th century, it was still as inflecting as Old High German, and Modern German, is, despite that the placement of the second verb (either in the infinitive form or conjugated to the perfect tense) in the sentence changed from the end of the sentence to the middle field. Old English then was influenced by the French language and took many words from it through use in government activities and in the court, when Great Britain was invaded by the French in the 11th century, which also marks the transition from Old English to Middle English. Further evidence of the French invasion is the introduction of "to," *à*. Before the French invasion, there was no use of preposition in the English language to refer to an indirect object (see 2.3.2.1.3.2 for more examples and detailed discussion). Old English, as Germanic as it was, used a dative case to signal the meaning of INDIRECT OBJECT.

It was the Middle English that made English closer to today's English language, which is influenced by the invasion of the Normans. In addition to the use of prepositions to show the dative case, prepositions too take over the responsibilities of locatives. In the Germanic languages, a genitive case and its accompanying inflection is used to express possession. In the Modern English, the preposition "of" appears frequently to show the relation of belonging, whereas the form "'s" will still be used, due to the incomplete replacement of the preposition.

Also, in Middle English, the Germanic inflecting system is strongly simplified. As in Modern English, there is no inflecting when word class changes. Whether a noun is the subject, object or indirect object of a sentence, the form of any modifying word preceding it will not change with the change of the case, a.k.a. there is no grammatical morpheme marking cases in English. Additionally, there is no gender assigned to English nouns any more, which also reflects the reduction in reflection that characterizes the English language.

Another grammatical simplification is the placement of the verb. A Germanic language has the conjugated verb in the second place in the main clause, but at the very end of the sentence if in a subordinate clause. A subordinate clause may be marked by a conjunction that requires a subordinate clause, such as *ob* 'whether,' *obwohl* 'although' and *dass* 'that,' or interrogative attributes, such as welch 'which,' was 'what' and *wieviel* 'how much.' However, in English, placing the conjugated verb to the end of a subordinate clause became obsolete.

Generally, Middle English absorbs more layers from the Romance languages, such as French, Latin, and so forth. In the light of morphology (in German *Wortbildung*), a considerable number of the Germanic nouns are able to show the meaning through spelling, in other words: they have motivation, while this is mostly lost in English, except for foreign coinages. For example, the English word "pork," of Latin origin, does not show from which animal the meat comes. But its German cognate *Schweinefleisch*, literally "pig meat," clearly indicates that pigs are the origin of the meat. It is surprising to note that its Chinese cognate *zhurou* 'pork,' literally "pig meat," has the same morphology as its German cognate has.

In the following sections, several categories of grammatical differences between the German and English languages are presented for discussion: such as the inflecting system.

2.3.2.1 Inflections

Inflection is defined to be modification of a word to show different categories, such as gender, case, tense and so on. The inflection of a verb is called verb conjugation, which can give information about the verb, such as tense, number, voice and mood. And the inflection of a noun can be called declension, which expresses gender, number, case for example. We have enough confidence to state that German is more inflecting than English, because there are two inflecting components that English does not have: gender and case. Another component that plays a role in the inflecting system is number, which is a component of the English language, but is not used to inflect a noun. A countable noun in German has its own plural form, unlike English, which usually attach the suffix -s or -es to a noun to show there are more than one items that are identical to each other. Moreover, English nouns do not inflect into two number categories (singular and plural) as the German nouns do, i.e. whether English nouns are in the singular or plural form, it does not change the form of the articles, adjectives or any modifying parts preceding them. Although "these" instead of "this" will be used to mark the plurality of the noun it is modifying, it is not considered a kind of inflection, for the reason that "this" and "these" do not belong to the same morpheme, which falls out of the definition of inflection.

In the previous section, I have listed all possible forms of the German demonstratives. The forms are different because they need to give information on gender, number and case of the noun following them. What gender is the noun? Is it a masculine noun, a feminine noun, or a neuter noun? Is it singular or plural? Which role does it play in the sentence it is in, for example: is it in the nominative case, genitive case, dative case, or accusative case?

2.3.2.1.1 Gender

A grammatical gender is assigned to each German noun. Some of the gender assignments can be understood to be determined by natural gender: such as *Bruder* 'brother' is a male noun, *Mutter* 'mother' is a feminine noun, and *Fenster* 'window' is a neuter noun, because it is an inanimate object. But most of the assignments do not correspondent to their natural origin. For example, *Mädchen* 'girl' is a neuter noun, but a girl should be considered a female object, whereas *Junge* 'boy' is a masculine noun, just as a boy is by nature a male. In all, "gender in German, is mostly a purely grammatical category, not motivated in any way by conceptual factors" (Köpke, Panther & Zubin, 2010, p,171).

In Köpke and Zubin's study (1996), there are several semantic fields that tend to be marked by a specific gender. Most of fruits are feminine, such as *Birne* 'pear,' *Orange* 'orange,' *Melone* 'melon' etc., with exceptions of *Apfel* 'apple' and *Pfirsisch* 'peach,' which are masculine nouns. Other examples include that almost all beers are neuter (including brand names), most of soft drinks are feminine and automobiles are dominated by the masculine gender. The above examples are often attributed to be partially motivated by "conceptual factors." Other factors may include "morphological factors" and "phonological factors." A noun with the diminutive suffix -lein or -chen is neuter, which is an example of the prior category. And a noun that starts with the phoneme /kn-/ is most likely masculine, whereas a noun that ends in the morpheme /-uːr/ is mostly feminine, for example *Uhr* 'clock.' These fall into the latter category of factors that may account for the motivation in gender assignment.

Agreement required between the noun and its modifying parts.

Both the noun and the modifying parts need to signal the same grammatical gender of the noun. There is no negotiation in this matter. For example:

    2.21a)   ein   klein-es   Mädchen
               [NEUT]   [NEUT]   [NEUT]
             'a little girl'
    2.21b)   *ein   klein-e   Mädchen
               [NEUT]   [FEM]   [NEUT]

(Köpke, Panther & Zubin, 2010, p.180)

Here the second example is not grammatically correct, since the indefinite article *ein* 'one' and the noun *Mädchen* 'girl' signal NEUTER, whereas the inflected form *kleine* 'small' signals FEMININE. This combination of forms signal meanings in different directions, which will confuse the hearer and fail to make sense. The first example, however, has forms that all signal NEUTER, and therefore there is no ambiguity with regards to the gender agreement.

In discourse, the grammatical gender of a noun may conflict with its conceptual gender in the issue of predicate nominals, for example:

    2.22)   Das   Mädchen   ist   Studentin   der   Medizin.
             [NEUT]   girl   be.3sg female student FEM   medicine
             'The girl is a medical student.'

(Köpke, Panther & Zubin, 2010, p.181)

In this example, the subject of the sentence *Mädchen* 'girl,' a neuter noun, is in conflict with the predicate *Studentin* 'female student,' a feminine noun. Köpke, Panther and Zubin (2010, p.181) explain it as "the natural gender FEMALE of the controller das *Mädchen* is most likely to determine the grammatical gender FEMININE of the predicate nominal (conceptual gender agreement)." If the natural gender of the noun agrees to the grammatical gender, there is "a tendency in the present German to specify the natural gender of human referents, especially when the noun denotes a profession," as shown in the following example:

2.23) Die   Frau   ist   Ärzt-in.
      ART.[FEM]   woman   be.3sg   doctor-[FEM]
      'The woman is a doctor.'

(Köpke, Panther & Zubin, 2010, p.181)

In the same study, Köpke claims that the question of agreement between the subject and the predicate does not arise, when "the predicate nominal is not semantically specified according to the gender." In order to support the argument, the following example is used as evidence:

2.24) Sein-e   Freundin   ist   Lehrling-Ø   bei   BMW.
      his-[FEM]   girlfriend be   apprentice-[Ø] at   BMW
      'His girlfriend is apprentice with BMW.'

The claim that the noun *Lehrling* 'apprentice' is not semantically specified according to the gender may be true because *Lehrling* does not necessarily mean that the apprentice is male (the natural gender is not shown), but is simply a grammatically masculine noun. On the other hand, it may also be because that there is no naturally gendered form of *Lehrling*, whereas other professions, such as *Arzt* 'doctor' has a male and a female form: *Arzt* 'male doctor' and *Ärztin* 'female doctor.' In my opinion, applying *Lehrling* to a female noun illustrates the notion of "using the least inappropriate" (cf. Kirsner, 1972; Diver, 1995). If there is no form in the language that corresponds to the notion of "most appropriate," a good strategy is to use the next most appropriate one. It is not wise to look for another word with a female form, because it will for sure automatically signal other meanings, either a different meaning than apprentice, which is the meaning one wants to signal, or additional meaning other than just apprentice. It will either mislead the hearer, or force the hearer to reflect longer to consider the real meaning of the alternative. In all, it is not worth replacing the word with an alternative that has gendered options but has a different meaning.

Köpke, Panther & Zubin (2010, pp. 182—191) explore the conflict between the grammatical gender of a neuter noun and its tracking modifiers, which may signal FEMININE, such as pronouns, possessive adjectives, relative clause and so forth. They examine texts and come to the conclusion that conceptual gender take place most frequently when referring to a noun that appears earlier in the sentence/context. Besides pragmatic factors such as context and capitalization, other factors that need to be taken into consideration are the linear distance between controller and target, their respective syntactic domains, the word class of the target, and the degree of syntactic embeddedness of the target relative to its controller.

When it comes to plural, the three genders collapse in the plural form: the definite article for any noun in the plural form is *die*, which is identical to the feminine article but behaves differently in terms of grammar. Plurality, in the light of gender, can be viewed as a fourth gender, which has its distinct rules of inflection, which results in extra inflected forms of modifying words preceding a noun.

2.3.2.1.2 Number

An essential component of the grammatical system, especially the semantic and typological system, is number. It marks the quantity of the noun, and illustrates whether it is a single item or more than one identical item of the same kind.

As mentioned above, each countable German noun has its plural form, which cannot be decided by either its gender, phoneme or morpheme. The plural form of a noun is autonomous.

Since the number of a noun will result in the inflection of the modifying parts that precede it, including demonstratives and articles, I will have a more detailed analysis in Chapter 3.

2.3.2.1.3 Case

There are four cases in the German language: the nominative case, the genitive case, the dative case and the accusative case. They mark the word class of the noun. They indicate that the noun is the subject, the processor of another item, the indirect object, and the direct object respectively. Although English does not show word class by inflection, it has a similar grammar system with regards to word order. As mentioned before, the English suffix -'s is its "adjusted" form of the German genitive case (see previous section this chapter). In addition, the German accusative case functions as the English direct object in the grammar system. In this section, I will only discuss the nominative case and the dative case. For the reason that the former does not have to be in the initial position in German, but has to be in the initial position, a.k.a. preceding verb, in English. And the latter in German does not equal to the indirect object in the English language.

2.3.2.1.3.1 The nominative case

If a noun is in the nominative case of a sentence, it is marked as the subject of the verb, a.k.a. the agent of the action, which is indicated by the verb. If the verb is in the passive voice, the nominative case is the receiver of the action.

Note that a different between the German and English is that in English, a predicate noun may not be in the nominative case, whereas in German, a predicate noun is always in the nominative case. For example:

    2.25) Der   Student   war   ich.
           DM (the)   student   be.past.1sg/3sg   I-NOM
           'The student was me.'

In this example, *ich* 'I' is in the nominative case, indicating that *ich* 'I' is equivalent to *der Student* 'the student.' Both *ich* and *der Student* are not receiver of any action, but are agents of the action "to be" or "to equal to." In the example, *ich* is not considered to be the subject of the sentence, because the verb *sein* 'to be' is not conjugated according to it, but rather according to *der Student*.

English, not as inflecting as German, needs to apply word order to indicate the word class of a word. It is impossible to have sentences like:

2.26a) * The ticket buy I.

However, in German, it is possible to have the subject not in the initial position:

2.26b) Die   Karte   kauf-e   ich.
        ART   ticket buy-1sg I

In German, it can be implied from the conjugated form of the verb which word is the subject of the sentence. The previous example clearly indicates that the subject is *ich*, instead of the ticket. If the ticket were the subject of the sentence, the verb *kaufen* 'to buy' should be conjugated to its third person singular form *kauft* to have the subject-verb or agent-action agreement.

According to Garcia (1979, p.35), nominative is a "natural candidate for the initial position," because nominative signals FOCUS and the noun in the nominative case is a noun that the speaker "views as important," and thus should be "mentioned more than once throughout the discourse" and becomes a familiar item (cf. Zubin, 1979). It is possible to have other cases in the initial position, but it would imply that the item, not in the nominative case but in the initial position, is of even more importance than the subject and urges the hearer to pay more attention to it. This is also supported by communicative economy in the way that "(hierarchically) first things (temporally) first" as they are "related to communication" (1979, p. 37).

2.3.2.1.3.2 The dative case

It is too restrictive to state that the dative case in the German language is used to mark indirect object in the sentence, because there are obviously other grammatical roles that dative case fulfills.

2.27a) Mir   ist   kalt.
       I.[DAT]   be.3sg   cold
       'I am feeling cold.'

In the example, *mir* 'I' is in the dative case, but is still the "agent" in the sentence: it is "I" that feel cold and share the subjunctive feeling with the hearer. Although there is no subject in the sentence, *mir* in the dative case functions as the agent of the indicated "feeling" action. If putting "I" into the nominative case, as in the following example:

2.27b) Ich   bin   kalt.
       I.[NOM]   be.1sg   cold
       'I am cold.' (a.k.a. the speaker's body temperature is low)

This example is different from the previous one in light of the fact that in this example, *ich* 'I,' is in the nominative case in a predicate structure sentence. This sentence means "I" is equivalent to "being cold," and thus is objective instead of being subjunctive.

Another use of dative case is to indicate location instead of direction. See examples:

2.28a) Ich   geh-e   in   das   Klassenzimmer.
       I.[NOM]   go-1sg   in   ART.[ACC]   classroom
       'I am going to the classroom.'

2.28b) Ich   bleib-e   in   dem   Klassenzimmer.
       I.[NOM]   stay-1sg in   ART.[DAT]   classroom
       'I am staying in the classroom.'

The examples show that if preceded by a locational or directional preposition, the noun in the dative case indicates that the speaker is in the classroom and will not change his/her location relatively in reference to the classroom. However, if the noun is in the accusative case, the speaker will change his/her location in reference to the classroom: previously the speaker is not in the classroom, but is approaching to the classroom and will enter the classroom upon arrival.

Last but not the least, dative is used to indicate the indirect object of the sentence. The difference between English and German is that in English, it is common to use a prepositional phrase to indicate indirect object, whereas in German, there is rarely any indirect object signaled by a prepositional phrase. Therefore, when it comes to second language acquisition, it is extremely important for students whose native language is English and who begin to study German to avoid using the German cognate *zu* when trying to use the prepositional structure 'to somebody' or 'to something.' They are tempted to apply *zu* whenever there is a 'to' preceding the indirect object in the sentence. On the other hand, they fail to process German sentences when there is an indirect object without *zu* preceding it. This problematic situation can be illustrated in Example 2.29:

2.29) Ich   geb-e   dir   ein   Buch.
       I.[NOM]   give-1sg   you.[DAT]   a   book
       'I give a book to you.' or 'I give you a book.'

In this example, when students are asked to translate the English sentence into German, they will inevitably translate it into *Ich gebe ein Buch zu dir*, or literally, 'I give a book to you.' And when asked to comprehend the German sentence, they sometimes are only able to proceed to get to the meaning of 'I give a book' and will look for the indirect object in vain, until they are told the dative pronoun *dir* 'you' is what they are looking for.

In addition, students may continue to use the structure of *zu* 'to' plus the verb, despite that the meaning of structure with *zu* differs from the meaning of the structure without *zu*.

2.30) a Ich   sag-e   zu   dir.
      b Ich   sag-e   dir.
         I.[NOM]   say-1sg   to   you.[DAT]
      a 'I say to you.'
      b 'I tell you.'

In example 2.30, although they understand that the first sentence means 'I say to you' and the second 'I tell you,' students always rely upon the first one, regardless of what meaning they gave in mind, if they are told that the structure with *zu* really does exist.

As mentioned above, English departed from a Germanic language when the Vikings, the French and the Norse invaded Great Britain. The French invasion in particular brought the prepositional dative into the English language. In this portion, I will look for evidence in Old English where indirect object is in the form of a synthetic dative noun phrase and then try to explain where a prepositional dative (necessarily *tō*-structure) is used and where a synthetic dative is used. And, at the end of this project, I will elucidate the reasons why "to-structure" is generally applied to precede indirect objects in modern English.

First, I will give a clear definition of the term "Dative" within the Germanic languages framework. Dative is usually considered the alternative term for the indirect object in modern English in most elementary German textbooks (see *Vorsprung*, *Na klar*! and *Stationen*). However, students may get confused when they are instructed that *helfen* 'to help' requires a dative object, because the act is directly extended to the helped. And they will encounter similar verbs at which point, their understanding of indirect object collapses. Thus, it is necessary to give a in-depth definition of "Dative":

> er [Dativ] bezeichnet im wesentlichen eine belebte Grösse, die in das vom Verb beschriebene Geschehen nur indirekt involviert ist, von ihm nicht verändert wird und den anderen Handlungsbeteiligten selbständig gegenübersteht. (Wegener, 1985, p. 321)
>
> 'Essentially the dative signifies a living entity, which is only indirectly involved in the action the verb describes, and is not changed by the action and is independent from all of the other elements of the action.'①

According to this passage, at least three principles of a dative noun phrase can be identified: first, it is "indirectly involved in the action described by the verb"; second, it is "not changed by the action"; and third, it is "standing opposite the other entities involved in the action" (Smith, 1987, p. 352). Thus, if we draw an action line to each sentence, there are two participants in every dative-containing sentence, namely an active participant, the nominative of the sentence, and a passive participant, the dative of the sentence. Their relationship can be illustrated in Table 2.4.

	Source Domain	Recipient Domain
Active Participant	Agent	Experiencer
Passive Participant	Instrument	Patient/Mover/Absolute

(Smith, 1987, p. 355)

Table 2.4

Unlike the active participant, which is required in every sentence, the passive participant of the action does not have to exist in every

---

① Translation credits given to Andre Schuetze and S. Kye Terrasi.

sentence. As in the example 2.30, the German verb *sagen* has two meanings: 'to say' and 'to tell' and requires a synthetic dative noun phrase, i.e. without zu, if meaning 'to tell.' This is because people prefer not to end the sentence with 'I tell,' but would prefer to add the actual indirect object to it, say 'you.' If the sentence ends with 'I tell,' the hearer will not assume that there will be more information added to the sentence and will wait for the speaker to continue. In contrast, if the speaker stops with the sentence 'I say' or 'I am saying,' the listener will not suppose there is more information coming when the pause is acknowledged. Therefore, the sentence has to have *zu* to incorporate a complement, which is not required by the verb, in order to add more information to the sentence.

In this way, there are two kinds of verbs in Germanic languages that mean "to say": one kind does require a dative case and the other kind does not, as described by Visser (1963, § 682):

> This construction [indirect object + direct object] is extremely common in Old English with verbs whose fundamental meaning is that of giving, bestowing, granting, imparting, etc. The indirect object demote, the person who 'receives' what is referred to by the direct object, which may be an answers news, a report, a communication, a refusal, a rebuke, a warning, a title, a rank, a confession, a direction, etc. The functional relation is clearly expressed by the indirect object appearing in the dative and the direct object in the accusative case.

To make this statement vivid and clear, I cite two examples from Old English.

2.31) To ðām wife   cwæð   God   ēac   swylċe
      To the woman.[DAT] say.3sg.past God   also alike
      "God also said to the woman likewise..."

(The fall of Adam and Eve: 19)

In this example, similar to the first sentence in example 2.30, consider taking out this part with 'God said' or 'God was saying' and then continues with what he actually said in a subordinate clause. However, in order to put the object to which God spoke clear, a complement, namely the woman, is added to the sentence. Since 'to say' is not a verb that has the meaning of "granting, bestowing or imparting," the passive participant of the action "saying" is introduced with the preposition *tō* preceding it.

The verb in the example 2.32 requires a dative noun phrase in the sentence, as following:

2.32) Æðeldryð wearð   þā   forgifen ānum ealdormenn   tō wife.
      Adeldryd become. 3sg. past then give-pp ART ruler. [DAT] to wife. [DAT]
      "Adeldryd became then given to a ruler to wife."

(The life of Æðeldryð: 3)

In this example, the Old English verb *forgifan* has the meaning of "to give." According to Visser, this verb requires an indirect object, i.e. dative noun phrase, in the sentence and does not need the preposition *tō* 'to' to precede it.

Visser lists 188 verbs in his book (1963, § 682) suggesting that all these verbs do use "three-place constructions" (Smith, 1987, pp. 360—369), i.e. they must have nominative, accusative and dative in the sentence when used. A three-place construction can be illustrated as follows:

⎧ 1) Agent: NOM
⎨ 2) Recipient: ACC
⎩ 3) Possessor, Indirect Object, Experiencer/Observer: DAT

In order to find statistical evidence to prove that Visser's 188 verbs incorporate a dative noun phrase within themselves and do not use the preposition *tō* to introduce dative, I use *The York-Toronto-Helsinki*

Parsed Corpus of Old English Prose[①] to count the total number of sentences where those verbs have dative noun phrase with the preposition *tō* preceding it and where those verbs have a synthetic dative in the sentence. In order to avoid stylistic employment of the synthetic dative in poems, only Old English prose is taken into consideration[②].

I have chosen six verbs from Visser's list to run the data, namely *agifan* 'to give, to deliver,' *forgifan* 'to grant, to give,' *gifan* 'to give,' *offrian* 'to offer,' *sceawian* 'to look, to examine' and *tellan* 'to tell.' Semantically they form three groups: the first four verbs have the meaning of "to give", the fifth "to examine" and the last "to tell." I take *forgifan* as the representative of the first semantic group and its distribution in the prose corpus is shown in Table 2.5:

	Nr. of co-existence with synthetic dative	Nr. of co-existence with prepositional dative
forgife	46	0
forgif	22	0
forgyfð/forgifð	52	3
forgifan	48	0
forgeaf	187	5
forgeafon	12	1
Total	367	9

Table 2.5

---

① Please refer to: http://ota.ahds.ac.uk/headers/2462.xml However, a request of using the corpus has to be approved.

② The number of co-existence counted in the statistic validation part only refers to sentences where the indirect object is either introduced by a synthetic or prepositional dative. Thus, sentence complements are not included in this corpus search. For example, in for ðan ðe ðū eart dūst and tō dūste gewyrst 'because you are dust and change into dust,' the use of prepositional phrase with a datuve noun *tō dūste* does not count as a prepositional dative in discussion, because "dust" is not the indirect object of the sentence, but rather a complement of future status.

This table illustrates that the verb *forgifan* is predominately used with a synthetic dative than with a prepositional dative.

The verb *sceawian* from the second semantic group is less used more in Old English than *forgifan*. Its most used conjugated forms are *sceawian* (infinitive), *sceawode* (first and third person singular past tense), *sceawodon* (plural past tense) and *gesceawiað* (plural present tense). And its statistics are shown in Table 2.6.

	Nr. of co-existence with synthetic dative	Nr. of co-existence with prepositional dative
sceawian	47	0
sceawode	41	0
sceawodon	19	0
gesceawiað	2	0
Total	109	0

Table 2.6

Here the verb *sceawian* shows a drastic contrast in its actual use in Old English: it never takes *tō* to introduce its dative noun phrase and clearly shows that the dative is incorporated in the action described by the verb. The dative is not a complement of the sentence, but a necessary participant in the original action.

The representative of the third group *tellan* is counted in the corpus as well. The result is shown in Table 2.7.

	Nr. of co-existence with synthetic dative	Nr. of co-existence with prepositional dative
tellan	7	5
telle	11	1
getelest	1	0

(Table 2.7 continued)

	Nr. of co-existence with synthetic dative	Nr. of co-existence with prepositional dative
tele	4	0
geteald	78	0
telleð	4	1
Total	105	7

Table 2.7

Though less significant, the result still supports the notion that the verb *tellan* tends to have a synthetic dative rather than a prepositional dative in the actual use.

To summarize the results of all six sample verbs from Visser's list, I provide a cumulative total of the results, as presented in Table 2.8.

	Nr. of co-existence with synthetic dative	Nr. of co-existence with prepositional dative
Total	937	21

Table 2.8

Table 2.8 is a strong statistical proof of Visser's argument and verb list. It is interesting to note how infrequently the *tō*-structure is used in Old English, although Visser (1963, §687) did suggest in his book that the *tō*-structure was not widely used until Middle English but did occasionally exist in late Old English. The common use of synthetic dative in Old English can be seen as a language characteristic of the Germanic languages from which languages such as German, Dutch and Afrikaans still employ synthetic dative to express the indirect object of the sentence, rather than a characteristic enforced by Latin. Above all, due to geographic isolation it was not possible for Latin to influence the English language. Certainly, Old English is not isolated from Latin influence. But there was neither evidence nor logical explanation for the English language to inherit the whole syntax from Latin at all. On one hand, Germanic languages themselves have the use of synthetic dative themselves. And on the other hand, since there were neither many authors nor readers who were educated to write or read works in Latin (Danchev, 1969). Thus, there is neither need nor possibility to produce works in a Latinized language rather than in the native language. In all, as stated by Visser (1969): "[there is] no need to use a language with constructions unfamiliar with readers" and the synthetic dative is genius of Old English.

However, the situation of synthetic and prepositional dative is totally different in the Middle English period, where the preposition $t\bar{o}$ became the main stream of introducing indirect object of the sentence. Visser (1963, § 624) attributes this phenomenon partly as the result of the French conquest and the influx of the French language at the beginning of the 14th century:

> In the course of the 14th and 15th centuries the number [of the use of prepositional dative] increases with striking rapidity, partly also on account of the adoption of numerous French verbs which were construed with $à$ before a noun-complement.

In my point of view, this is a possible explanation. The adoption of numerous French verbs into Middle English is only one aspect of the whole language change under the influence of another language. First, the writers changed in the Middle English period. Not only Middle English writers, but also French writers at that time were able to have their works published. French writers, however, were primarily proficient at French where there was and is a predominance of using prepositional dative, i.e. to have the preposition $à$, which is the cognate of 'to' in French, preceding indirect object. Second, the audiences were different, too. With the conquest many French came to England and settled there. They exercised a great influence on the English and their language. As a result, many of them were able to read and write fluently in French. Through the communication of the two languages, the use of prepositional dative, which already existed in Old English but had not been widely utilized until then, was later more frequently used and was fixed into the grammar frame of Middle English. This process is an on-going process, not a drastic one, but an effective one, and can be explained by Hopper's Emergent Grammar (1998, p. 156):

> The notion of Emergent Grammar is meant to suggest that structure, or regularity, comes out of discourse and is shaped by discourse in an ongoing process... Its forms are not fixed templates but emerge out of face-to-face interaction in ways that reflect the individual speakers' past experience of these forms, and their assessment of the present context, including especially their interlocutors, whose experiences and assessments may be quite different."

In conclusion, the use of synthetic dative to incorporate the indirect object in an Old English sentence overrides the application of synthetic dative. German, like Old English, too favors to employing synthetic dative for the indirect object if three-place construction verbs are used. But with the French conquest, the disadvantaged and less common use of prepositional dative became frequently used and later fixed into the grammar frame of Middle English through the communication between English and French in discourse. And it is for this reason that there is an overt use of the prepositional dative to indicate indirect object in the English language, while German, as Germanic as it is, only employs synthetic dative in its discourse.

2.3.2.2 Focus system of the cases

Zubin (1979, p. 473) mentions two properties of human perception that are hypothesized to build up "a cognitive basis for the semantic substance SPEAKER'S FOCUS OF INTEREST in German": selective attention and the egocentric bias. These two properties are based on the fact that human beings, unlike computers, have a limited capacity of focus and memory, and naturally prefer to pay more attention to specific items. Because of this, one should now suppose either the speaker or the hearer is able to include all useful information, but one could expect that there are communicative strategies that the speaker can use to approach to his/her communicative goal. And the focus system is a device of the strategies, because it, along with its cognitive roots, is "of particular importance in investigating how speakers construct their discourse plans."

A quantitatively validated grammatical system of the German case forms is the system of degree of contribution (Zubin, 1977, 1978; cf. Diver, 1984; Garcia, 1975; Kirsner, 1977; Reid, 1977; Gildin, 1979). In this system, the case forms are interlocked in a system where the degree of contribution is signaled, a.k.a. how much does each case participates as the agent in the action. Nominative, subject of a verb and a sentence, is usually considered the agent of the action, with exceptions of passive sentences, and therefore signals HIGH CONTRIBUTION. Dative, indirect object of a sentence, is considered partly a participant and partly a receiver of an action, and signals MID CONTRIBUTION for partial contribution. And accusative, direct object of a sentence, does not have any active participation in an action, is a pure receiver of the action, and signals LOW CONTRIBUTION. Please note that the genitive case is not included in the system, due to the fact that it does not have a meaning that is related to contribution (Zubin, 1979, p. 474). Similarly, the genitive case too does not signal any meaning related to FOCUS and is also not included in the focus system.

A later postulated system of the case forms is called the focus system (Zubin, 1979, p. 474), which denotes which component of the sentence is of speaker's focus of interest in an action/event. It differs from the system of contribution not only in the way of meaning, but also in the way of degrees: there is no high *deixis* or low *deixis* in the system, but rather only FOCUS or NONFOCUS. Nominative is the only case form that is in the speaker's focus, and both dative and accusative are not in the speaker's focus of interest. Note that nominative, dative and accusative are considered within one sentence with respect to one action. One cannot compare an item in the nominative case in one sentence to another item in the accusative case in another sentence. Because on one hand, both items may be the same item in different actions and cannot be in the speaker's focus and not in the speaker's focus at the same time; and on the other hand, there is no point to talk about the speaker's focus in several actions: they are disconnected to each other and are not subject to each other's discourse importance. There is only one thing that accounts for the speaker's most interest at the discourse level in a particular action, other things being equal, with the rest of the participants of the action not at the center of the speaker's focus. And saying that the noun in the nominative case is at the "center" of the speaker's focus does not mean that other participants are not of the speaker's interest at all. All participants in an action will be of more or less importance to the speaker, as long as they still take part in the action. There is no absolute full focus implied by the nominative case. Also, there is no absolute lack of focus signaled by the dative and accusative case. This grammatical-semantic system instructs relatively more focus to the entity in the nominative case and relatively less focus to the entities in the dative and accusative case.

The two properties, selective attention and egocentric bias, which are mentioned at the beginning of the section, play an important role in selecting an entity and putting it in the nominative case. They suggest that "a human speaker is likely to select either (a) the entity most salient to him at a specific point in discourse; or (b) the entity most like himself—namely himself, or another human being—for encoding in the nominative case" (Zubin, 1979, p. 477). Therefore, according to psychological principles, a speaker would pay the most attention to himself, some less attention to the hearer, some less attention to other human participants in the action, some less attention to nonhuman participants and the least amount of attention to abstract entities in the action (cf. Clark and Begun, 1971; Frishberg, 1972; Creamer, 1974; Hawkinson & Hyman, 1974; Garcia, 1975; Kuno, 1976; Zubin, 1976).

2.3.2.2.1 Focus system in a relative clause

A relative clause is a subcategory of subordinate clauses. In a relative clause, the relative pronoun refers to an entity or a place in the main clause, is grammatically dependent on the referent and provides more information about the referent. A typological difference between German and English is that in a subordinate clause, including relative clause, the conjugated verb is usually placed at the end of the clause. A relative pronoun can either be in the nominative case, the genitive case, the dative case or the accusative case.

   2.33a) ...der Professor, der   seine Tochter nicht mag.
       ...ART professor ART.[NOM] his daughter not like. 3sg
     '... the professor, who his daughter does not like.'

2.33b) ...der   Professor, den   seine Tochter nicht mag.
       ...ART   professor   ART.[ACC]   his   daughter not   like. 3sg
       '...the professor, whom his daughter does not like.'

In both examples, the relative clauses provide more detailed specific information about the professor, not about his daughter. From the first example, we can infer that the professor is more salient to the speaker: "professor" is the topic of the relative clause, and we are provided with more identifying information. Admittedly, a more descriptive information is provided by the relative clause in the second example as well, but "professor" is no longer the "topic" of the sentence, i.e. "professor" will no longer be in the topic chain of the conversation and no further discussion will be carried out about him.

Based on the abovementioned properties, principles and attention hierarchy, in a relative clause, the relative pronoun is most likely in the nominative case, if the noun, which is modified by the relative clause, is "of the high salience of the relativized entity" and "most akin to himself [the speaker]" (Zubin, 1977, p. 479).

Zubin (1977, pp. 480—482) did a quantitative study of the frequency with which the more salient entity or the more ego-like entity is in the nominative case in relative clauses. He arrives at the result that in 96% of the clauses in the sample, either a more salient entity or a more ego-like entity, i.e. a "demonstrably focus-deserving entity" (1977, p. 481) has been placed in the nominative case. If both categories coincide, the relative pronoun is no doubt in the nominative case. This indirectly provides a validation for the case assignment in the focus system: nominative signals FOCUS, in contrast to dative and accusative, which signal NONFOCUS.

2.3.2.2.2 Frequency of mentioning and topic chain

An entity can be mentioned quite regularly in discourse. First it is important to find out whether it is a frequent mention or the topic of the discourse. If the entity is frequently mentioned but not the topic discussed in the discourse, then it is a frequent mention, not the topic of the sentence.

A more frequently mentioned entity is placed more in the nominative case than a rarely mentioned entity. Zubin (1979, pp. 483—488) uses the hypothesis "production strategy" to explain how discourse plans have an effect on syntactic and morphology selection. If an entity needs to be mentioned in the discourse now and then, the more frequent it is mentioned, the more prominent it is to the speaker, and thus more in the focus of the speaker and should rather be more placed in the nominative case. Zubin did a pilot questionnaire to test how native speakers tend to describe a more frequently mentioned entity in a paragraph. And as in the result, 72% of the native speakers placed the more frequently mentioned entity in the nominative case. This obviously supports the notion that a more frequently mentioned entity tends to be placed more in the nominative case.

If an entity is successively adjacently referred to in the discourse, this demonstrates that the entity is the topic of the discourse. A topic determines the nature of the discourse and how it is arranged. The closer the discourse is organized according to the topic, the more prominent the topic is rooted in the discourse, and thus the more frequently the speaker tends to mention it. Unlike Chinese, which tends to leave out the subject in a topic chain in discourse, German has to have a subject in every grammatically correct sentence. And if there is continuous mention of the topic, it tends to appear more frequently in the nominative case, as opposed to either the dative case or the accusative case (for quantitative validation, see Zubin, 1979, pp. 491—

495; cf. Li & Thompson, 1979, 1981).

2.3.2.2.3 Range of reference

There is a conflict in the Columbia School theory between Reid (1978) and Diver (1995), where the former posts that plural entities require more attention from the hearer in order to be clear with each individual item of the plurality, whereas according to Diver, it is necessary to pay more attention to a single item, because it is easier for the hearer to understand.

Zubin (1979, p. 491) put forward the idea of narrowing of focus, which states that a singular noun phrase (NP) tends to occur mostly in the nominative, a plural NP tends to be occur less frequently in the nominative case and NP series occur the least in the nominative case. This is psychologically logical (see the two properties), because it is impossible for human beings to multi-task and keep everything in mind. It may be possible for human beings to pay attention to a series of complicated various entities for a very short period of time, but with time the task will get harder, not to mention that each of the entities may change with time. Therefore, it is natural and logical for human beings to choose one from the plurality and focus on it. And the rest of the plurality will be paid less attention and will not be learned to great detail. In Zubin's quantitative validation, the proportion of a singular NP in the nominative in the discourse is 57%, a plural NP 44%, and NP series 17%. The percentage drop provides evidence for the theory of narrowing attention, which "appears both in the planning of individual clauses (the skewing to singular NPs in the nominative) and in the planning of discourse (the limitation of the nominative to relatively few different entities)" (1979, p. 491).

Chapter 3 The German Demonstratives

In a grammatical system where a referent is differentiated from other entities and then located, there are certain morphological units. These units are articles and demonstratives, and constitute signals that indicate meaning in a system of oppositions that exhaustively classifies the semantic field of DIFFERENTIATION (Diver, 1969; Kirsner, 1972). Given that the participants in a conversation are native speakers and that they use language most efficiently to communicate, one would expect that they tend to use coherent combinations rather than incoherent combinations to convey, with statistical significance, certain meanings more often in actual conversations or texts. Since certain meanings are semantically closer than other meanings in such a system, one could also expect, in general conversations and texts, that such meanings would be applied with statistical significance more often than other meanings whose messages are not quite appropriate. Therefore, it can be expected from such grammatical systems that the distribution of any combination of signal-meaning will be highly skewed.

In this chapter, I will validate the grammatical system of DIFFERENTIATION in the German language, in which articles and demonstratives are included. I will follow three steps in the validation process: first, I will validate definite articles and indefinite articles in a subsystem of NUMBER; second, I will validate definite articles and demonstratives in a subsystem of DIFFERENTIATION; and third, I will validate proximal and non-proximal demonstratives in a subsystem of FOCUS. In each of the steps, I will first provide all possible combinations of grammatical and lexical meanings and compare their efficiency in signaling the meaning in question, a.k.a. qualitative validation. In addition, I will provide an analysis of the nature of the message itself. Moreover, at the end of each analysis, I will supplement the qualitative study with a quantitative study.

Kirsner's study of the frequency of combinations of the English tenses and their accompanying lexical items referring to different time frames (1972, p. 72) supports Diver's theory (Diver, 1969). Diver claims that a combination of a grammatical meaning and a contradicting lexical meaning will occur at a low frequency, while a combination of grammatical meaning and a non-contradicting lexical meaning will occur at a relative high frequency. In Kirsner's (1972) study, the following examples are used to illustrate that the English present perfect and simple past tense occur more frequently with lexical items referring to past time, and far less frequently with lexical items denoting present or future tense.

3.1a) John has lectured in New York recently.

3.1b) *John has lectured in New York next month. (p. 72)

In this example, "has lectured" is a present perfect tense, which indicates that it is an event that is already completed and therefore requires a lexical meaning that refers to a time frame in the past. "Recently" refers to a time period in the past that is not far from the present, while "next month" denotes a time that has not yet come, a.k.a. the future. Therefore, "recently" fits in a sentence in the present perfect tense, while "next month" will confuse a hearer in such a sentence due to contradicting signals in the time expression.

3.2a) * John lectures in New York recently.

3.2b) John lectures in New York next month.

Here the verb form "lectures" signals the meaning NON-PAST and therefore needs a lexical meaning of NON-PAST with which it can co-occur. Hence, "next month" denotes a time frame in the future and is more acceptable to co-occur with the verb form "lectures" rather than the past tense denoting "next month." This and the above examples support the idea that "the non-occurrence of a signal-meaning complex results from direct semantic incompatibility" (Kirsner, 1972, p. 72).

Kirsner (1972) mentions two situations (in this study, there are three situations) where non-occurrence of a signal-meaning complex does not necessarily result from direct semantic incompatibility. One example that Kirsner cites is that there may be more than one meaning in the system that can transmit the message in question equally well. Each meaning can apply, as they do not contradict the existing lexical meanings in the sentence. For example in German:

3.3a)   Er   geh-t   morgen   nach   Deutschland.
        He   go-3sg   tomorrow to   Germany
        'He is going to Germany tomorrow.'

3.3b)   Er   wird   morgen   nach   Deutschland   gehen.
        He   will.3sg   tomorrow to   Germany   go
        'He will go to Germany tomorrow.'

In the case, both sentences can be used to indicate the fact that a male subject is going to Germany the day after today. In the first sentence, the verb form *geht* is a third person singular present tense conjugation. In the second sentence, the future tense *wird gehen* is used. The conjugations may differ from each other in meaning, but the final choice of either one does not result from direct semantic incompatibility, but instead from a particular meaning the speaker wants to signal or simply due to arbitrariness.

Another situation that needs to be taken into consideration, but will be excluded from the material used to validate the hypothesis, is when the message to be transmitted may "span the oppositions between the available meanings" (Kirsner, 1972, p. 73). In other words, lexically the meaning may move from one grammatical meaning to another grammatical meaning. Since it is not possible to have both forms in the same sentence, the choice of one does not mean that the other contradicts the present lexical meaning; rather, this choice is the result of arbitrariness. See the example below:

3.4) Er   leb-t   seit   zwei Jahren in   der   Stadt.
     He   live-3sg   since two   years   in   ART (the)   city
     'He has lived in the city for two years.'

In the example, the event of the male subject living in the city has started in the past, continues until now, and is still happening. The tense spans from the past to the present. In the German tense system, either the present or the present perfect can be employed to signal NON-PAST. The present tense is available to apply to an event in the present. However, in this sentence, only the present tense is used to apply to an event that starts in the past and continues on at least into the present. Again, this is not due to semantic incompatibility, but is instead arbitrary. In contrast, a sentence such as "He lives in the city since two years" is not possible. This provides evidence of the arbitrary nature of the process of choosing a semantic meaning from all possible meanings.

The third situation is when a speaker does not finish the sentence grammatically or does not "spell out all the details of the message" (Kirsner, 1972, p. 75). 'This' functions in a similar way to the Chinese zero anaphora, i.e. certain parts in a sentence can be left out when they can be inferred from the context. If this situation can be categorized as "communicative needs," another situation may be added to it: a particular grammatical or lexical meaning choice or a zero-anaphora of certain sentence parts results from communicative strategy. It is impossible to predict which part or which content of a sentence would be left out, since it is impossible to predict the joint platform of the speaker and the hearer, their backgrounds, and the communicative goal of the conversation. However, inconsistency between the meaning in question and the meaning literally proposed by the speaker is not due to semantic incompatibility. Therefore, when choosing examples and texts, extra-linguistic factors need to be considered first. The analysis of a certain sentence within a specific context is, therefore, tentative and contingent on the context itself. When any of the variables of a context change, it is plausible that the word choice or its meaning may change. As a result, "it will also be clear that, in beginning the investigation of a particular problem, the analyst may indeed be obliged to make plausible but unsupported working assumptions about the lexicon and the contribution to messages of other unanalyzed systems" (Kirsner, 1972, p. 77).

3.1 The System of NUMBER

When a grammatical system needs to be validated, it is necessary to validate all the components in the system. In the system of DIFFRENTIATION in this study, there are two categories: the articles and the demonstratives. Each category has two subcategories. The articles consist of definite articles and indefinite articles, *der*, *die*, *das* and their declined forms, and *ein* and its declined forms, respectively.

Furthermore, two kinds of demonstratives fall within the German demonstrative category: the proximal *dies-* and its declined forms, and the non-proximal *jen-* and its declined forms (see Chapter 2 for more possible forms of demonstratives). The following table provides the possible forms of German definite and indefinite articles.

ART	Possible Forms
der	*der, des, dem, den, die*
die	*die, der, den*
das	*das, des, dem, die, der, den*
kein	*kein, keine, keiner, keines, keinen, keinem*
ein	*ein, eine, einer, eines, einen, einem*

Table 3.1

In order to analyze a system of DIFFERENTIATION, it is first necessary to define the semantic meaning of a system of DIFFERENTIATION. In such a system, components signal DIFFERENTIATION to different degrees. When differentiation is made, it means the differentiated entity or place is one of the same kind. If differentiation is required but not made, it may because the entity or place in question is the only one of its kind. Finally, if differentiation is not required and not made, it indicates that there are several identical items of the same kind and that each of them would qualify to participate in the targeted action. Thus, one could conclude that it is essential to discuss whether an entity or a place is singular or plural before assigning them to the appropriate category. As such, in this section I will discuss German definite and indefinite articles, analyzing them in a system of NUMBER.

The semantic scope of the system of NUMBER spans from singular to plural (here non-existence is categorized as singular, since "none of something" can be paraphrased as "not a single something") and deals with the quantity of the targeted entity or place. If the entity or place is singular, it means that "the lexical item in question is to be taken as a single thing"; if plural, the entity or place is "to be taken as any number of entities other than one, i. e. as more than just a single thing" (Kirsner, 1972, p. 78). In this study, I will employ Kirsner's terms used for the two categories in the system: ONE and OTHER. While a singular noun stays in its uninflected form and is unmarked to signal the semantic meaning ONE, a plural noun will be marked by its unique plural affix.

According to Köpke (1988, 1998), there are several plural affixes that are possible for the German nouns (cf. 1988, p. 307):

plural-morpheme	Examples		
	noun (singular)	noun (plural)	English translation
-e	Fisch, MASC	Fische	fish
-en	Tür, FEM	Türen	door
-er	Kind, NEUT	Kinder	child
-s	Auto, NEUT	Autos	car
umlaut	Bruder, MASC	Brüder	brother
umlaut+-e	Sohn, MASC	Söhne	son
umlaut+-er	Volk, NEUT	Völker	people
-n	Decke, FEM	Decken	cover
-∅	Fenster, NEUT	Fenster	window

Table 3.2

Since there are several plural morphemes (PM) in the table and it is difficult and confusing to list them all in the hierarchy of system of NUMBER, in the following graphs, PM will be used to stand for plural morphemes. Therefore, the German system of NUMBER can be graphed as follows:

$$\text{NUMBER} \begin{cases} \text{-}\emptyset\text{: ONE} \\ \text{-PM: OTHER} \end{cases}$$

Figure 3.1

3.1.1 Quantity specified by a numeral

In the German grammatical system of NUMBER, the combinations that signal ONE and OTHER are fairly straightforward when mentioning the exact quantity of the referred entity or place: for ONE, number+noun+-∅; for OTHER, number+noun+-PM. Obviously, in order to signal one, the number should be one, and not any numbers other than one (the number zero, as discussed before, is included in the category of ONE). In contrast, to employ the latter combination to signal OTHER, one needs to have a number that is greater than one. The occurrence of the number one with a noun with PM would result in a semantic contradiction and confuse the hearer in the sense that the hearer would not be able to decide whether a singular or a plural entity is being referred to. For example:

3.5a) Meine   Familie   ha-t   ein   Haus.
       my   family   have-3sg   ART (one) house
       'My family has a house.'

3.5b) *Meine   Familie   ha-t   ein   Häuser.
       my   family   have-3sg   ART (one) houses
       *'My family has a houses.'

3.5c) Meine   Familie   ha-t   drei   Häuser.
       my   family   have-3sg   three   houses
       'My family has three houses.'

3.5d) *Meine   Familie   ha-t   drei   Haus.
       my   family   have-3sg   three   house
       *'My family has three house.'

In the examples, an attempt is made to test for the co-ocurance of a quantity (either ONE or OTHER) and a noun (either singular, without PM, or plural, then with PM). It proves that direct semantic incompatibility will result in semantic confusion and, thus, in low frequency in the co-occurrence (in the sense that a noun without PM does not occur with a number more than one frequently). Similarly, a noun with PM that signals OTHER rather than ONE does not frequently occur with a number that denotes ONE.

There are two facts that may account for the strict number-PM agreement in the German language. One fact is that there is no fluid subject-verb agreement, nor are there any "collective" nouns that signal OTHER while in their singular forms in the German language. For example:

    3.6a)   Meine   Familie   reis-t   nächstes   Jahr   nach   Italien.
              my   family   travel-3sg   next   year   to   Italy
            'My family will travel to Italy next year.'

    3.6b)   *Meine   Familie   seh-en   gerne   fern.
              my   family   watch-pl   like   TV
            *'My family like to watch TV.'

As we can see, the German noun *Familie* means "family" or "family members" and when it stands by itself, i.e. it does not have any PM, in the subject position of a sentence, it requires a third person singular conjugation of the verb. In contrast, the English word for *Familie*, family, can be either a singular noun meaning, simply, "family" or has a lexically plural noun reading meaning "family members." As such, the English "family" can be followed by either a third person singular conjugated verb or a plural conjugated verb.

There are, of course, German nouns that have a collective meaning. In these cases, affixes such as *Ge-*, *-werk* and so forth can signal this collective meaning, as in the nouns *Gebirge* 'group of mountains' and *Schuhwerk* 'footwear.' Notice that both words are singular and require a third person singular conjugation of verbs.

Another factor to consider is the way that German compounds are formed according to German morphology. Preece and Schulze (1999), in their book on modern German grammar, suggest that there is no standard "one-size-fits-all" rule for compound formation. In some cases, a genitive form of the first element of the compound will be used to attach it to the second part. Sometimes, the plural form of the first element will be used to combine words together. Finally, sometimes there is zero linkage bonding the first part and the second part together. For example:

 3.7a) die Tagesschau

   'review of the day' [formation: Tag-es-Schau, GEN of "Tag" 'day']

 3.7b) der Stundenplan

   'study grid/daily schedule' [formation: Stunde-n-Plan, PM of "*Stunde*" 'hour']

 3.7c) die Telefonnummer

   'phone number' [formation: Telefon-Ø-Nummer, zero linkage]

Despite the fact that there are different methods of forming a compound and there is no one-applies-to-all standard rule for choosing certain morphemes as linkage words that connect both parts of a compound; there is, however, a rule for a subcategory of compounds that are formed by two nouns with the first part in its plural form. This rule states that the first noun in its plural form always retains the plural form in a compound if it is not the head of the compound, as in the second compound in the above example: *Stunden* is the plural form of *Stunde* 'hour.' For instance, if one plans a day and then has a schedule for the whole day, it is definitely not based only on a specific hour of the day, but based on the whole day: twenty-four hours. Here *Stunden* takes the form of plurality and marks the plurality of the first part of the compound. Other examples can be found throughout the German language. I will illustrate another example here in addition to *Stundenplan*:

3.8a) das Dreiländereck

'joint point of three countries' [formation: drei-Land-umlaut + er-Eck, PM of "Land" 'country,' 'land']

3.8b) * das Dreilandeck

In addition, when using a noun to modify another by putting it right before the noun modified, if the noun signals a meaning of plurality, the noun should appear in its plural form. For example:

3.9a) ein Vier-Stunden-Unterricht

'a four hour class'

3.9b) ein Drei-Monate-Studium

'a three month study'

From the English translation of the abovementioned examples, one could conclude that German departs from English with regard to the formation of compounds. If the first part, the modifying part, has a meaning of plurality, the German compounds tend to keep the plural form, while in English, the plural form gets dropped and replaced by the singular form of the noun. In other words, German compounds show the plurality of the modifying component, if any; in contrast, an English compound, the plurality of the modifying part, if any, however, is not marked by its PM.

3.1.2 The nature of the nouns

In the Germanic languages, a noun, if countable, should have two forms: a singular form and a plural form. A countable noun is an entity that can be separated into identical items and modified by numerals. An uncountable noun is an entity that cannot be separated into disparate elements, nor can it be modified by numerals or classifiers. Since an uncountable noun cannot be counted, it takes neither a singular form nor a plural form, and therefore does not signal the meaning ONE if it is not marked by a PM for plurality.

Given that all the countable nouns have a singular form and a plural form, they can either take the singular form -Ø to signal ONE or the plural form -PM to signal OTHER freely in the system. Generally speaking, both forms should occur with similar frequency, since either form is available when needed in the context. But there are always certain nouns that appear more frequently in one form and less frequently in the other form. It is understandable that some nouns are rarely seen in the plural form, i.e. with their PM, to signal the meaning OTHER, since they are commonly seen as a single item and do not really exist in a collection. For example, unique entities, if in their plural forms, will give the hearer contradicting signals: the lexical meaning signals that the noun is a unique entity in the world, a.k.a. the only one of its kind, while the grammatical meaning signals that there is more than one item of the same kind, i.e. an entity that is non-unique. A good example of this is *die Sonne* 'sun,' which is a concept unique to the world. However, while the plural form *Sonnen* 'suns,' exists, it does not make sense because there is only one sun in existence and there are no other suns to use as a point of reference. Therefore, *Sonnen* can only exist in very specific situations where it is used for specific or metaphoric purposes, but can not refer to actual referents in the world. In this case, one could expect *Sonnen* 'suns' to appear with very low frequency in actual conversations or texts. ① On the other hand, there are certain German nouns that frequently appear in the plural form, but not in the singular form. For example, *Geschwister* 'siblings,' meaning brothers and sisters, does not have a singular form, since the word itself already bears plurality in its lexical meaning: brother and sister. Even just one set of "brother and sister" includes two individuals. Therefore, it is always the case that *Geschwister* co-occurs with a low-to-no frequency with the meaning of ONE.

Other examples that favor the singular form over the plural form are those of a discipline. A discipline is usually seen as a theory and its practice as a set in a whole. If one applies the plural to it, it does not mean that there are several such disciplines, but rather different theories within the same discipline. *Philosophie* 'philosophy,' for instance, means the discipline dealing with general and fundamental problems on earth, such as reality, value, and minds. The plural form *Philosophien* does not mean the discipline itself anymore, but different theories within the discipline of philosophy, as in: *Vergleich mit anderen Philosophien* 'compare to other philosophies,' ② in which the author, say, compares Buddhism to other religious theories.

When using the word *Philosophie*, however, one would expect that it refers to the discipline rather than different philosophic theories. Therefore, *Philosophie* in its singular form is usually regarded as a set of theories and practices, rather than subfields of philosophy. In other words, "one would expect the totality of a given field of inquiry (all

---

① Of course, *Sonnen* may appear in many cases but it is not a plural form. It is spelled this way when forming compounds with many feminine nouns that end in an -*e*.

② Example from "*Buddhistische Philosophie*," Wikipedia, last modified February 21 2013, http://de. wikipedia. org/wiki/Buddhistische _ Philosophie # Vergleich _ mit _ anderen _ Philosophien.

instances of what the discipline is) to be regarded more fittingly as ONE than as OTHER, more properly a whole, a unit, than a collection of more than one distinguishable thing" (Kirsner, 1972, p. 84). In contrast, a person who is practicing the discipline of philosophy, a *Philosoph* 'philosopher,' is not a unique noun, nor a discipline, and should be able to co-occur with both the singular form -Ø and the plural form -*en* freely. In order to demonstrate this, I counted the instances of both words *Philosophie* 'philosophy' and *Philosoph* 'philosopher' in my own mini-corpus, which has about 320,000 German words in total, consisting of about 80,000 words from news and reports, 140,000 words from novels and stories, and 100,000 words from academic articles. I have compiled this mini-corpus in the hope that the result can be applied to a general German-speaking environment. The results are as follows:

	+-Ø	+-PM
Philosophie	6	0
Philosoph	1	1

Table 3.3

In the table, there are six instances of the singular form of *Philosophie* and no instance of its plural form. In contrast, there is one instance of the singular form of *Philosoph* and one instance of its plural. This evidence supports the above statement that the word *Philosophie* is more commonly regarded as a discipline rather than as different theories within the discipline.

There are nouns that do not have their own plural forms and are either attached to a word or receive a prefix that lends meaning to them. For example, *Rat* 'advice; suggestion' is a masculine noun, which does not have its own plural form. When one needs a German word that means 'suggestions' or 'advices,' *Rat* becomes *Ratschläge* 'suggestions.' In order to co-occur with the meaning OTHER, the word *Rat* is not marked by a PM, but by another word *Schlag* with its PM. Additionally, the noun *Wasser* 'water' is an uncountable noun and can only be preceded by certain classifiers, as in the NP *ein Glas Wasser* 'a glass of water.' When trying to form its plural to have a meaning similar to the English 'waters,' the word *Wasser* changes to *Gewässer* 'waters; stretch of water.' Though possessing a plural meaning, the word itself is a singular noun. For more information on this topic, see the above discussion of the prefix *Ge-*.

Similarly, there are words in the German language that are singular but whose cognates in English are in the plural form. See the table below:

German		English	
Brille	singular	glasses	plural
Hose	singular	pants, trousers	plural
Schere	singular	scissors	plural

Table 3.4

Note that this table does not suggest that German words such as *Brille*, *Hose*, and *Schere* do not possess a PM or do not co-occur with the meaning OTHER. Each of these words does have its PM; here they all have the PM *-n*. When they co-occur with their PMs, they mean 'more than one pair of glasses,' 'several pairs of pants' and 'some pairs of scissors,' respectively.

Conversely, there are German words that are plural but have singular English cognates. As mentioned before, *Geschwister* 'siblings' is always plural, while its English cognate "sibling" can have both singular and plural forms. Similarly, in English, one can use the word "parent" to either refer to his/her mother or father, but in German, the noun *Eltern* 'parents' does not have a singular form or reading.

Kirsner (1972) calls this the concept of the spanned opposition (pp. 64—68, 88). Although German and English are two very different languages (see Chapter 2), each of them has a system of NUMBER of the noun, where an exhaustive classification of all possible numbers of entities arranges them into two categories: ONE and OTHER. Because they are different languages, it is possible that native speakers of German and native speakers of English view certain entities from different perspectives. For example, when viewing a pair of pants, a German speaker may view it as a whole, as a single entity that can be put on as a bottom wear, while an English speaker may focus on the two trouser legs, and thus consider it plural. That said, not all nouns would cause confusion in classifying a noun's NUMBER. Most objects are clear and unambiguous, as in table, bed, book, and so forth. Only if a noun's numerical status is not clear enough, a speaker from one culture may conceive it as a whole, while a speaker from another culture may focus on the fact that it is composed of several identical parts. The particular choice to signal ONE or OTHER is indeed unpredictable and arbitrary and may provide further evidence for language determinism (see Chapter 5).

As a conclusion to this section, there are words in German that only co-occur with either the meaning of ONE or the meaning of OTHER, a.k.a. singular *tantum* and plural *tantum*. Because those nouns do not have the opposition of ONE and OTHER and always only co-occur with either ONE or OTHER, they should be excluded from the corpus in the qualitative and quantitative validation.

3.1.3 Noun as classifiers

Kirsner (1972) notes that "grammars of Modern Standard Dutch typically point out that with nouns of quantity, measure, weight, money, and time preceded by a cardinal number greater than one, the singular is used 'even though the word has a plural meaning,'①" such as *uur* 'hour' in an NP such as *drie uur slaap* 'three hours of sleep' (p. 90). However, this is not always the case in the German language.

I will start with nouns to classify different categories of measure, since quantity is a bigger frame compared to measure, weight, money, and time. Quantity is a vague word not as well specified as the other four: by mentioning the quantity of an entity, one still does not have any idea of what kind of classification it takes or how the entities are itemized. For example, if one wants to itemize water, despite the fact that water is not countable, one has the option to itemize water into drops, cups, glasses, jars, or bottles etc.. Therefore, I will refrain from discussing quantity for now, and will address this issue at the end of this section.

A noun that can be used as a measure includes possibilities like measure of length, such as *Meter* 'meter'; measure of temperature, such as *Grad* 'degree'; measure of calorie, such as *Kalorie* 'calorie'; and so on.

3.10a) Es   ist   heute   vier   Grad-∅   Celsius.
        It   be.3sg   today   four   degree-SG   celsius
        'It is four degrees today.'

3.10b) *Es   ist   heute   vier   Grad-e   Celsius.
        It   be.3sg   today   four   degree-PM   celsius

---

① As cited in Rijpma and Schuringa, 1962, p.167.

In the above example, the only difference between sentence *a* and sentence *b* is that in sentence *a*, the word *Grad* is in the singular form, while in sentence *b*, it is in the plural form. Sentence *b* demonstrates that when *Grad* 'degree' is preceded by a cardinal number and used to refer to temperature, one should choose the singular form *Grad* instead of the plural *Grade*, even though 'degrees' indicates a plural meaning, as shown by the PM -s in the English translation 'degree-s.' However,

  3.11a) Eine Tafel Schokolade ha-t 500 Kalorie-n.
      ART (one) bar chocolate have-3sg 500 calorie-PM
      'A bar of chocolate contains 500 calories.'
  3.11b) *Eine Tafel Schokolade ha-t 500 Kalorie-Ø.
      ART (one) bar chocolate have-3sg 500 calorie-SG

Unlike *Grad*, which takes its singular form to signal a plural meaning, *Kalorie* 'calorie' takes the plural form and has a plural meaning.

  In the classification of weight, there are options such as *Gramm* 'gram' and *Tonne* 'ton.'

  3.12a) Ich brauch-e 250 Gramm-Ø Fleisch.
      I need-1sg 250 gram-SG meat
      'I need 250 grams of meat.'
  3.12b) *Ich brauch-e 250 Gramm-e Fleisch.
      I need-1sg 250 gram-PM meat

In this example a German speaker would choose to use the singular form of *Gramm* 'gram' despite the fact that the meaning is plural (250 grams is indeed more than ONE). But when referring to a much heavier object and talking about its weight, one needs to use the plural form of *Tonne* 'ton' when the object exceeds one ton:

  3.13a) Unbekannte hatt-en zwei Tonne-n Metall gestohlen.①
      unknown have.past-pl two ton-PM metal steal.pp

---

  ① Über zwei Tonnen Metall gestohlen. (2013, February 23)

'Unknown people had stolen two tons of metal.'

3.13b) *Unbekannte   hatt-en   zwei   Tonne-Ø   Metall   gestohlen.
        unknown   have.past-pl   two   ton-SG   metal   steal.pp

As for money, most of the currencies are masculine nouns in German, such as *Franken* 'franc,' *Euro* 'euro,' *Pfennig* 'penny,' and so forth, while the old German currency *Mark* 'mark' itself is feminine. The next example shows that only the singular form of either *Euro* or *Mark* can be used, when referring to money as a measuring unit.

3.14a) Das   Buch   kost-et   drei   Euro-Ø.
        ART (the)   book   cost-3sg   three   euro-SG
        'The book costs three euros.'

3.14b) Das   Buch   kost-et   drei   Mark-Ø.
        ART (the)   book   cost-3sg   three   mark-SG
        'The book costs three marks.'

3.14c) *Das   Buch   kost-et   drei   Märk-er.
        ART (the)   book   cost-3sg   three   mark-PM

Here it is clear that any measure of currency, no matter its gender in German, does not use the plural form to signal plural, but rather co-occurs with the singular form -Ø to mean plurality. One exception is:

3.14d) Ich   hab-e   nur   noch   ein   paar   Märk-er[①].
        I   have-1sg   only   still   a   some   mark-PM
        'I only have few marks left.'

In this specific example, *Mark* 'mark' takes its plural form and means several marks. One explanation for the phenomenon is that *Mark* is not preceded by a cardinal number in the sentence and therefore does not fall into the category of classifiers. Another additional possible explanation is that this sentence is extremely colloquial and should not be taken into

---

① Example from *De Han Ci Dian* [The German-Chinese Dictionary]. (1982, p.808)

account. The reason it should be disregarded is that there are stylistic concerns present in actual conversation: the use of the plural form is used ironically—that is, to indicate that the speaker does not have much money left and wants to impress this point upon his/her audience. In this way, the plural form is used as a means to exaggerate the amount.

In the category of time, I have already discussed the issue of *Stunde* 'hour' which co-occurs with the meaning OTHER when the time span exceeds one hour. Here I will provide two more examples, one with *Jahr* 'year,' a neuter noun, and the other one with *Monat* 'month,' a masculine noun.

3.15a) Der   Schwarzfahrer   muss   drei   Jahr-e   in   Haft[①].
       ART (the) fare dodger   must.3sg   three year-PM in   custody
       'The fare dodger must be put in custody for three years.'

3.15b) *Der   Schwarzfahrer   muss   drei   Jahr-Ø   in   Haft.
       ART (the) fare dodger   must.3sg   three year-SG in   custody

3.16a) Ihr   drei   Monat-e   altes Baby
       your   three month-PM   old   baby
       'your three month old baby'

3.16b) *Ihr   drei   Monat-Ø   altes Baby
       your   three month-SG   old   baby

As these examples demonstrate, time-related measure words, either masculine, feminine or neuter, use their plural form if preceded by cardinal numbers.

Finally, if a noun indicates the quantity of an object, it has a broader frame of measurement than weight, money and time, due to the fact that the category of the measure is not specified. In my effort to include all the possible instances within several examples, I have

---

① 16-jähriger Schwarzfahrer muss fast drei Jahre in Haft. (2103, January 29)

selected the following classifiers: *Stück* 'piece,' as a measure of solid; *Flasche* 'bottle,' as a measure of liquid; and *Glas* 'glass,' for exceptions.

    3.17a)   Er   kauf-t   zwei   Stück-Ø   Kuchen.
                  he   buy-3sg   two   piece-SG   cake
                  'He buys two pieces of cake.'

    3.17b)   *Er   kauf-t   zwei   Stück-e   Kuchen.
                  he   buy-3sg   two   piece-PM   cake

In the example, *Kuchen* 'cake' is an uncountable noun, except for the meaning of "cupcake," where it is countable. Both sentences show the meaning of plurality of the object "cake." But sentence *b* however, does not exist in actual German texts, where *Stück* 'piece' is signaling plurality in its plural form.

    3.18a)   Sie   trink-t   zwei   Flasche-n   Wein.
                  she   drink-3sg two   bottle-PM   wine
                  'She drinks two bottles of wine.'

    3.18b)   *Sie   trink-t   zwei   Flasche-Ø   Wein.
                  she   drink-3sg two   bottle-SG   wine

As seen in the example, *Flasche* 'bottle' needs to be in its plural form in order to co-occur with the meaning OTHER.

    3.19a)   Ich   möcht-e   gern   zwei   Glas   Wein.
                  I   would like-1sg like   two   glass-SG wine
                  'I would like to have two glasses of wine.'

    3.19b)   Neben   ihnen   steh-en   zwei   Gläs-er   Bier.
                  next to them   stand-pl   two   glass-PM beer
                  'Next to them stand two glasses of beer.'

(Di et al., 2012, p.191)

In the second sentence of this example, the plural form of *Glas* 'glass' is used to indicate the existence of two full glasses of beer on the table. One might argue that the NP *zwei Gläser Bier* 'two glasses of beer' has a different meaning as the NP *zwei Glas Bier* 'two glasses of beer'; that is, the former NP refers to the glasses rather than the beer in them, while the latter NP clearly refers to the beer, which is contained in the glasses. Admittedly, *Glas* in the former NP is more an object than a classifier. But both the singular form and the plural form of *Glas* 'glass' would work in the first sentence, with a different indication of how the wine is ordered and served. ① If there are two guests who each order one glass of wine, they will order *zwei Gläser Wein* 'two glasses of wine' with *Glas* in the plural form. But when one guest orders two glasses of wine for him/herself one after the other, he/she will order *zwei Glas Wein* 'two glasses of wine' with *Glas* in the singular form. A possible explanation is that if the two glasses of wine are required to be itemized by object boundaries, the plural form is needed to split the boundaries of the entities; if the two glasses of wine do not need to be itemized, for instance if they are consumed by the same person, the singular form is used.

To conclude this section, based on the examples I have analyzed, when a feminine noun is used as a classifier, and if it is preceded by a cardinal number and signals OTHER, it will most likely be in its plural form (with the exception of *Mark* 'mark'). If a masculine or neuter noun is used as a classifier, and if it is preceded by a cardinal number and signals OTHER, it will most likely be in its singular form. Although there are possible explanations for the exceptions and unusual usages, it is better to conclude that the assignment of NUMBER is arbitrary and not based on logic.

---

① I consulted three native German speakers at work who corroborated this usage.

3.2 The System of DIFFERENTIATION

In the German grammar, articles, including the definite articles *der*, *die*, *das* and their inflected forms, and the indefinite articles *ein*, *kein* and their inflected forms, "signal meanings exhaustively classifying the substance degree of differentiation from others" (Kirsner, 1972, p. 112). In other words, "degree of differentiation" suggests the use of articles to signal whether an entity or a place NEEDS to be differentiated from other entities or places and whether it IS differentiated.

Therefore, two questions need to be answered when considering the use of articles. First, is differentiation required? And second, is differentiation made? Three meanings are automatically created through the different combinations of the answers to the questions: the first meaning would be DIFFERENTIATION NOT REQUIRED, which is a rejection of the first question, and if so, there is no need to ask the second question. This meaning implies that the lexical item refers to an entity or a place that does not have to be differentiated from all other entities or places. The second meaning is DIFFERENTIATION REQUIRED BUT NOT MADE, which implies a positive answer to the first question and a negative answer to the second question, which means the lexical item refers to an entity or a place that needs to be differentiated from all other entities or places but is not differentiated. The third meaning can be DIFFERENTIATION REQUIRED AND MADE, indicating that the answers to both questions are positive, meaning that the lexical item refers to an entity or place that needs to be and is differentiated from all other entities or places. Thus, we arrive at the system illustrated below:

$$\text{Differentiation} \begin{cases} \text{Differentiation Not Required} \\ \text{Differentiation Required} \begin{cases} \text{Differentiation Made} \\ \text{Differentiation Not Made} \end{cases} \end{cases}$$

Figure 3.2

This figure shows that there are several degrees of differentiation, which can be achieved according to the speaker's wish. In any case, it should be noted that the degree of differentiation is related to the substance of number, meaning that if anything is to be differentiated, it cannot be only the thing by itself. There should be at least one other entity, from which the entity in question is being differentiated. Otherwise, the entity or place in question is considered a unique entity and therefore is automatically differentiated.

Kirsner (1972) claims that "a lexical item refers to a plurality of entities and implies that the entities are separate things requiring differentiation from others, even if such differentiation is not achieved," and further states that "the meaning OTHER of the system of number, raising as it does the issue of sufficient differentiation, would not readily combine with the meaning DIFFERENTIATION NOT REQUIRED" (pp. 113, 114).

Logically, the plural form of a noun indicates that there are several separate independent identical items of the same entity. If one is able to point them out, it automatically means that they are already differentiated from other items; otherwise it is not possible to make clear "which" entities belong to the collection. Being differentiated, however, does not necessarily mean that they are itemized, which depends on whether the collection is seen as separate individualized items and each of them is identified and requires differentiation.[1] Depending on one's point of view, the speaker may see a collection of the same entities as a whole, or as individual items. If one views the collection from a totality's point of view, one would not differentiate each item of the collection, but rather the collection as a whole. If one considers each item of the collection, each component of the collection is thus differentiated from other items. Therefore, the first situation conveys the meaning of DIFFERENTIATION REQUIRED AND NOT MADE, while the second situation signals DIFFERENTIATION REQUIRED AND MADE. See the following example:

3.20a) He has been living there for the past three decades.
3.20b) Three decades is a long period of time.

Clearly, the three decades in sentence 3.20a are differentiated, since one would know when each of these decades occurred. In contrast, the three decades in sentence 3.20b are not differentiated, since here the decades denote a general and unspecified period of time (i.e. one would not be able to discern the three specific decades to which the sentence refers).

When adding the system of NUMBER to the system of DIFFERENTIATION, we should be able to see the semantic interlock of the two systems and the way in which signals in both systems contribute to the form-meaning relationships of each system. The following table demonstrates the semantic interlock of the two systems in the German language (cf. Kirsner, 1972, p. 114):

---

[1] cf. Reid (1977), Diver (1995) on whether high *deixis* is put on singular or plural nouns.

		NUMBER	
		ONE	OTHER
DIFFEREN-TIATION	Not Required	Ø+____-Ø	N/A
	Required, Not Made	ein-①+____-Ø	Ø+____-PM
	Required, Made	d-②+____-Ø	d-+____-PM

Table 3.5

According to the table, there are five meanings that need to be discussed in this section: a singular entity that is not required to be differentiated; a singular entity that is required to be differentiated but is not differentiated; a plural entity that is required to be differentiated but is not differentiated; a singular entity that needs to be differentiated and is differentiated; and finally, a plural entity that needs to be differentiated and is differentiated. By using the noun *Student* 'student,' the five meanings can be illustrated by the following examples:

3.21a) Er   ist   Student-Ø.
        he   be.3sg   student-SG
        'He is a student.'

3.21b) Ein   Student-Ø   geh-t   aus   dem   Zimmer.
        ART (one) student-SG   go-3sg   out of   ART (the)   room
        'A students goes out of the room.'

3.21c) Da   komm-en   Student-en   ans   Fenster.
        there   come-pl   student-PM   to DM (the)   window
        'There come students to the window.'

3.21d) Der   Student-Ø   kenn-t   niemand   hier.
        ART (the) student-SG   know-3sg no one   here
        'The student does not know anyone here.'

---

① Here "ein-" refers to the indefinite article *ein* and its inflected forms, see Chapter 2.

② Here "d-" refers to the definite articles such as *der*, *die*, *das*, and their inflected forms, see Chapter 2.

3.21e) Sie   ha-t   die   Student-en   gern.
       she   have-3sg   ART (the)   student-pl   like
       'She likes the students.'

In the following discussions, I will analyze each example and the meaning it illustrates.

3.2.1 The signal Ø+____-Ø and its meaning

In example 3.21a, we know that the subject is a student from a vocational perspective. The noun *Student* 'student' does not have any articles or demonstratives preceding it, and is co-occurring with the meaning ONE. According to the signal Ø+____-Ø, the referent of the lexical item *Student* is not required to be differentiated from the other potential pool of *Student*, i.e. "without depicting the referent... as a distinct entity of some kind" (Kirsner, 1972, p. 161). As a contrast, consider the following examples:

3.22a) * Er   ist   ein   Student-Ø.
         he   be.3sg   ART (one)   student-SG
       'He is a student.'

3.22b) Er   ist   der   Student-Ø.
        he   be.3sg   ART (the)   student-SG
       'He is the student.'

The difference between sentence 3.21a and the above two sentences is that sentence 3.21a does not require differentiation, while these two sentences do. In sentence 3.21a, any student from the kind would work because no differentiation is required. Therefore, *Student* 'student' in the sentence actually refers to the general characteristics that make anyone a student, such as going to school and taking exams. As in the example 3.22a, the signal ein-+____-Ø has the meaning of DIFFERNTIATION REQUIRED AND NOT MADE. As such, the student in this example is one of the students that needs more information following it to differentiate the student from other students[①]. Furthermore, in sentence 3.22b, the meaning signaled is DIFFERENTIATION REQUIRED AND MADE; this means that the subject, a male individual, is a known student, which is previously specified in the context and may be followed by repeated information and new information. The opposition between meanings can be illustrated by the following table:

Signal	Need Information?	Information location
Ø+___-Ø	no	N/A
ein-+___-Ø	yes	After
d-+___-Ø	yes	before, can have additional after

Table 3.6

Another way to verify the opposition among meanings is to test the subject-verb agreement in different combinations of meanings in sentences:

3.23a)　Peter　und　Martin　sind　Student-Ø.
　　　　 Peter　and　Martin　be.pl　student-SG
　　　　 'Peter and Martin are students.'

3.23b)　*Peter　und　Martin　sind　ein　　　Student-Ø.
　　　　 Peter　and　Martin　be.pl　ART (one)　student-SG
　　　　 '*Peter and Martin are a student.'

3.23c)　Peter　und　Martin　sind　Student-en.
　　　　 Peter　and　Martin　be.pl　student-PM
　　　　 'Peter and Martin are students.'

---

① This example, however, is perfect by itself. It is better to form the sentence as *Er ist ein guter Student* 'He is a good student,' otherwise the sentence may occur with very low frequence (for explanations please refer to following examples and sections).

3.23d) *Peter und Martin sind der Student-Ø.
Peter and Martin be.pl ART (the) student-SG
'*Peter and Martin are the student.'

3.23e) Peter und Martin sind die Student-en.
Peter and Martin be.pl ART (the) student-PM
'Peter and Martin are students.'

In the above example, sentence 3.23d clearly provides contradicting information in the sense that Peter and Martin are two people, while the part with which they are equated is a differentiated singular non-collective entity. It is impossible for both Peter and Martin to be the student at the same time. Similarly, in sentence 3.23b, it is also not possible for Peter and Martin to be a student that will be differentiated at the same time, in the sense that Peter and Martin signal the meaning of OTHER, while the signal ein-+____-Ø has the meaning of ONE.

However, though *Student* 'student' signals the meaning of ONE in sentence 3.23a, in contradiction with the meaning OTHER signaled by the subject Peter and Martin, the sentence is not grammatically wrong. As discussed before, Ø+____-Ø contains the meaning of features that any item of its kind would possess, since *Student* does not need to be differentiated. Moreover, if a differentiation is not needed, the singular-plural opposition, which depends on the differentiation, is no longer valid. And therefore, the form Ø+____-Ø "takes no cognizance of the distinction" between singular and plural and this fact, then, supports the claim that Ø+____-Ø signals DIFFERENTIATION NOT REQUIRED.

I would like to use another example as supporting evidence:

3.24) Als Student-Ø muss-t ihr hart arbeiten.
as student-SG must-2pl you guys hard work.inf
'As students you need to work hard.'

Again the entity *Student* in this sentence signals the meaning

DIFFERENTIATION NOT REQUIRED with its form Ø+____-Ø. The referent that Student denotes to is *ihr* 'you guys' in the sentence, which is a second person plural pronoun. This, too, provides evidence that Ø+____-Ø "may well be used in reference to a plurality" (Kirsner, 1972, p. 162)①.

However, general characteristics are not the only explanation or limitation of using the signal Ø+____-Ø. There are lexical limitations we need to include in the analysis. In the previous example, *Student* 'student' is a very general lawful profession: a person studying at a school. If a profession is characterized as unlawful, as *Dieb* 'thief' is in the following example, it cannot co-exist with the form Ø+____-Ø.

3.25a)　　＊Er　　ist　　　　Dieb-Ø.

　　　　　　he　　be.3sg　　thief-sg

3.25b)　　Er　　ist　　　　ein　　　　　Dieb.

　　　　　he　　be.3sg　　ART (one)　thief

　　　　　'He is a thief.'

Another lexical limitation is that if the noun already shows its characteristics in the spelling, it is mostly impossible to co-occur with Ø+____-Ø because the grammatical meaning of the signal Ø+____-Ø is DIFFERENTIATION NOT REQUIRED. This contradicts the lexical meaning with specific characteristics, which is to some extent already differentiated from other entities of the same kind by its characteristics.

3.26a)　　＊Er　　ist　　　　Taugenichts.

　　　　　　he　　be.3sg　　good-for-nothing

---

① This may provide a validation for the capitalization and so-called "nominalization" of some originally separate verbs, such as *Auto fahren* 'to drive a car,' originally written and recognized as *auto/fahren*. Since *Auto* is part of the verb, it is understandable that *Auto* 'car' is not differentiated nor required to be differentiated, because *Auto fahren* is an action, designating to the general auto-driving action, not to a subject, not to mention to which subject.

3.26b) Er   ist   ein   Taugenichts.
        he   be.3sg   ART (one)   good-for-nothing
        'He is worthless.'
3.27a) Sie ist   Empfangsdame.
        she be.3sg   receptionist.FEM
3.27b) *Sie ist   eine   Empfangsdame.
        she be.3sg   ART (one)   receptionist.FEM
        'She is a receptionist.'
3.27c) *Sie ist   Empfangsmädchen.
        she be.3sg   reception girl
3.27d) Sie ist   ein   Empfangsmädchen.
        she be.3sg   ART (one)   reception girl
        'She is a reception girl.'

In light of these examples, we can surmise that ∅ + ____ -∅ does not work with the lexical items such as *Taugenicht* 'a worthless person' and *Empfangsmädchen* 'reception girl.' The common feature of both lexical words is that they both add characteristics or features to the general semantic meaning. For example, *Taugenicht* adds the "worthless" feature to the human being kind and *Empfangsmädchen* adds a young feature to the general occupation "receptionist" by having a diminutive marker *-chen* attached to the basis word of the compound. Adding either feature to the word would more or less indicate the speaker's attitude toward the referent in question, or would comment on the age, height, or size of the entity mentioned. Therefore, the adding process implies comparison or differences, serving as a kind of differentiation and taking the entity in question from a general common category to a more specified level.

In conclusion, the signal ∅ + ____ -∅ can be used with either singular or plural subjects that fall into the category of general common profession without further indication of specified characteristics.

3.2.2　The signal ein-+＿＿-Ø and its meaning

In the system of differentiation, we claim that the signal ein-+ ＿＿-Ø bears the meaning of DIFFERENTIATION REQUIRED AND NOT MADE. In the interlock with the system of NUMBER, it also bears the meaning ONE. Provided that they do not contradict one another, the combination of the grammatical meaning with a lexical item should refer to an individual of a certain kind, "either an individual example of what is named by the lexical item or something singular with respect to it" (Kirsner, 1972, p.179). Previous examples provide evidence for this statement. For instance sentence 3.21a is coherent and sentence 3.23b is not coherent.

Further examples from previous sections are listed here:

3.25b)　Er　　ist　　　　ein　　　　　Dieb.
　　　　he　be.3sg　ART (one)　thief
　　　　'He is a thief.'

3.26b)　Er　　ist　　　　ein　　　　　Taugenichts.
　　　　he　be.3sg　ART (one)　good-for-nothing
　　　　'He is worthless.'

3.27d)　Sie　　ist　　　　ein　　　　　Empfangsmädchen.
　　　　she　be.3sg　ART (one)　reception girl
　　　　'She is a reception girl.'

We can infer from the examples that the signal ein-+ ＿＿-Ø does not refer to a general category of human beings, but rather emphasizes the individual with his/her personality, comments on it, and expresses a personal attitude towards it. In addition, it also indicates that entities similar to the entity in question do exist. If there is a collection or a group of similar entities and the referent is one of them, it suggests that the referent in question shares the characteristic of the collection that makes the collection unique to other entities or groups. Therefore, the referent in question should be a member of such a collection or group and can serve as an actual member to represent the collection or group. Consider the following example:

    3.28a) Er ist Philosoph.

    3.28b) Er ist ein Philosoph.

        'He is a philosopher.'

The opposition of the signals ein-+____-Ø and Ø+____-Ø illustrated in the above example shows that in the first sentence the speaker says that a male character serves as a philosopher: one who thinks about issues of the world, logic, and mind etc., just as all other philosophers do. The second sentence indicates that the male character is one of the philosophers and thus he knows something about philosophy, or has issues similar to those other philosophers would have. In other words, while the signal Ø+____-Ø gives the hearer the impression that the subject is to an abstract degree a philosopher, a profession other than teacher or professor, the signal ein-+____-Ø, combined with the lexical item *Philosoph* 'philosopher,' is expected to emphasize the personality, feature, or behavior of the referred *Philosoph* as opposed to other items in the group that are referred to by the lexical item *Philosoph*.

    3.29) An **einem** Abend gerieten Sophie und ich bei der Heimfahrt in **ein** Gewitter und stellten us im Neuenheimer Feld, in dem damals noch nicht Gebäude der Universität, sondern Felder und Gärten lagen, unter das Vordach eines Gartenhauses. (Schlink, 1995, p. 73)

    One evening Sophie and I got caught in **a** thunderstorm on our way home and took shelter under the overhang of a garden shed in Neuenheimer Feld, which had no university buildings on it then, just fields and gardens. (Schlink, 1997, p. 75)

This example clearly illustrates the opposition of the signals ein-+____

-Ø and Ø+____-Ø. In the example, ein-+____-Ø is used to co-occur with both lexical items *Abend* 'evening' and *Gewitter* 'thunderstorm' to refer to an individual time period that is later in the day and typically dark, and a weather phenomenon that is rainy and windy, respectively. If ever the signal Ø+____-Ø can be used here, it would mean a time period between five o'clock and ten o'clock in the afternoon. Therefore, Ø+____-Ø would be inappropriate here, because it would not denote to an individual evening and a single independent thunderstorm. In contrast, ein-+____-Ø is used to refer to a time that has the characteristics of the word "evening" and a single weather phenomenon that has the features necessary to be defined as "thunderstorm."

When we return to examples 3.25b, 3.26b and 3.27d again, we will find that the sentences do not indicate their subjects' professions, but rather describe what kind of characteristics or personalities they have or what kind of typical behavior they display that categorizes them in a certain group of people. For example, in 3.25b, *Dieb* 'thief' is not a profession, but a category of people. As a member of such a group, one is characterized as someone who steals (not for a living). In the other two examples, the subjects of the sentences are characterized as worthless, in the general category of human beings, or as young, in the category of receptionist.

One final piece of evidence should be mentioned before concluding this section. In the German language, the indefinite personal pronoun *man* 'one' changes to *einem* in the dative case and *einen* in the accusative case. Diver's theory on the Columbia School of linguistics contains the main idea of "one form one meaning," and both *einem* and *einen* can be seen as declined forms of the indefinite article *ein* 'a/an.' We would suppose that *ein* has the meaning of 'one,' leaving the head of the potential NP open, a.k.a. one of the group of what is following. In contrast to the signal Ø+___-Ø, which puts more weight on the group as a whole and perceives it at a more abstract level, the signal ein-+___-Ø is more concerned with the referent as an individual of a certain kind.

3.2.3 The signal d-+___-Ø and its meaning

In this section, I will analyze the signal d-+___-Ø and its meaning. In previous sections, examples with the lexical item *Student* 'student' have illustrated the opposition between d-+___-Ø and other signals with the interlocking meaning of ONE. By employing d-+___-Ø, the lexical item in question is not only required for differentiation, but is also differentiated from other potential referents. This indicates that first, there are other potential referents; and second, that the referent in question is not a neutral or general member of the potential group, but is explicitly differentiated from other potential referents. When stating that the referent is differentiated, it does not mean that the referent is emphasized to a greater extent, but rather that the referent in question stands out due to specific reasons: either it has features that others do not have, or it is the only option of that kind that is available.

 3.30a) Pommern ist eine Region in Deutschland und Polen mit Ølanger Geschichte. ①

 3.30b) Pommern ist eine Region in Deutschland und Polen mit **der** langen Geschichte.

  'Pomerania is a region in Germany and Poland with long history.'

---

① "Geschichte Pommerns." *Wikipedia*. www.de.wikipedia.org/wiki/Geschichte_Pommerns. (2012, January 1)

Three German informants point out the difference between the two sentences in the example. They explain that *Geschichte* 'history' is more general, more random, and not specified in the first sentence. In the second sentence, the word *Geschichte* 'history' is more concrete, specific, and representative. The second sentence indicates that *Geschichte* should have been mentioned and described before, while the history in the first sentence is just a general mention, not necessarily related to any specific history. The first sentence assigns Pomerania a long history, as it is clearly separated from other potential long histories in the second sentence.

 3.30c) Pommern ist eine Region in Deutschland und Polen mit **einer** langen Geschichte.

 'Pomerania is a region in Germany and Poland with **a** long history.'

The Pomeranian history in this sentence, associated with the signal ein- + ___ -Ø, is meant to be one of the long histories. Although this sentence does not show much difference from 3.30a, it puts more focus on the fact that the Pomeranian history is an individual member of the collection of all long histories.

 Due to the fact that d-+ ___ -Ø signals DIFFERENTIATION REQUIRED AND MADE and Ø+ ___ -Ø signals DIFFERENTIATION NOT REQUIRED, there are some lexical items that can only go with one, not both. Otherwise their meanings would be changed to fit into the grammatical-lexical meaning association.

 3.31a) Nächste Woche haben wir ØSonne.

 3.31b) Nächste Woche haben wir **die** Sonne.

 'We will have the sun next week.'

Both sentences are grammatically and semantically correct and have almost the same meaning: stating that the sun will start to come out next week. However, we cannot assume *Sonne* 'sun' in the first sentence as the star travelling in the galaxy. It is because by co-occurring with Ø+____-Ø, *Sonne* would be understood as "all kinds of suns," which is impossible because there is only one sun existing in the world. That is why *Sonne* in the first sentence can only be translated as "sunshine." If one limits the meaning of *Sonne* to the star providing warmth to the earth, the first sentence does not work anymore. At any rate, it is impossible to use *eine*① 'one' to refer to the sun. First, *eine* would exclude the possibility that *Sonne* could mean "sunshine," since *eine* restricts the entity in question to "one individual item," while sunshine is indivisible and unquantifiable; second, using *eine* would automatically create the assumption that there are a group of possible referents with the one in question simply as one member of them, which contradicts the common sense that there are no other suns.

In addition to *Sonne*, I will examine the opposition between d-+____-Ø and other signals such as Ø+____-Ø with another noun *Ursache* 'cause,' which will have the same meaning associated either with d-+____-Ø or Ø+____-Ø.

3.32a) Mediziner entdecken ØUrsache für Nervenleiden ALS. ②
   'Doctors discover cause for ALS nerve-suffering.'

3.32b) Mediziner entdecken **die** Ursache für Nervenleiden ALS.
   'Doctors discover **the** cause for ALS nerve-suffering.'

3.32c) Mediziner entdecken **eine** Ursache für Nervenleiden ALS.
   'Doctors discover **a** cause for ALS nerve-suffering.'

In the first sentence, the *Ursache* 'cause' is characterized as a cause of the nerve suffering, leaving the question open as to whether

---

 ① Here "*eine*" is an inflected form of *ein* and is inflected to agree with the noun "sun," which is a feminine accusative singular noun in the above example.
 ② "Mediziner entdecken Ursache für Nervenleiden ALS." *Zeit Online*. http://www.zeit.de/wissen/gesundheit/2011-08/ursache-amyotrophe-lateralsklerose. (2011, August 22)

this *Ursache* is the only cause or if there are many other causes for the same issue. Once it is determined whether it is the only cause or one of the causes, the form Ø+____-Ø will be eschewed in favor of either d-+____-Ø or ein-+____-Ø, as illustrated by the second and third sentence. The second sentence indicates that scientists have already excluded any other possibility before making the statement that there is only one cause. In the third sentence, it is assumed that there are some other causes in addition to the one mentioned, and the cause in the sentence qualifies as one of those causes. Therefore, if there are contexts providing more information about the cause, the options will be limited to one of d-+____-Ø or ein-+____-Ø.

  3.33a) ? Es ist Ursache für Nervenleiden ALS. Es gibt keine andere Möglichkeiten.

    '? It is cause for ALS nerve-suffering. There are no other possibilities.'

  3.33b) ? Es ist **eine** Ursache für Nervenleiden ALS. Es gibt keine andere Möglichkeiten.

    '? It is **a** cause for ALS nerve-suffering. There are no other possibilities.'

  3.33c) Es ist **die** Ursache für Nervenleiden ALS. Es gibt keine andere Möglichkeiten.

    'It is **the** cause for ALS nerve-suffering. There are no other possibilities.'

The first two sentences in this example are grammatically correct, but contradict the information in the sentence (that there is no other possible cause). Therefore, the third sentence, by stating that the cause needs differentiation and is differentiated, is preferable in the given context.

  Moreover, there are certain verbs that prefer to associate with d-+____-Ø, like *erfinden* 'to invent.'

3.34a) * Edison hat ØGlühbirne erfunden.
'Edison has invented light bulb.'

3.34b) * Edison hat **eine** Glühbirne erfunden.
'Edison has invented **a** light bulb.'

3.34c) Edison hat **die** Glühbirne erfunden.
'Edison has invented **the** light bulb.'

The second sentence is obviously ambiguous, because its grammatical meaning, signaled by ein-+____-Ø, claims that the light bulb is not one of its kind, while its lexical meaning, as the verb "invent" indicates, states that there are no other candidates. The first sentence does not work as well, in the sense that the form Ø+____-Ø signals DIFFERENTIATION NOT REQUIRED and thus means "all kinds of," when it is possible for anyone to invent all kinds of light bulbs at a time. The third sentence with d-+____-Ø clearly indicates that Edison has invented the light bulb, which has been created at that time, in a specific way, and of specific materials; in other words, the light bulb he invented is limited to the technology of that time. Another possible explanation is that all future production will constitute "instances of that single invention" (Kirsner, 1972, p.191).

3.2.4 The opposition between Ø+____-PM and d-+____-PM

Admittedly, Ø+____-PM and d-+____-PM are the plural forms of ein-+____-Ø and d-+____-Ø, respectively. Taking the noun *Bett* 'bed' for example, one would recognize *Betten* 'beds' with meaning OTHER parallels to *ein Bett* 'a bed' with meaning ONE in the system of DIFFERENTIATION, and *die Betten* 'the beds' to *das Bett* 'the bed.' In the previous sections, I validated the individual signal-meaning complexes of the system of DIFFERENTIATION, with its interlock with the meaning ONE of the system of NUMBER. However, it is not justifiable to apply my previous findings to this section and its discussion of the plural form. The messages transmitted by Ø + ___-PM in opposition to those transmitted by d-+ ___-PM do not necessarily parallel the messages transmitted by ein-+ ___-Ø in opposition to those transmitted by d-+ ___-Ø. Therefore, a separate validation of the plural signals is necessary and will be able to indicate how the uses of the signal-meaning complexes with the meaning OTHER differ from those with the meaning ONE, not only in the opposition between the meaning OTHER and ONE, but also in aspects other than the opposition between OTHER and ONE.

Another justification of a separate validation is that validating the opposition between the two signals in question within the system of OTHER is different from validating the opposition between a signal with the meaning ONE and its parallel signal with the meaning OTHER. The latter can be illustrated by different forms, such as verb conjugation and the affix PM added to the noun, and their related difference of meaning. For example, *ein Bett* 'a bed' means one of all kinds of beds, as opposed to *Betten* 'beds,' meaning more than one kind of all beds, in the same ways that the latter NP objectively refers to several individual members of the category "bed." The opposition here is more obvious and straightforward than the opposition in the following example:

 3.35a) In **den** nächsten Tagen hatte die Frau Frühschicht. Sie kam um zwölf nach Hause, und ich schwänzte Tag auf Tag die letzte Stunde, um sie auf dem Treppenabsatz vor ihrer Wohnung zu erwarten. Wir duschten und liebten uns, und kurz vor halb zwei zog ich mich hastig an und rannte los. Um halb zwei wurde Mittag gegessen. Am Sonntag gab es das Mittagessen schon um zwölf, begann und endete aber auch ihre Frühschicht später.
 (Schlink, 1995, p. 33)

'For **the** next few days, the woman was working the early shift. She came home at noon, and I cut my last class every day so as to be waiting for her on the landing outside her apartment. We showered and made love, and just before half past one I scrambled into my clothes and ran out the door. Lunch was at one-thirty. On Sundays lunch was at noon, but her early shift also started and ended later.' (Schlink, 1997, p. 32)

3.35b) In Ø nächsten Tagen hatte die Frau Frühschicht. Sie kam um zwölf nach Hause, und ich schwänzte Tag auf Tag die letzte Stunde, um sie auf dem Treppenabsatz vor ihrer Wohnung zu erwarten. Wir duschten und liebten uns, und kurz vor halb zwei zog ich mich hastig an und rannte los. Um halb zwei wurde Mittag gegessen. Am Sonntag gab es das Mittagessen schon um zwölf, begann und endete aber auch ihre Frühschicht später.

'For following days, the woman was working the early shift. She came home at noon, and I cut my last class every day so as to be waiting for her on the landing outside her apartment. We showered and made love, and just before half past one I scrambled into my clothes and ran out the door. Lunch was at one-thirty. On Sundays lunch was at noon, but her early shift also started and ended later.'

The second passage only differs from the first passage due to the lack of *den* 'the' in the first sentence.① As shown in the translation, the difference in meaning is that the textual reference to "the next few days" in the first passage feels shorter than the description of the "following days" provided in the second passage. However, in the context, the author does not provide extra-linguistic background to make a strong case for either option, i.e. the author does not provide "enough redundant information to justify the choice of a particular form-meaning complex in a particular instance" (Kirsner, 1972, p. 131). Therefore,

---

① Here *den* 'the' is an inflected form of the definite article *die*, to agree to the plural dative noun *Tagen* 'days.'

this example does not necessarily provide evidence for the opposition between Ø+____-PM and d-+____-PM.

What we could conclude from the previous example is that Ø+____-PM, signaling DIFFERENTIATION REQUIRED AND NOT MADE, works on a larger scope than d-+____-PM, which signals DIFFERENTIATION REQUIRED AND MADE. Here I will provide more examples to examine the opposition between them.

3.36a) Ich esse gerne **Ø** Eier.

'I like to eat eggs.'

3.36b) Ich esse gerne *die* Eier.

'I like to eat **the** eggs.'

In this example, the first sentence indicates that the speaker, generally, likes to eat eggs and leaves the specific category of eggs open, whereas the second sentence, with the use of d-+____-PM, suggests that the speaker likes to eat the eggs, which need to be differentiated and are differentiated. The second sentence, therefore, unlike the first sentence, is not a general statement about what category of food the speaker likes to eat, but rather what specific kind of eggs the speaker likes.

From the example, we may suppose that the signal Ø+____-PM tends to associate better with lexical items with a generic or general meaning, and the signal d-+____-PM fits more with a lexical item or sentence that has a specialized or quasi-generic meaning. I will now add lexical items to our examples and see how they work with both signals. The lexical items I have selected are *beide* 'both' and *alle* 'all.' If what we just supposed is correct, we can further suppose that Ø+____-PM is incoherent when associated with *beide*, if there are no other modifying parts, such as numerals, preceding the noun that the signal is modifying.

3.37a) *ØZwei Brüder arbeiten beide bei Mercedes.
   'Two brothers both work at Mercedes.'
3.37b) **Die** zwei Brüder arbeiten beide bei Mercedes.
   '**The** two brothers both work at Mercedes.'
3.37c) *ØBrüder arbeiten beide bei Mercedes.
   'Brothers both work at Mercedes.'
3.37d) **Die** Brüder arbeiten beide bei Mercedes.
   '**The** brothers both work at Mercedes.'

The lexical item *beide* 'both' refers to a known, and therefore definite, plurality of exactly two items①. In the first two sentences, because of the presence of the numeral *zwei* 'two,' both signals can co-occur with *beide*, which could further intensify the number of the subject of the sentence②. However, when the numeral is absent, as shown in sentence 3.37c and 3.37d, Ø+____-PM, without differentiating the items in the plurality in advance, is incoherent, whereas d-+____-PM, signaling DIFFERENTIATION MADE, is more coherent when it co-occurs with *beide*. The explanation for this is clear. If a numeral is present and provides the hearer with the exact number of the referent, the referent is then differentiated because its quantity is given. But if a numeral is absent, the hearer does not have further information regarding the referent. The quantity of the referent is then missing in the context, if co-occurring with Ø+____-PM or d-+____

---

① as explaned in *Duden*: *die zwei zusammen* 'the two together.' It may also provide an evidence that *beide* refers to a known definite set of two.

② Sentence 3.37a does not have a definite group of two, to which *beide* refers. A possible correction may be: *Zwei Brüder arbeiten bei Mercedes, sie sind beide 18 Jahre alt* 'Two brothers work at the Mercedes. They both are 18 years old.' To the contrast, sentence 3.37c lacks the matching quantity (therefore only has near-to-zero possibility to mean "there are only two brothers"), and cannot be grammatically correct with the same modification: * *Brüder arbeiten bei Mercedes, sie sind beide 18 Jahre alt*. This is not the main topic of this section and will not be discussed further here.

-PM, or as already specified, if co-occurring with d-+____-PM. In the latter case, *beide* and d-+____-PM create a coherent meaning. They occur as an intensifier of the quantity of the referent, namely *zwei* 'two.' In the former case, if co-occurring with d-+____-PM, it is obvious that the plurality in question is already differentiated, because the referent is differentiated. However, if *beide* co-occurs with Ø+____-PM in the former case, it is incoherent because of the absence of a numeral and lack of differentiation of the referent. This results in the quantity of the referent being unknown, thereby transmitting a contradicting message, as *beide* is used as an intensifier of the quantity of the referent in question. Given that *beide* is only appropriate if the referent in question is definite and consists of exactly two entities, it is only compatible to co-occur with d-+____-PM, not Ø+____-PM.

In the following example, the lexical item *alle* 'all' will be discussed in co-occurrence with both signals.

3.38a) **Ø**Kinder sind alle süss.
'Children are all sweet.'

3.38b) **Die** Kinder sind alle süss.
'**The** children are all sweet.'

The lexical item *alle* 'all' means each from the mentioned category. Unlike *beide*, it does not require a specified quantity. In this example, both sentences have coherent messages signaled by grammatical and lexical meanings. In the first sentence, the signal Ø+____-PM means DIFFERENTIATION REQUIRED AND NOT MADE, makes the subject of the sentence unmarked and indicates that generally, all children are sweet, without any exception. The second sentence, with d-+____-PM signaling DIFFERENTIATION MADE, does not mean that all children are sweet, but that each child from a specific, mentioned/known collection is sweet.

3.39a) Diebe müssen alle ins Gefängnis.

    'All thieves must be put in jail.'

3.39b) Die Diebe müssen alle ins Gefängnis.

    'The thieves must all be put in jail.'

It is common sense or a part of folk wisdom that thieves should be sent to jail, without exception. No thief should be forgiven for whatever reason, as long as he/she is a thief. This is a generic statement described by 3.39a. The second sentence, however, with the meaning DIFFERENTIATTION MADE signaled by d-+____-PM, automatically segments a part from the whole category of thieves, who are not part of the thieves, who have to go to jail. Therefore, the second sentence, though grammatically correct, goes against the common sense or folk wisdom, and hence cannot apply generally. It is then only correct when there is a specific context, say a girl points to a certain amount of thieves and means that they should all be sent to prison. To any extent, for sentence 3.39b, a generic reading is not possible.

From the above examples, I conclude that the signal d-+____-PM is relatively restricted and cannot be combined with relative generic or unrestricted statements, but rather favors generalizations: that is, statements that do not require that a feature apply to each of the category without exception, but only that it remains true for the majority or the main part of the entities of a category. In contrast, the signal Ø+____-PM, meaning DIFFERENTIATION REQUIRED AND NOT MADE, is preferred in *bona fide* generic and unrestricted statements, where any entity of a category is defined, without any exception.

3.2.5 Referencing and co-referencing with Ø+____-PM and d-+____-PM

Both signals Ø+____-PM and d-+____-PM are used to refer to referents in question. The question of which signal to use depends on "whether the linguistic and non-linguistic context is consonant with the inference" (Kirsner, 1972, p.139). Considering that Ø+____-PM favors generic unrestricted statements and d-+____-PM is appropriate in general statements, I will examine additional passages to ascertain whether and how the two signals, if combined with the same lexical item, refer to the same referent with no ambiguity. As an example, I will take part of the pear story video clip[①] and reproduce the story from a first person's perspective. The transcription of the video clip is as follows: "I go to pick up pears and there I see two boys walking towards me. While I am picking pears, they steal my pears." The signals are examined in association with the two boys who walk towards "me" and steal "my" pears. This will allow us to examine whether and how the two signals, when combined with the same lexical item, can refer to the same referent in question with no ambiguity. There are four possible combinations of the two signals. The examples illustrating the four possibilities are as follows:

3.40a) Ich gehe Birnen pflücken. Da sehe ich **Ø** zwei Jungen, die mir gegenübergehen. Während ich Birnen pflücke, gehen **die** zwei Jungen meine Birnen stehlen.

[I go to pick up pears. There I see **Ø** two boys, who walk towards me. While I am picking up pears, **the** two boys go steal my pears.]

3.40b) Ich gehe Birnen pflücken. Da sehe ich **Ø** zwei Jungen, die mir gegenübergehen. Während ich Birnen pflücke, gehen **Ø** zwei Jungen

---

① This video clip can be found at www.pearstories.org.

meine Birnen stehlen.

[I go to pick up pears. There I see Ø two boys, who walk towards me. While I am picking up pears, Ø two boys go steal my pears.]

3. 40c) Ich gehe Birnen pflücken. Da sehe ich **die** zwei Jungen, die mir gegenübergehen. Während ich Birnen pflücke, gehen **die** zwei Jungen meine Birnen stehlen.

[I go to pick up pears. There I see **the** two boys, who walk towards me. While I am picking up pears, **the** two boys go steal my pears.]

3. 40d) Ich gehe Birnen pflücken. Da sehe ich **die** zwei Jungen, die mir gegenübergehen. Während ich Birnen pflücke, gehen Ø zwei Jungen meine Birnen stehlen.

[I go to pick up pears. There I see **the** two boys, who walk towards me. While I am picking up pears, Ø two boys go steal my pears.]

The first sentence serves as the standard version of the example. It clearly describes that the two boys who steal the pears are the same ones who walk towards the speaker. In the second sentence, it is not necessarily true that the boys who steal the pears are the ones who walk towards the speaker, due the fact that Ø + ____-PM is used twice, which indicates that the referent in question has not been differentiated. This suggests that either the boys refer to a single undifferentiated plurality or to two undifferentiated pluralities, which does not necessarily indicate that the boys are the same referent. The third sentence, by using the signal d-+ ____-PM twice, asserts twice that the referent has been differentiated, and most likely signals the same referents, despite the subtle difference in meaning that is created when the two boys are differentiated at the very beginning of the sentence. As in the fourth sentence, it cannot be interpreted as having the same referent, because the first reference already indicates that the referent is differentiated. If two signals have the same referent, it is not possible that the referent is differentiated at first mention, but changes to undifferentiated the second time it is mentioned. Therefore, the second combination in the fourth sentence is most likely used to refer to a new plurality.

In the example, the two referents are supposed to be the same in order to examine whether combinations of the two signals are able to refer to the same referent. Also, the two referents in question, namely two boys, exclude the possibility that the first referent is part of the second referent. In the following example, I will change the second referent to Swiss in order to enable the possibility of the first referent being part of the second. This will allow us to examine how the two signals, Ø+____-PM and d-+____-PM, co-reference each other.

3.41a) Ich gehe Birnen pflücken. Da sehe ich Ø zwei Jungen, die mir gegenübergehen. Während ich Birnen pflücke, gehen **die** Schweizer meine Birnen stehlen.

[I go to pick up pears. There I see Ø two boys, who walk towards me. While I am picking up pears, **the** Swiss go steal my pears.]

3.41b) Ich gehe Birnen pflücken. Da sehe ich Ø zwei Jungen, die mir gegenübergehen. Während ich Birnen pflücke, gehen Ø Schweizer meine Birnen stehlen.

[I go to pick up pears. There I see Ø two boys, who walk towards me. While I am picking up pears, Ø Swiss go steal my pears.]

3.41c) Ich gehe Birnen pflücken. Da sehe ich **die** zwei Jungen, die mir gegenübergehen. Während ich Birnen pflücke, gehen **die** Schweizer meine Birnen stehlen.

[I go to pick up pears. There I see **the** two boys, who walk towards me. While I am picking up pears, **the** Swiss go steal my pears.]

3.41d) Ich gehe Birnen pflücken. Da sehe ich **die** zwei Jungen, die mir gegenübergehen. Während ich Birnen pflücke, gehen Ø Schweizer meine Birnen stehlen.

[I go to pick up pears. There I see **the** two boys, who walk towards me. While I am picking up pears, Ø Swiss go steal my pears.]

In the first and second sentences, there is very little evidence to equate the boys with the Swiss who steal the speaker's pears. The boys are associated with the Ø+____-PM, which means DIFFERENTIATION REQUIRED AND NOT MADE, and are therefore not differentiated; in other words, the two boys are random boys without any differentiating features or characteristics. If the boys are not differentiated, it is not logical to state that they have anything to do with being Swiss. In this way, whether or not the boys are connected to the Swiss figures depends upon whether identified or unidentified Swiss are involved.

If the Swiss are associated with d-+ ____-PM, they have been differentiated. In this case, there are three possibilities in the sense of co-reference: first, the Swiss consist exclusively of the two boys aforementioned; second, the Swiss consist of the two boys mentioned and some other members; and third, the Swiss are a completely different plurality. The question of which example provides the most accurate information will depend on the context and the information about the origin of the two boys.

If the Swiss are associated with Ø + ____-PM, they need to be differentiated but are not yet differentiated. Hence, it is impossible that the Swiss consist exclusively of the two boys. First, the quantity of the Swiss is unknown; second, the age range of the Swiss could be any range, and not necessarily between ten and twenty. Therefore, the only possible options are either the two boys are part of the Swiss, or the boys are not of Swiss origin and the Swiss are a different plurality.

In either case, more information about the boys and/or the Swiss is needed in the context to make the co-reference clear.

3.3 The System of DEIXIS

In this section, I will present an analysis of German demonstratives based on the Columbia School linguistic theory and show that German demonstratives serve as signals of the meaning DEIXIS, which is an instruction that urges the hearer to approach the referent in question (see Chapter 1). Similar to Dutch (Kirsner, 1979) and Chinese demonstratives (see Chapters 2 & 4), German demonstratives are not limited to providing spatial information about referents, but should be analyzed in the hierarchy of DEIXIS. Other terms related to such a system may include Gorup's system of FOCUS, which gives a more precise meaning to the Serbo-Croatian demonstrative *se*, which signals CENTRAL PARTICIPANT FOCUS (Gorup, 2006; cf. Davis, 2000). This analysis, however, does not reject the system of DEIXIS, but rather provides an alternative to it, the reason being that if the speaker urges the hearer to put more attention on an entity, it should be the central focus of the speaker and the hearer.

Langacker's definition of demonstratives provides further explanation of Gorup's system of FOCUS:

> Demonstratives represent a conventionalized, grammaticalized means of connecting nominal referents to the subjects of conception. It is thus intrinsic to their value and function that they invoke the ground as a kind of 'viewing platform' from which to seek out a referent and establish it as a mutual focus of attention. Metaphorically, the speaker and addressee can be portrayed as looking out from their shared platform, the direction of their gaze determining which portion of their surroundings will fall within their field of view. (1997, p. 246)

Langacker's definition, too, does not reject *deixis*. It provides the background of a referring event; there is a joint platform of both the speaker and the hearer, and there is the direction to the referent, which starts from the speaker's ego and needs to take the hearer's background into consideration. This definition is an analysis of the referring process in terms of the communicative goal and strategy.

In this section, I will take two steps to validate the German demonstratives in the system of DEIXIS: first, I will give some basic examples; second, I will validate the analysis with qualitative and quantitative data.

3.3.1 Basic use of the German demonstratives

In addition to the German definite articles *der*, *die*, *das*, and their inflected forms, the German demonstratives *dies-*, *jen-*, and their inflected forms are also used to differentiate the referent in question from other potential referents. They go one step further, in so much as they also provide spatial information that directs the speaker to locate the referent. The opposition between the proximal demonstrative *dies-* and non-proximal demonstrative *jen-* can be demonstrated as follows:

3.42a) dieses   Jahr
        DM (this) year
        'this year'

3.42b) jenes   Jahr
        DM (that) year
        'that year'

3.42c) das   Jahr
        ART (the) year
        'the year'

This example consists of three NPs with the head *Jahr* 'year.' In the first one, *Jahr* is preceded by the proximal demonstrative *dies-* and in this way denotes the year that the speaker is in. In the second NP, *Jahr* is modified by the non-proximal demonstrative *jen-* and hence refers to a year quite far in the past. The last NP is an association of the definite article *das* with *Jahr*. It is obvious that the year the NP refers to is a differentiated year, but the lack of further information makes the hearer unable to locate it based on the current information in the NP.

Since the referent will be automatically located based on the speaker's relative position, the use of demonstratives should be closely examined so as not to include contradicting messages in a sentence. In the following example, the speaker is trying to direct the hearer's attention to the balloons on the horizon, as in Nena's song, "99 Luftballons" '99 balloons.'

3.43a) * Seh-en Sie diese Ballon-s am Horizont?
see-pl you.formal DM (this) balloon-PM on the horizon
'Do you see these balloons on the horizon?'

3.43b) Seh-en Sie jene Ballon-s am Horizont?
see-pl you.formal DM (that) balloon-PM on the horizon
'Do you see those balloons on the horizon?'

3.43c) Seh-en Sie die Ballon-s am Horizont?
see-pl you.formal ART (the) balloon-PM on the horizon
'Do you see the balloons on the horizon?'

In the first sentence, the information provided by the grammatical signal *diese* 'these' and lexical item *am Horizont* 'on the horizon' is contradicting, for they direct the hearer's attention to different locations. For example, the sentence implies a location that is close to the speaker and far away on the horizon (unless, of course, the speaker is referring to a picture, or if the speaker is quite close to the horizon). The information in the third sentence is coherent, in the sense that a definite article is unmarked with respect to location, i.e. it does not provide any information regarding location. Therefore, preceded by the definite article *die* 'the,' the balloons can refer to any balloons that are available and differentiated.

Note that, in the current modern German language, the two demonstratives are to some extent obsolete (see Chapters 1 and 2) and are mostly replaced by a combination of a definite article and a locative. For example, *dies-* 'this' is mainly replaced by d-+___+*hier*, such as *das Buch hier* 'this book,' or 'the book here' literally. In this case, if we replace *diese* with d-+ ___ + *hier* in the first sentence of the example, it would be clearer that there are potential contradicting messages.

3.43a') * Seh-en Sie   die   Ballon-s   hier   am   Horizont?
        see-pl   you. formal ART (the) balloon-PM here   on the horizon
        'Do you see the balloons here on the horizon?'

When "used in pointing out and differentiating separate referents referred to with multiple occurrences of the very same noun," information about the referents' location is essential (Kirsner, 2011, p. 102).

3.44a) Ich nehm-e   diesen   Apfel und diesen   Apfel.
        I   take-1sg DM (this)   apple and DM (this)   apple
        'I will take this apple and this apple.'

3.44b) Ich nehm-e   jenen   Apfel und jenen   Apfel.
        I   take-1sg DM (that)   apple and DM (that)   apple
        'I will take that apple and that apple.'

3.44c) ? Ich nehm-e   den   Apfel und den   Apfel.
          I   take-1sg ART (the)   apple and ART (the)   apple
        '? I will take the apple and the apple.'

The third sentence in this example is confusing to the hearer, for the reason that both apples are differentiated but not located. The hearer has two referents that are of the same kind, but does not know their absolute or relative position. If there is more than one separately differentiated entity, it is impossible for anyone to point out each one. This task is similar to asking someone to differentiate each item from a collection without providing any further information on how each item is differentiated from the others. With regard to the third sentence, the speaker must use other means to indicate the location. One efficient way is to point to the item individually and place stress on the articles[①].

Another way to examine the opposition between articles and demonstratives is to test whether they can be used as pronouns, i. e. whether they can take place in sentences independently, without any nouns following them, and refer to the referent at the same time. This is feasible, for the reason that a demonstrative not only refers to a noun, but also to a location, while a definite article only refers to an entity or a place, but not both. If the lexical item is left out in actual text, it would make the article lose its referent. As a *xuci* 'empty word,' an article would be meaningless if not co-occurring with a *shici* 'lexical items.' In contrast, a demonstrative will not end in the same way as an article, because it at least refers to a location, i. e. it still has a place to refer to. The following example is supposed to express the speaker's attitude towards a *Rock* 'skirt,' a masculine noun in German. Note that there is no previous mentioning of the referent in question, i. e. the name of the referent is not supposed to be called before. All three sentences should be the first-mention of the referent "Rock."

  3.45a) Dieser ist so teuer!
       DM (this) be. 3sg so expensive
       'This is so expensive!'

---

  ① And if so, the speaker would change *jenen* 'that' to *diesen* 'this.'

3.45b) Jener   ist   so   teuer!
        DM (that)   be.3sg   so   expensive
        'That is so expensive!'

3.45c) *Der   ist   so   teuer!
        ART (the)   be.3sg   so   expensive
        'The/It is so expensive!'

The third sentence loses its actual subject and thus is not able to refer to anything. Again, here we need to provide more information on what the referent is. If we want to keep this sentence as it is, we need to point to the actual referent in question and/or stress the article, which is the first word of the sentence①.

As a conclusion to this section, it appears that articles provide less information than demonstratives. Demonstratives, on the other hand, not only differentiate the referent from other potential ones, but also make it possible for the hearer to locate the referent. And "no matter how useful and traditional labels such as 'articles' and 'demonstratives' are, they simply reflect the purely message-oriented character of traditional grammar as an aid to translation and language-learning and provide, at best, only the raw material for analysis within a sign-based linguistics theory, one which postulates that the basic units of language are not messages but rather signals of meanings (cf. Huffman, 1997,

---

① If the noun is already mentioned in the context, then the third sentence is acceptable. Take a conversation between A and B for example: A: *Wie findest du den Rock hier*? 'How do you like this skirt?' B: *Der is so teuer*! 'It is so expensive!' In this conversation, B shares his/her mind with A and wants to keep on commenting on the skirt. *Rock* 'skirt' is omitted here, and *der* no longer serves as an article, but rather as a definite pronoun that is referring to *Rock*. However, if the noun is not mentioned in the context, the left out of the noun is grammatically not acceptable as it is in 3.45c). On the other hand, if B wants to end the topic (which is the Rock) and switches to another item (say, *eine Bluse* 'a blouse'), B would use a personal pronoun to refer to the *Rock*: B: *Er is so teuer*! 'It is so expensive!' or even: B: *Er is zu teuer*! 'It is too expensive!'

2006; Reid, 2006; Kirsner, 2011).

3.3.2　The system of deixis

In this section, the German demonstratives are demonstrated in the system of *Deixis*, where messages of proximity and non-proximity are held to be pragmatic inferences from the meaning HIGH DEIXIS and LOW DEIXIS, where *Deixis* is, as discussed in Chapter 1, an instruction to urge the hearer to seek out the referent. In the previous section, we validated that German demonstratives do not need to be followed by a noun to refer to them, but can be independently used, because they refer to location, whereas a definite article needs to be accompanied by a noun, unless otherwise specified. Therefore, if we extend the system of DIFFERENTIATION by adding demonstratives to it, the extended part of the system of DIFFERENTIATION can be illustrated as follows:

$$\text{DIFFEREN-TIATION MADE} \begin{cases} \text{NOT LOCATED}: \text{d-}+\underline{\quad}+\text{-}\emptyset/\text{-PM} \\ \text{LOCATED} \begin{cases} \text{PROXIMAL}: \text{dies-}+\underline{\quad}+\text{-}\emptyset/\text{-PM} \\ \text{NON-PROXIMAL}: \text{jen-}+\underline{\quad}+\text{-}\emptyset/\text{-PM} \end{cases} \end{cases}$$

Figure 3.3

Note that d- in the graph refers to the German definite articles, *der*, *die*, *das*, and their inflected forms. A definite article, if stressed or provided with other information about the referent, may also function in the same manner as the demonstratives. We can postulate that the meaning of a definite article, according to the Columbia School linguistic theory, is a hint for the hearer to seek out the referent in the speaker's mind. This is because definite articles signal DIFFERENTIATION REQUIRED AND MADE, and the lexical item associated with them is differentiated from other potential referents, or because "the referent simply deserves extra attention" (Kirsner, 2011, p.105).

However, we still should not include definite articles in the system of *Deixis*. Admittedly, if stressed and provided with extra information about the referent, definite articles can demonstrate "demonstrativity" to a greater extent than when they are without stress and further information①. This is because they can better instruct the hearer to differentiate the referent from others by providing more information that the referent is "within the visual or conceptual field (in which case an accompanying lexical item, a noun, may be brought into play)" (Kirsner, 2011, p. 107). If ever a definite article is used to signal any demonstrative meaning, instead of using a demonstrative, it is suggested that there is extra meaning beyond the word's original meanings. Otherwise, other forms, which are more appropriate and semantically closer, should be used instead of taking an alternative that is less appropriate.

3.46a) Die   Frau   ha-t   viel   Geld.
       ART (the) lady   have-3sg   much   money
       'The lady has a lot of money.'

3.46b) Die   ha-t   viel   Geld.
       ART (the) have-3sg   much   money
       'The one/She has a lot of money.'

3.46c) Diese   Frau   ha-t   viel   Geld.
       DM (this) lady   have-3sg   much   money
       'This lady has a lot of money.'

3.46d) Diese   ha-t   viel   Geld.
       DM (this) have-3sg   much   money
       'This one has a lot of money.'

3.46e) Sie   ha-t   Viel   Geld.
       PRON (she) have-3sg   much   money
       'She has a lot of money.'

---

① Please refer to 3.45c footnote where *der* serves as a definite pronoun.

In the above example, all sentences refer to a female character with a lot of money. The first sentence differentiates the character from other characters with the definite article *die*. The third and fourth sentences use the proximal demonstrative to locate the lady by indicating that the lady is within the speaker's perception of vicinity. The last sentence uses a personal pronoun to refer to the rich lady. Among the four sentences, the last sentence urges the hearer to give the least amount of attention to the lady, since "she" only signals the meaning of a female character, without differentiating her from other possible characters, such as female teachers. In contrast, the third sentence urges the hearer to put the most emphasis on the referent, because it provides the most information about the character; and, according to Diver (1987), the more the speaker is interested in the referent, the more information he is expected to provide about the referent. Therefore, scaling from low interest to high interest, the speaker is provided with sufficient options to choose from and does not have to turn to a less frequent and less appropriate option. For example, in the second sentence, the definite article *die* 'the' is used to communicate a demonstrative message, which, however, works only as a definite pronoun and shows up in the first place of the sentence (i. e. as topic in the topic chain of the topic, which in Chinese can be characterized as the zero anaphora phenomenon).

3.47a) Die   Frau   ha-t   das   Geld.
       ART (the) lady   have-3sg ART (the) money
       'The lady has the money.'

3.47b) Die   ha-t   das   Geld.
       ART (the) have-3sg ART (the)   money
       'The one/She has the money.'

3.47c) *Die   Frau   ha-t   das.
       ART (the) lady   have-3sg   ART (the)

'The lady has the/it.'

3.47d)　Die　　　　　Frau　　ha-t　　　es.
　　　　　ART (the)　lady　have-3sg　PRON (it)
　　　　　'The lady has it.'

In this example, the third sentence has the definite article *das* 'the' as the object in the sentence, which makes it very difficult for the hearer to seek out what the exact object is. Similar to what has already discussed in the previous section, *das* can only be grammatically right to use if it is a definite pronoun here and is used to keep the topic chain moving on. In this case, it has to show up in the first place of the sentence. If das is used alone in a sentence or at the end of a sentence, the hearer will usually turn to the last mentioned noun if there is no lexical item associated with the definite article. In sentence 3.46c), however, the noun preceding *das* is *die Frau* 'the lady,' which is the subject of the sentence; this makes it impossible for it to be the object of the sentence at the same time.

Since German is a highly inflected language and does not rely solely on word order to decide word class, the object of a sentence may also appear at the beginning of the sentence. In this case, an object can also be referred to with a definite pronoun (which has the same form of the corresponding definite article), without being followed by a noun.

3.47c')　Das　　　　　ha-t　　　die　　　　　Frau.
　　　　　PRON (the)　have-3sg　ART (the)　lady
　　　　　'The one/It, the lady has.'

In this sentence, the object can also be considered the topic of the conversation (so that the hearer is able to refer to the lexical item), and the rest of the sentence a comment to it.

3.48a)　Viele　lern-en　　die　　　　　Sprache　　in　der　　　　　Schule.
　　　　　many　study-pl　ART (the)　language　in　ART (the)　school

'Many (people) study the language in school.'

3.48b)　　＊Viele　lern-en　　die　　　　in　der　　　　　Schule.
　　　　　many　　study-pl　ART (the)　in　ART (the)　school
　　　　'Many study the/it in school.'

In this example, the noun *Sprache* 'language' must be in the sentence to indicate exactly what it is worth paying attention to. Without the noun, the sentence would be ungrammatical; the definite article *die* 'the' is glossed as an article, but not pronominally as "the one" to function as a nominalized phrase. Therefore, in most cases, we would agree that a definite article signals "article" kinds of messages and should not be included in the system of DEIXIS.

Based on the conclusions drawn in this section, the system of DEIXIS can be illustrated as in the following figure:

$$\text{DEIXIS} \begin{cases} \text{HIGH: dies-}+\underline{\quad}+\text{-}\emptyset\text{/-PM} \\ \text{LOW: jen-}+\underline{\quad}+\text{-}\emptyset\text{/-PM} \end{cases}$$

Figure 3.4

3.3.3　The opposition between HIGH DEIXIS and LOW DEIXIS

In the process of pointing, there are two participants, namely the speaker and the hearer. The speaker is trying to direct the hearer's attention to the referent in question and make sure that the hearer is able to differentiate and locate the referent in question (see Chapter 1). Therefore, in order to make sure that this communicative goal will be achieved, the speaker needs to take the hearer's background knowledge into consideration, which can be called communicative strategy.

There are several pragmatic factors involved in the pointing event. First, the speaker is the starting point of the pointing. Whether the referent is near or far depends on the speaker's perception. An entity that is in proximity in one's mind can be in non-proximity in another's feeling. Also, the described distance between the speaker and the referent is relative in two ways: first, the distance is relative to the speaker's standpoint; and second, the distance depends on how the speaker perceives it and how the speaker wants to perceive it. In any case, the distance is not related to the physical distance between the speaker and the referent at all (cf. Diessel, 1999, 2006).

A second factor is that the speaker is the one to decide what to talk about. No one would be willing to start with an unpleasant topic and carry on a conversation about such a topic. Most of the time (excluding times where one has to talk about unfavorable topics) a speaker will tend to take the conversation in a direction that pleases him/her or that he/she feels comfortable with. Based on the natural egocentricity, which claims that everyone is egocentric and wants to be the center of focus, subjects would prefer to talk about themselves, their personal experiences or favorite subjects: the things closest to that individual. It is understandable that the speaker would want the hearer to focus on the things the speaker himself is interested in. And therefore, the speaker would urge the hearer to put more effort into seeking out the referent and more attention on the referent.

A third factor is that a referent can be pointed out and located relatively easily and more efficiently, if the referent is relatively closer to the speaker or, as stated earlier, if the referent is close to the speaker's preference, experience, and interests. If the referent in question is in the vicinity of the speaker, it can be clearly seen and precisely located. But if the referent is out of the speaker's sight it would be difficult for the speaker to ascertain its absolute or relative location and, thus, difficult for the speaker to describe. In this way, it would be even more difficult for the hearer to seek out the referent. Similarly, if a referent matches the speaker's interests, it could be described by the speaker in a more precise, informative, and efficient way, so that the hearer would be able to locate the referent based on the relatively abundant information provided.

3.3.3.1 Proximity and non-proximity

The Columbia School linguistic theory hypothesizes that in a system of DEIXIS, *dies-* and its inflected forms, with their explicit nearness to the speaker, signal HIGH DEIXIS and urge the hearer to pay more attention to the referent in question. Conversely, *jen-* and its inflected forms, with their explicit non-nearness to the speaker, signal LOW DEIXIS and do not urge the hearer to focus much attention on the referent in question.

Due to the nearness associated with the demonstrative *dies-* and its inflected forms, the speaker would tend to use them to refer to entities that are in the vicinity of the speaker and can be described with more information and thus extra precision. This is congruent with a message of calm assessment (cf. Kirsner, 2011, p. 112), which is a more objective description of an entity rather than a subjective perception or feelings of excitement with exclamatory messages.

3.49a) Ich hätt-e gern dieses Stück Kuchen.
I have.subj-1sg like DM (this) piece cake
'I would like to have this piece of cake.'

3.49b) ? Ich hätt-e gern dieses beste Stück Kuchen.
I have.subj-1sg like DM (this) best piece cake
'? I would like to have this best piece of cake.'

The second sentence of this example is grammatically correct (according to three native speakers of German) but sounds strange. A possible reason is that the piece of cake is differentiated and close to the speaker and thus does not need extra dramatic description (in the example, the speaker uses a superlative). In addition, if the dramatic description is a subjunctive evaluation (such as "outstanding"), it semantically contradicts the proximal demonstrative *dieses* 'this,' which bears the meaning of calm assessment and is rather objective, so that the hearer is able to detect and locate the referent. The use of the word "outstanding" is a subjunctive assessment of the cake, for which there is no standard and depends on individual's preference and assessment.

In contrast, the non-proximal demonstrative *jen-* and its inflected forms, and the non-nearness associated with them, indicate that the referent is not in the vicinity of the speaker and moreover, lack precise information on the referent's location and features. Therefore, if the non-proximal demonstrative modifies a referent that is provided with detailed and explicit information, the grammatical and lexical meanings will be incoherent.

3.50a) Mag-st du jene, die weit von hier wohn-en?
like-2sg you DM (that) who/that far from here live-pl
'Do you like those, who live far away from here?'

3.50b) ? Jenes Baby ist heute 31 Tage alt.
DM (that) baby be.3sg today 31 days old
'? That baby is today 31 days old.'

However, the German demonstratives no longer signal proximity or non-proximity, because they are replaced by the combination of a definite article and a locative. For example:

3.51a) Der Herr hier arbeite-t in einer Schule.
ART (the) man here work-3sg in ART (one) school
'This gentleman works at a school.'

3.51b) Das Rad da ist kaputt.
ART (the) bike there be.3sg broken.

'That bike is broken.'

In order to explore how the German demonstratives provide information about relative location, as similar to English and Chinese demonstratives, I researched the frequency of the total instances of the demonstratives that transmit the message of relative location. The following result is based on the book *Der Vorleser* 'The Reader' (Schlink, 1995).

DM	Location of Refernt		Total	% of Location Given
	Given	Not Given		
dies-	5	41	46	10.9%
jen-	0	2	2	0%

Table 3.7

The next table illustrates whether the demonstratives in Table 3.7, which have messages related to relative location, can be replaced by a combination of a definitive and a locative, i.e. whether the demonstratives, which have something to do with relative location, are only used to refer to a relative location.

DM	Replaceable	Not Replaceable	Total	% of Replaceable
dies-	0	5	5	0%

Table 3.8

We can conclude from the table that instances of *dies-* in actual texts, although they may be related to proximity, transmit other messages.

3.52) Keine wie **diese**, obwohl es **diese** Teedosen damals auch schon gab, sondern eine mit kyrillischen Schriftzeichen, der Deckel nicht zum Reindrücken, sondern zum Drüberstülpen. (Schlink, 1995, p. 202)

'Not like **this**, although **these** sorts of tea tins already existed, but one with Cyrillic letters, not one with a top you push in, but one you snap shut.' (Schlink, 1997, p. 214)

In this example, both *diese* are translated into this/these, but neither of them can be replaced by the combination of the definite article *die* 'the' and the locative *hier* 'here.' As for the first *diese*, although it refers to the tea tin right in front of the speaker, it cannot be replaced by the previously mentioned combination. Due to the lack of the lexical item to which the combination refers, the definite article *die* 'the' in the combination cannot direct the hearer's attention to the tea tin. The second *diese* cannot be replaced by the combination either, because *diese* is not referring to the tea tin in front of the speaker, but to the tea tins of the same kind as the tea tin in front of her. As suggested in the English translation, *diese* is better understood as 'such' or 'of this kind,' which clearly, indicates a place that is in close proximity to the speaker (cf. Diessel, 1999, 2006)

3.3.3.2 HIGH DEIXIS and LOW DEIXIS

As discussed, definite articles differ from demonstratives in the sense that they do not signal location, which are signaled by demonstratives. In the German language, the demonstratives signal more than the differentiation of the referent from other entities, which could be accomplished by the definite articles alone. In the last example, *diese* denotes a specific kind of tea tins that date to the Second World War. This, however, cannot be achieved by definite articles, which are defined as "pure attentionworthiness" according to Kirsner (2011, p. 112). It means that the articles are "instrumental rather than representational," compared to demonstratives in communicating messages (Kirsner, 2011, p. 113; cf. Huffman, 1997). The reason is that "the grammatical and lexical hints which the speaker presents to the hearer in an utterance do not so much say exactly what the speaker wants to communicate but rather do *not* say what he does *not* want to communicate" (Kirsner, 2011, p. 113).

Because *dies-* and *jen-* both provide more information on the referent's relative location, they may be considered more precise than the definite articles. Furthermore, since "the more precise the hints, the less freedom is given to the hearer's imagination" (Kirsner, 2011, p. 113), *dies-* is able to provide even more precise information than *jen-*, assuming that there are fewer locations in proximity of the speaker than in non-proximity of the speaker (see Chapter 1); and that more precision can be more easily achieved when the referent is in sight rather than out of sight, which leads to the fact that speakers tend to be willing to talk about things they know and that are related to themselves (see previous section). As a result, *dies-* 'this/these' refers to the entities that are either more familiar to the speaker or of the speaker's interest. In either circumstance, the speaker would want the hearer to seek out the referent in a more engaging and efficient way and to focus more attention on it. In contrast, *jen-* 'that/those' refers to the entities that are out of the speaker's interests and are hard for the speaker to find information about. It is logical then that the speaker would not want to initiate and participate in a conversation on entities he/she is not familiar with or not in his/her interests. Therefore, most likely the speaker will also be unwilling to have the hearer focus on the unfavorable entities. As a result, the proximal demonstrative *dies-* is expected to signal HIGH DEIXIS, and the non-proximal demonstrative *jen-* LOW DEIXIS.

Diver (1984, 1987, 1995) has argued in his discussion of number in the Homeric Greek noun that the more the speaker is interested in an entity or a place, the more information he will tend to provide. The following examples are from the German novel *Der Vorleser* 'The Reader.'

 3.53) Ich hatt-e nicht nur diesen Streit verloren.
    I have.past-1sg not only DM (this) fight lose-pp
                    (Schlink, 1995, p. 50)
  'I have not only lost this fight.'
                    (Schlink, 1997, p. 49)

  The demonstrative *diesen* 'this' refers to the first fight the speaker has gone through with his girlfriend Hanna at that time. It was very fierce. The speaker not only discusses this fight, but also how it started, what the possible reason was for it, how it ended, who compromised, and what kind of influence the fight had on their relationship. The speaker spent several pages (45—50) examining the entire course of the fight, and the next few chapters focusing on the chain effect of this fight. This fight is a milestone in the relationship between the speaker and Hanna, and is no doubt of great interest to the speaker. This example proves Diver's argument on the relation of the speaker's interests and how much information the speaker would want to provide.

 3.54) Wenn ich mich an das Arbeiten in **jenen** Wochen erinnere, ist mir, als
    hätte ich mich an den Schreibtisch gesetzt und war an ihm sitzengeblieben,
    bis alles aufgeholt war, was ich während der Gelbsucht versäumt hatte,
    alle Vokabeln gelernt, alle Texte gelesen, alle mathematischen Beweise
    geführt und chemischen Verbindungen geknüpft. (Schlink, 1995, p. 42)
    'When I think about the work I did in **those** weeks, it's as if I had sat
    down at my desk and stayed there until I had caught up with everything
    I'd missed during my hepatitis, learned all the vocabulary, read all the
    texts, worked through all the theorems and memorized the periodic
    table.' (Schlink, 1997, p. 41)

  Here the speaker uses the non-proximal demonstrative *jenen* 'those' to refer to the weeks, in which he was studying very hard in order to pass his class. However, the speaker does not give further description of exactly how he worked, but rather only gives a very vague analogy to the intensity of his work. What is more, there is only one mention in the book of these four weeks of hard work. One possible reason may be that the four weeks are not a pleasant memory for the speaker because Hanna refused to allow him to visit her and request that he pass the class in order to qualify to see her. As in love as the speaker was, four weeks of not seeing Hanna at all was torture and not something that he wanted to dwell on.

Kirsner (2011) postulates two ways to test the hypothesis of the opposition between HIGH DEIXIS and LOW DEIXIS in system: the first is to "examine the kind of nouns which turn up with each demonstrative," and the second is to "examine the use of the demonstratives to refer to items in earlier discourse" (p. 114).

In order to examine what kind of nouns turn up with each demonstrative, we need to seek "any support for the notion of a *de facto* degree of precision of reference" (Kirsner, 2011, p. 114). In our corpus, the novel *Der Vorleser*, I have only found two instances of the non-proximal demonstrative *jen-*, both referring to the plural form of *Wochen* 'weeks.' Since it is harder for the hearer to take care of the features of each item of a plurality than of a single entity, the precision of a singularity is generally higher than of a plurality. Therefore, it can be expected that an entity of singularity, more than an entity of plurality, will indicate a higher degree of precision, and would tend to co-occur more frequently with the more specific and precise demonstrative *dies-* 'this.' Going over all the instances of demonstratives, we can come to the statistic result as demonstrated in the following table:

DM	instances of sg.	instances of pl.	Total	sg. instances %
dies-	36	9	45	80%
jen-	0	2	2	0%

Table 3.9

This table shows that the non-proximal demonstrative does not co-occur with singular entities, while the proximal demonstrative co-occurs frequently with a singular entity. This confirms the hypothesis that a proximal demonstrative signals precision. One may argue, however, that the two instances of the non-proximal demonstrative may not be taken into account due to the limited instances, which may not qualify for a statistical significance test. Nonetheless, it at least confirms that *dies-* co-occurs more frequently with singular entities, which serves as the confirmation of the hypothesis that the more precise demonstrative co-occurs with more precise lexical items, thereby supporting the idea that *dies-* signals HIGH DEIXIS.

The second method Kirsner (2011) identifies for testing the hypothesis is concerned with the use of demonstratives to refer to entities that have been mentioned earlier. We can expect that in actual texts, as the discourse proceeds, there are entities that are continuously mentioned. Among the entities, there are some that are simply repeated and others that will be "reinterpreted, rephrased and developed" (Kirsner 2011, p. 115; cf. Kirsner & van Heuven, 1988, pp. 223—231). Kirsner further states that, "it would be absurd to have an essay in which the precisely same referent is referred to in precisely the same way again and again" (2011, p. 115). If an entity is precisely mentioned in the same way, it is being referred to in a purely instructional or instrumental manner, not in a representational one. This is the "article-like" use, rather than the "demonstrative-like" use. If a speaker uses a demonstrative as if it were an article, it means that either there is something he would like the hearer to pay extra attention to, or it is simply a misuse.

If an entity is rephrased, reinterpreted, or developed along the discourse, it indicates that more information has been added to the referent, making it more precise. Also, if an entity has been developed throughout the discourse, the referent is expected to be in the speaker's focus. That being said, an entity that is mentioned earlier and developed in the discourse will tend to co-occur with the proximal demonstrative *dies-* rather than the non-proximal demonstrative *jen-*. In addition, if an entity is solely repeated, an article should be utilized to refer to it.

> 3.55) So verstellt **dieser** erste Streit und überhaupt unser Streiten was—alles, was unser Ritual des Vorlesens, Duschens, Liebens und Beianderliegens öffnete, tat uns gut. (Schlink, 1995, p. 51)
> 'As sham as our first fight and indeed all our fights were, everything that enlarged our ritual of reading, showering, making love, and lying beside each other did us good.' (Schlink, 1997, p. 51)

Like example 3.53, this example again refers to the first fight between the speaker and Hanna. When first mentioning it, the speaker provides information on when and how it started. As the story develops, the speaker slowly begins to release more information. He talks about the influence of the relationship on his life, how he must constantly make compromises with Hanna, and how Hanna deals with their complex relationship. In the book, this first fight spans throughout the book and whenever it is mentioned, the precise demonstrative *dies-* is used to refer to it.

The following table demonstrates how the demonstratives are associated with entities, which are rephrased, reinterpreted, or developed in the discourse, in the novel *Der Vorleser*.

DM	w/ developed	w/o developed	Total	w/ developed %
dies-	34	11	45	76%
jen-	0	2	2	0%

Table 3.10

This table confirms that the demonstrative *dies-* co-occurs more frequently with entities that are developed in the discourse.

What we can also conclude from the aforementioned tables is that there are not many instances that are associated with the non-proximal demonstrative *jen-*. This, too, can be a proof that *jen-* signals LOW DEIXIS in system in several ways. First, it is understandable that if an entity is being talked about and developed after its introduction, it is in the speaker's focus and will appear less frequently with the non-proximal demonstrative *jen-*, which signals the meaning LOW DEIXIS. If an entity is marked by LOW DEIXIS, it is out of the speaker's attention; and when it is mentioned in the discourse after its introduction, the speaker would not further develop it or even re-mention it. Therefore, the only option for the speaker to refer to an entity with *jen-* is to move from one entity to the next entity. This also implies that the non-proximal demonstrative *jen-* will rarely be used, for there are limited circumstances under which the speaker can use *jen-*. It is therefore not surprising that there are few instances of *jen-*. As shown in the aforementioned tables, there are only two instances of it.

Since the proximal demonstrative *dies-* signals HIGH DEIXIS, it is expected that *dies-* would be used for more important referents than *jen-*. Important referents include things that are turning points in one's life. For example, in *Der Vorleser*, both turning points in the speaker and Hanna's relationship are marked by *dies-*. Besides the first fight, which has already been discussed, the other important "milestone" in their relationship, *der Geruch* 'the smell,' is also referred to continuously by *dies-*. The following example is a summary of the association of *dies-* and *Geruch*.

3.56) Unter **diesen** frischen Gerüchen lag noch ein anderer, ein schwerer, dunkler, herber Geruch. (Schlink, 1995, p. 185)

'Under **these** fresh smells was another, heavy, dark, sharp smell.' (Schlink, 1997, p. 171)

Oft habe ich an ihr geschnüffelt wie ein neugieriges Tier, habe an Hals und Schultern angefangen, die Frisch gewaschen rochen, habe zwischen den Brüsten den frischen Schweißgeruch eingesogen, der sich in den Achselhöhlen mit dem anderen Geruch mischte, fand **diesen** schweren, dunklen Geruch um Taille und Bauch fast pur und zwischen Beinen in einer fruchtigen Färbung, die mich erregte, habe auch ihre Beine und Füße beschnuppert, die Schenkel, an denen sich der schwerer Geruch verlor, die Kniekehlen, noch mal mit leichtem frischem Schweißgeruch, und die Füße, mit dem Geruch von Seife oder Leder oder Müdigkeit. (Schlink, 1995, p. 185)

'Often I would sniff at her like a curious animal, starting with her throat and shoulders, which smelled freshly washed, soaking up the fresh smell of sweat between her breasts mixed in her armpits with the other smell, then finding **this** heavy dark smell almost pure around her waist and stomach and between her legs with a fruity tinge that excited me; I would also sniff at her legs and feet—her thighs, where the heavy smell disappeared, the hollows of her knees again with that light, fresh smell of sweat, and her feet, which smelled of soap or leather or tiredness.' (Schlink, 1997, pp. 196—197)

Ich weiß nicht, was **diesen** Geruch ausmacht, den ich von Großmüttern und alten Tanten kenne und der in Altersheimen in den Zimmern und Fluren hängt wie ein Fluch. (Schlink, 1995, p. 186)

'I don't know what makes up **this** smell, which I recognize from grandmothers and elderly aunts, and which hangs in the rooms and halls of old-age homes like a curse.' (Schlink, 1997, p.197)

In the example, *der Geruch* 'the smell' is the turning point of the speaker's attitude towards Hanna. It first draws the speaker to Hanna because she smells mysterious and sexually feminine. That is one of the reasons why the speaker used to be so attracted to Hanna, who is almost twenty years older than the speaker. The age difference at first did not influence the speaker's psychological feeling. In fact, the novel suggests that Hanna's age allows her to be more open; she doesn't hold back and, because of that, helps the speaker also open up and begin to express himself. The speaker was very shy at his young age and was very eager to explore everything with Hanna, who never held back her feelings. After many years being apart from each other, the speaker eventually saw Hanna in court where she was being sentenced for the part she played in the murder of a group of Jewish women during the war. While Hanna was in jail, the speaker began to read for her again. It was not until these visits, when he found out that Hanna had become much older, like an average elderly lady, and had a different unpleasant smell, that he realized that she was no longer young and attractive. She had changed into an old lady, while the speaker was still a young man. The speaker could no longer accept the great difference in their ages, as all of the features he had once liked in her had faded away. *Der Geruch* 'the smell' is a sign that reflects the speaker's emotion towards Hanna. Therefore, *dies-* is used to refer to this important entity.

Other important kinds of referents include everything that is associated with human beings and their activities (cf. Kirsner, 2011, p.120). It is egocentricity that causes human beings to pay more attention to entities that are close to them or similar to them. It is thus expected that lexical items related to human beings or human activities would tend to co-occur more frequently with *dies-* than *jen-*. Based on the novel *Der Vorleser*，the frequencies of human related lexical items co-occurring with demonstratives and non-human related lexical items associated with demonstratives are shown in the next table:

DM	human-related instances	non-human related instances	Total	human-related instances %
dies-	35	10	45	78%
jen-	0	2	2	0%

Table 3.11

Based on the table, we may agree that *dies-* tends to refer to more important entities than *jen-*. This also indicates that the non-proximal demonstrative *jen-* has potential "negative" implications, which include any non-positive attitudes, less crucial characters, and entities that do not count as main roles (cf. Kirsner, 2011, p.121).

Chapter 4　The Chinese Demonstratives

In this chapter, I will analyze the Chinese demonstratives using the Columbia School linguistic theory framework, as well as cognitive linguistic theory. The two frameworks differ in the sense that the prior focuses on working out a general meaning for each word, whereas the latter concentrates on the mental process associated with each word.

4.1　A Language Without an Article System

As discussed in the second chapter, there are no articles in the Chinese language. Because of this, the function of the article must be taken over by other grammatical categories. There are two possibilities in Chinese that parallel the article system: the unpreceded, and the system of demonstratives. Both of these possible systems will be discussed below. Note that the combination numeral+classifier+noun does not qualify here as part of the differentiating system, because it does not signal any meaning of DIFFERENTIATION (cf. Chapter 3), but only to transmits the message of how many items of a kind are present. For example:

4.1a) Do you have **a** younger brother?

　　　'ni　　you　　didi　　　　　　ma?'
　　　you　　have　　Ø younger brother　QS

4.1b) Do you have **A** younger brother?

'ni   you   yi   ge   didi   ma?'

you   have   one   CL   younger brother   QS

In sentence 4.1a, the question asks whether the hearer has any younger brothers, and the word "a" in the sentence does not mark the quantity of younger brothers, but signals DIFFERENTIATION NOT MADE, transmitting the message of any younger brother. It does not have to be a smart younger brother or a handsome younger brother. Any of the younger brother kind, i.e. any male relative who has the same parents as the hearer and is younger than the hearer, will qualify. In the Chinese translation, the combination of numeral + classifier + noun is not employed to signal this meaning. In contrast, in sentence 4.1b, where the numeral + classifier + noun combination is used, the question, with the stressed "A" pronounced as the letter "A," asks about the quantity of the hearer's younger brother. However, in the English rendering, the word "A," though written as "a" just as it is in sentence 4.1a, functions not as an article, but as a numeral. That is to say, it does not have any differentiating function, but only marks the quantity "one." In the following sections, we will only discuss instances where "a" is an indefinite article. "A" as a numeral will be excluded in this study, because it does not signal any differentiation.

4.1.1 Unpreceded Ø

If "a" functions as an indefinite article, nothing would be used to precede the noun to signal the meaning DIFFERENTIATION NOT MADE. In addition, there are other situations where an article would be used to differentiate the lexical item but these situations remain unpreceded in Chinese.

The first situation, when a lexical item is literally unique, it will be preceded by the definite article "the" in English, but will be unpreceded in Chinese.

  4.2) **The** sun rises in the east.

    'taiyang cong dongfang sheng qi.'

    Ø sun from east   rise VC

In this example, the sun is unique, and is thus referred to by the definite article "the," which signals DIFFERENTIATION MADE. In the Chinese translation, it is unpreceded.

  The second situation is when a lexical item is associated with the signal of the unpreceded plural in English. In these cases, it most likely will be unpreceded in Chinese.

  4.3) Ø Dogs are man's best friends.

    'gou shi renlei   zui hao de pengyou.'

    Ø dog be human being most good MM friend

In this sentence, "dogs" refers to a general category of animal, not to any individual dog, and is unpreceded in English to signal the meaning DIFFERENTIATION NOT MADE. These cases will be unpreceded in Chinese as well.

  The third situation is when a lexical item is singular and unpreceded in English. These cases will be unpreceded in Chinese as well.

  4.4) I like to eat **Ø** chicken.

    'wo xihuan chi jirou.'

    I like eat Ø chicken

Here chicken is singular and not preceded by any articles, as is *jirou* 'chicken' in the Chinese translation.

  To summarize this section, if an entity in English is not preceded by a definite article, it most likely will be unpreceded in the parallel Chinese sentence. The only contrary case is when an entity is unique. In such cases, the entity will be preceded by the definite article in English, but will be unpreceded in Chinese. In conclusion, if an entity is associated with the meaning DIFFERENTIATION NOT MADE, either signaling DIFFERENTIATION REQUIRED or DIFFERENTIATION NOT REQUIRED, it will be unpreceded in Chinese. In addition, any entity that does not have potential peer referents, i. e. it is unique, will be unpreceded in Chinese as well. In the latter situation, although the entity is preceded by the definite article "the" in English, meaning DIFFERENTIATION MADE, there is no actual differentiating process, in the sense that there are no practical potential "competitors" present. Therefore, the *unprecededness* in Chinese may be characterized to signal NO DIFFERENTIATION.

4.1.2 Preceded by demonstratives

It is logical to postulate that in contrast to the meaning NO DIFFERENTIATION signaled by unprecededness, being preceded by a demonstrative will automatically show that the entity following it is differentiated from other entities. The nature of demonstrative bears the connotation DIFFERENTIATION MADE, because a demonstrative not only differentiates an entity from other entities, but also provides information on the relative location and distance from the speaker.

Basically, there are two situations in which demonstratives are used in Chinese. The first is when a singular entity is preceded by the definite article "the" in English and is not unique.

4.5) **The** student who is watching TV is American.

'<u>na</u>   ge   zai   kandianshi de   xuesheng shi meiguoren.'
DM (that) CL   at   watch TV   MM   student   be   American

In this sentence, the TV-watching student is preceded by the definite article "the," and is therefore differentiated from other students. And in Chinese, the student is preceded by the non-proximal demonstrative *na* 'that.'

The other situation is when the entity is in the plural and preceded by the definite article "the."

4.6a) **The** professors from California are very nice.

'<u>naxie</u>　　　cong　Jiazhou　lai　de　jiaoshou　hen　hao.'
DM (those)　from　California　come　MM　professor　very　nice

4.6b) Ø Professors from California are very nice.

'cong　Jiazhou　lai　de　jiaoshou　**dou**　hen　hao.'
Ø from　California　come　MM　professor　**all**　very　nice

In sentence 4.6a, "professors" is preceded by the definite article "the" and is differentiated from others. In its Chinese translation, it is preceded by the non-proximate demonstrative *na* 'that.' Sentence 4.6a means that a certain group of professors from California are nice, or some professors from California are nice. In contrast, sentence 4.6b does not have any article preceding "professors," which suggests that, in general, most or all professors from California are nice, which is obviously a generalization, not a specification as in sentence 4.6a. In this case, "professors" is not preceded by any demonstratives in Chinese. In addition, the adverb *dou* 'all' illustrates the difference between sentences 4.6a and 4.6b in meaning. By using *dou*, sentence 4.6b suggests that each one of the aforementioned group is applicable to the description generated by the sentence, which, in this case, suggests that every Californian professor is very nice (in contrast to the specific group of professors referred to by sentence 4.6a).

To summarize, if an entity is preceded by the definite article and is not unique, it would be preceded by the non-proximal demonstrative *na* 'that' in the parallel Chinese sentence, signaling DIFFERENTIATION.

Furthermore, we may also hypothesize that *na* takes over most of the function of the definite article for good reason. If an entity is associated with the definite article "the," without indicating its location, it means that either the location of the entity is not known, or the location of the entity is not worth mentioning. In either case, using the proximal demonstrative *zhe* 'this' to refer to it would generate contradicting messages. Because *zhe* only refers to limited space in the vicinity of the speaker, it is impossible for an entity to be in the vicinity of the speaker and at the same time have its location indicated as unknown or not worth mentioning. If so, it would simply reject egocentricity, which is a psychological principle of the human mind. Therefore, *na* is a less inappropriate option (cf. Diver, 1995), as it refers to space not close to the speaker and can expand infinitely throughout the universe. In any case, locations that are not in the vicinity of the speaker may be out of the speaker's sight and thus may be less precisely known by the speaker. Because of this, *na* contradicts neither the unspecificity of nor the unconcern with mentioning the referent's location suggested by use of the definite article and is therefore a less inappropriate option.

4.1.3 Use of demonstratives

In the traditional view of Chinese grammar (Wang, 1959), the demonstratives *zhe* 'this' and *na* 'that' signal the meanings NEAR and FAR. There is no boundary to decide whether an entity is objectively near or far because it is the speaker who decides and communicates the distance of the entity. That is to say, any absolute distance between the speaker and the entity is not the only standard, and the speaker's perception should be taken into consideration.

4.7a) zhe   shi   wode   pingguo.
       DM (this)   be   my   apple
       'This is my apple.'

4.7b) na   shi   nide   xiangjiao.
       DM (that)   be   your   banana
       'That is your banana.'

In the above example, it is obvious that the apple is near the speaker and the banana is farther than the apple. We may come to the following conclusion (Wang, 1959):

$$\text{Demonstratives:} \begin{cases} \text{NEAR} \begin{cases} \text{SINGULAR: } zhe, zhege \text{ 'this'} \\ \text{PLURAL: } zhexie \text{ 'these'} \end{cases} \\ \text{FAR} \begin{cases} \text{SINGULAR: } na, nage \text{ 'that'} \\ \text{PLURAL: } naxie \text{ 'those'} \end{cases} \end{cases}$$

Figure 4.1

The Chinese demonstratives can also differentiate temporal distance between a time point or an event in the past and the narrative time. For example:

4.8) zhexie   nian, rizi   hao   guo   le   henduo
     DM (these)   year   life   good   live   PFV   much
     huixiang   qi   jiefang   qian   naxie   kunan
     recall   CRS   emancipation before DM (those)   difficulty
     jingran   ye   ting   le   guolai.
     surprisingly also   suffer   PFV   manage

'Life has improved a lot these years. Upon reflection of those [*naxie*] hard times before the Emancipation, we surprisingly survived.'

This example claims that life after the Emancipation is better than life before it. Life before the Emancipation is referred to by the demonstrative *na*, whereas life after the Emancipation by *zhe*. Taking the emancipation as the reference point, any time before it should be temporally farther than any time after it. The demonstrative *zhe* can refer to an earlier time point or period, and *na* to a later time or period.

Note that both *zhe* and *na* can be used in situations where they function other than as demonstratives, such as gap-fillers (Hayashi & Yoon, 2006). Since this study only focuses on the demonstrative nature of both words, situations where they do not function as demonstratives are excluded in this study. Also, those instances will be screened out of the corpus and will not play any role in either qualitative or quantitative study.

4.2　The Problem

There are, however, inadequacies if we simply state that *zhe* 'this' signals NEAR and *na* 'that' signals FAR, as this provides no explanation for why *zhe* sometimes refers to the same item as *na* does, or for why *zhe* sometimes even refers to something which is farther from the speaker than that which *na* refers to. The following examples are from Qian Zhongshu's novel *Weicheng* (*Fortress Besieged*) and show that *zhe* and *na* are not limited to the meanings NEAR and FAR.

In the following example, Fang Hung-chien[①], the central character of the novel, is invited by Su Wen-wan, the girl who is pursuing Fang, to a dinner with her friend Chao Hsin-mei. They sit around the table, and Su introduces Hung-chien and Hsin-mei to each other. Su tells Hsin-mei that she and Hung-chien were on the same ship returning to China:

---

① For the sake of consistency, all names from the book *Weicheng* will be in Wade-Giles instead of pinyin because the English translation (Kelly & Mao, 1979) uses Wade-Giles.

Chapter 4 The Chinese Demonstratives 175

4.9) | Na | Chao | Hsin-mei | benlai | jiu | shenqihuoxian, | | |
|---|---|---|---|---|---|---|---|
| DM (that) | Chao | Hsin-mei | originally | already | arrogant | | |
| ting | Su | Xiaojie | shuo | | | | |
| hear | Su | Miss | say | | | | |
| Hung-chien | que | shi | gen | ta | tongchuan | huiguo | de, |
| Hung-chien | really | be | with | she | same boat | return | NOM |
| tade | biaoqing | jiu | fangfu | | | | |
| his | face | just | seem | | | | |
| Hung-chien | hua | wei | xidan | de | kongqi, | | |
| Hung-chien | change | become | thin | MM | air | | |
| yanjing | li | mei | you | zhe | ge | ren. | |
| eye | in | not | have | DM(this) | CL | person | |

(Qian, 1954, p. 50)

'[na] Chao Hsin-mei looked smug to begin with, and after hearing Miss Su confirm that Hung-chien indeed came home with her on the same ship, he acted as if Hung-chien had turned into thin air and ignored [zhe] Hung-chien completely.' (Qian, 1979, p. 54)

In this example, *na* refers to Chao Hsin-mei and *zhe* refers to Fang Hung-chien, but both are eating at the same table. Although *na* should connote that Chao is further and *zhe* that Fang is closer, it is not reasonable to state that Chao Hsin-mei is far and Fang Hung-chien is near. In the following example, both *zhe* and *na* refer to one person in the same situation.

4.10) | bici | jieshao | zhihou, | | | |
|---|---|---|---|---|---|
| each other | introduce | after | | | |
| Hung-chien | cai | zhidao | | | |
| Hung-chien | not until | know | | | |
| na | wei | gong | le | bei | de |
| DM (that) | CL | bow | PFV | back | MM |
| shi | zhexuejia | Ch'u | Shen-ming. | | |
| be | philosopher | Ch'u | Shen-ming | | |

...zhe	wei	Ch'u	Shen-ming	yuanming		Ch'u	Chia-pao,
...DM(this)	CL	Ch'u	Shen-ming	original name		Ch'u	Chia-pao

chengming	yihou	xian	Chia-pao	zhe		mingzi
get famous	after	mind	Chia-pao	DM(this)		name

bu	fuhe	zhexuejia	shenfen,
not	match	philosopher	status

ju	Sibinnuosha	gaiming	de	xianli,
according to	Spinosa	change name	MM	example

huan	cheng	Shen-ming
change	become	Shen-ming

qu	"shen-si-ming-bian"		de	yisi.
take	"carefully-think-clearly-tell"		MM	meaning

(Qian, 1954, p. 81)

'During the introductions, Hung-chien learned that the [*na*] hunchback was the philosopher Ch'u Shen-ming. ... [*zhe*] Ch'u Shen-ming's orginal name was Ch'u Chia-pao. After attaining fame he found Chia-pao (literally, family treasure) unsuitable for a philosopher and changed it, following the precedent set by Spinosa, to Shen-ming (literally, careful and clear), taken from the expression "consider carefully and argue clearly."' (Qian, 1979, p. 83)

In this example, *na* is used first and *zhe* second, but both refer to the philosopher Ch'u Chia-pao. The referent stays the same, but two different demonstratives are used to refer to him in the same situation. There is no way that the referent is both NEAR and FAR at the same time and at the same place. Therefore, in this example, the use of *zhe* 'this' and *na* 'that' conflicts with the common-sense interpretation of NEAR versus FAR. Thus, the demonstratives may no longer be limited to a spatial or temporal description.

4.3 The Hypothesis

Based on both examples, we can no longer claim that *zhe* and *na* are solely related to spatial and temporal distance. Rather, they are "instructions concerned with directing the hearer's attention to the particular referent of the noun which the speaker has in mind" (Kirsner, 1993, p. 88). So *zhe* 'this' is said to signal the meaning HIGH DEIXIS, and *na* 'that' is said to signal the meaning of LOW DEIXIS. The system is diagrammed in Figure 4.2, in contrast to Figure 4.1.

$$\text{DEIXIS} \begin{cases} \text{zhe} = \text{HIGH DEIXIS} \\ \quad \text{(requires more attention of the hearer to the referent)} \\ \text{na} = \text{LOW DEIXIS} \\ \quad \text{(requires less attention of the hearer to the referent)} \end{cases}$$

Figure 4.2

Let us refer back to examples 4.9 and 4.10. In example 4.9, Chao Hsin-mei is a peripheral character in the book, while Fang Hung-chien is the central character. It makes sense to give more attention to the main character and less on others because the book is Fang Hung-chien's story and the author does not want to distract the reader's attention with other supporting roles. In example 4.10, the author assigns different demonstratives to the same person based on the descriptive proximity: in the first sentence, Ch'u Shen-ming is mentioned for the first time. Every first impression of him is as a hunchback, with no other information provided. The second sentence, however, includes an anecdote about changing his name from the original out-of-fashion and rural name to the philosophy-related one. The reader is provided with more and new information and therefore needs to pay more attention to that. Another explanation of example 4.10 is that the style of the story is ironic. The character Ch'u Shen-ming, a so-called "founder of new Chinese philosophy," gained his fame by writing sycophantic letters to world-famous philosophers and received their replies either in words or in gift books, and he told others that he was familiar with those celebrities, using their replies as evidence. The truth is that he personally did not have any idea what philosophy was or what it dealt with, beyond possessing an appropriately philosophical name. To make this scene and his meaning clear, the author uses demonstratives to encourage the hearer to perceive the satirical tone of his anecdote.

4.4 Qualitative Validation

In this section, I will provide examples from the novel *Weicheng* and look for qualitative evidence to support that *zhe* signals HIGH DEIXIS and *na* signals LOW DEIXIS. When analyzing each demonstrative, I will provide examples of situations that exemplify the usage of these demonstratives.

4.4.1 Demonstrating HIGH DEIXIS

There are several situations that require the hearer's focused attention and signal HIGH DEIXIS in actual discourse: a positive attitude towards or high familiarity with an entity, contrast with previous information, co-existence with a superlative, ego-centricity, reiteration of the main argument, and the introduction of an important entity.

4.4.1.1 Speaker's positive attitude

When discussing something that is favorable to the speaker, the speaker wants the hearer to pay more attention to that entity. This is because if one likes an entity, it is natural that he/she knows a lot about it and would like to talk about it. In addition, he/she would also want the hearer to like the entity just as he/she likes it. If unable to emphasize his/her subject, the speaker would have difficulty encouraging the hearer to pay specific attention to the referent. As a result, it is unlikely that the hearer display interest in the referent and will not come to like the referent as much as the speaker does.

> 4.11) wenshuke zhuren kanjian yuanxin, xiang dongjia dada gongwei zhe wei wei guomende guye wenli shufa dou hao, bingqie dui sizhe qingci shenzhi, xiangjian tianxing jihou, ding shi ge yuandaozhiqi. (Qian, 1954, p. 8)
>
> 'When Chief-secretary Wang read Fang Hung-chien's letter, he had high praise for [zhe] his boss's would-be son-in-law, remarking that the young man's calligraphy and literary style were both excellent, and that the expression of his feelings for the deceased was deep and genuine, indicative of a very kind heart and talent that would take him far.' (Qian, 1979, p. 11)

In this example, Fang Hung-chien's would-be wife passed away when he was studying abroad. Before her death, Hung-chien did not like her and had even written a letter to his father asking to cancel the engagement, but his father did not agree. This made Hung-chien angrier about his future fiancé, and he wished her bad luck. Hung-chien was very well-written, but his words were not kind-hearted. He received money from his would-be father-in-law and went to study abroad, but failed to attain a degree after four years. In order to avoid remonstration, he bought a fake degree from an Irish man. The degree was from a European university with an American university's name. He did not notice this, even though he had spent four years in Europe. He also did not have any deep or affectionate feelings for his deceased wife-to-be; he hid her photo at the bottom of his suitcase and, later, was not able to tell whether the color of the picture had faded. The reality of Hung-chien's attitude toward his fiancé is very much at odds with the secretary's evaluation. To draw greater focus from the reader and to make the irony evident, the author uses *zhe* 'this' to precede the noun, which refers to the main character Hung-chien, which strengthens the intonation and highlights the irony. If the noun were preceded by *na* 'that,' the secretary's approval for Hung-chien would likely go unmarked. In addition, the reader would lack the emphasis that makes the irony of the Chief-secretary's shameless praise for Hung-chien's non-existant love for his deceased would-be wife apparent.

The following example describes a lady and her servant Ah Fu, who sit together in the bus. Hung-chien meets them on his trip to the university at which he is going to teach. The lady, well-dressed and enthusiastic, is in fact not a particularly good person or a moral character. She poisoned her husband to hide her affair with another man. In contrast, the servant, Ah Fu, gives a bad first impression because of his greasy hair and clothing, but is later proven to be loyal, protective, and quite insightful.

4.12) <u>na</u> guafu xiang Li Mei-ting yanzhu yi liu, zui yi che dao:"nai xiansheng zhen shi haoren!"... <u>zhe</u> nanren youtouhuamian, xiang jin you de pipahe, chuan jian qingbu dagua, gen nüren bingjian er zuo, kan bu chu shi yongren. (Qian, 1954, p. 163)

'The [*na*] widow threw him a glance and, giving her mouth a tug at the corners, said, "You are such a good man."... With his slick, greasy hair and shiny face, [*zhe*] Ah Fu looked like an oil-soaked loquat seed. As he was dressed in a blue cotton robe and was sitting next to the woman, one would not have guessed that he was a servant.' (Qian, 1979, p. 173)

The first impressions of the two characters are precisely contrary to their natures. The young widow behaves as an appreciative, decent and considerate lady with good manners, when, in fact, she is frivolous, an adulteress, and a murderer. In contrast, the servant looks like an oil-soaked loquat seed and is not dressed appropriately for his station. From these rather negative descriptions, the reader would not expect him to be upright and responsible, and yet, he both warns the widow of potential danger and protects her throughout their journey. Therefore, the use of both demonstratives provides a hint of the real traits of the both characters.

In the next example, the use of the demonstrative *zhe* 'this' shows the speaker's direct appreciation and positive attitude without reservation.

4.13) zhexie haizi rexin de bu dong daoli. (Qian, 1954, p. 184)

'Those [*zhexie*] kids are too enthusiastic for their own good.' (Qian, 1979, p. 195)

Here, Li Mei-ting comments on the luxurious welcome party thrown by his would-be students. Upon his arrival, Li Mei-ting found out that the students in his department were holding a party in his honor, and his companions immediately congratulated him on his popularity. Li wanted to show pride at his accomplishment, but did not want to appear arrogant. There are at least two reasons for this: First, it is not favored in traditional Chinese philosophy to praise or show pride in oneself; second, the person who is conspicuously more skilled or more loved than his peers will be a target for gossip and slander, as in the Chinese proverb "*qiang da chutou niao*" 'The bird, whose head first appears, will be shot' and "*gaochu bu sheng han*" 'The higher one climbs, the colder one feels.'[①] In order to balance displaying his appreciation and

---

① This is not just a Chinese cultural phenomenon and has such English equivalents as "the tallest blade of grass is the first to be cut."

avoiding the costs of fame, Li Mei-ting criticizes his students' enthusiasm even though he is pleased by it at the same time. Replacing *zhe* with *na* changes the meaning from acting entitled to showing contempt, and even though there is only a tiny change in mood, the usage of *zhe* reveals his real attitude toward his welcome party.

4.4.1.2 High familiarity

Generally, if an entity is close to the speaker, the speaker is more familiar with it in comparison to other entities. This is because the speaker has more opportunities to familiarize himself with entities that are closer to him. In addition, the entities are more accessible and, thus, will not be overly difficult for the speaker to explore.

If the speaker is very familiar with an entity, it makes sense that he would want the hearer to pay more attention to it. It would not be illogical for the speaker to show indifference to an entity with which he is acquainted.

In the following example, Hung-chien and Hsin-mei, are gossiping about Miss Su's husband, Ts'ao Yüan-lang. Neither of them believes that Ts'ao is a good choice for Su: he is not physically attractive, nor does he have a degree from a prestigious college, nor does he come from a wealthy family (these are believed to be the three most important factors when selecting one's future husband). Neither Hung-chien nor Hsin-mei likes Ts'ao, but for different reasons: Hung-chien does not care for him because he is from a similar background; Hsin-mei dislikes him because he himself had wanted to ask Miss Su to marry him and hates anyone marrying her but him. By way of background, Hung-chien has met Ts'ao before and Hsin-mei has not.

 4.14) "keshi wo dao xianzai ye bu zhidao <u>na</u> xing cao de shi shenmeyang'r de ren."

  "wo dao kanjian guo <u>zhe</u> ren, keshi wo xiang bu dao su xiaojie hui kan zhong ta. " (Qian, 1954, p. 120)

'"But I still don't know what sort of guy that [na] Ts'ao fellow is. "

"Well, I've met [zhe] him before, but I never thought Miss Su would go for him. "' (Qian, 1979, p. 124)

Hsin-mei has not met Yüan-lang before and is incapable of giving any further information about him and, as such, uses *na* to refer to him. In contrast, Hung-chien has had dinner with Yüan-lang and Miss Su together and knows about his work and character; thus, he is able to talk about him if asked, and points to him by using *zhe*. Hsin-mei also uses *na* to refer to Yüan-lang because he has been in love with Miss Su for more than ten years, but failed to propose. He thought the failure resulted from Hung-chien, his imaginary rival in love. In fact, the lady Hung-chien fell in love with was T'ang Hsiao-fu, not Miss Su. As one is not supposed display favor for a rival for love, Hsin-mei use *na* to show his disrespect and disdain for Yüan-lang.

4.15) chuan shang zhe ji wei, you zai faguo liuxue de, you zai yingguo, deguo, biguo deng dushu, dao bali qu zengzhang yeshenghuo jingyan, yinci ye zuo faguo chuan de. (Qian, 1954, p. 2)

'Although some of those [zhe] on board had been students in France, the others, who had been studying in England, Germany, and Belgium, had gone to Paris to gain more experience of nightlife before taking a French ship home. ' (Qian, 1979, p. 4)

This example provides more information about the students on board the ship. Hung-chien is on the same ship, but has never spoken to them. This example, however, gives detailed information about their background. The author wants the reader to have more information about the general quality of the students who are going abroad; that is, he wants his readers to understand how brilliant the study-abroad students seem from the outside, but know how hollow they actually are. With this kind of background information, the reader can predict what kind of life Hung-chien might lead after returning to China and thus, is psychologically prepared for Hung-chien's tragedy: a man without profound knowledge and social skills will not succeed in war time.

In the next example, both Hung-chien and Mrs. Chou refer to the same piece of news which appears in a local newspaper. The news is about Hung-chien returning to China with a degree from a famous American university. In fact, Hung-chien did not receive a degree from any university. In order to hide this fact from his would-be parents-in-law, who had financially sponsored his stay in Europe, Hung-chien bought a fake diploma from an Irish man. Understandably, he feels nervous when the news is published. Ignorant of the truth, Mrs. Chou is happy to praise her son-in-law-to-be to others.

    4.16) zai chuan shang cong mei gen su xiaojie tan qi xuewei de shi, ta kan dao zhe xinwen hui duanding ziji chuiniu pianren. (Qian, 1954, p. 28)

    'While on the ship he had never discussed degrees with her, but when she saw this [zhe] item, she would conclude that he was a deceitful braggart.' (Qian, 1979, p. 31)

    Chou taitai kan Fang Hung-chien peng bao lao zhe zhe lian, xiao dui zhangfu shuo:"ni qiao Hung-chien duo deyi, na tiao xinwen kan le ji bian hai bu fangshou." (Qian,1954, p. 28)

    'Noticing how son-in-law kept holding the paper before his face, Mrs. Chou said to herhusband with a smile, "See how pleased Hung-chien is. He's read the [na] itemseveral times and still can't put it down."' (Qian, 1979, p. 31)

Hung-chien's would-be father-in-law posted the notice in the newspaper without Hung-chien's permission. As previously explained, Hung-chien's Ph. D. degree was a fake. His would-be father-in-law had no idea about this, though, and wrote in the article that Hung-chien had newly received his Ph. D. from a German university (with the name of an American school). In so doing, he inadvertently revealed Hung-chien's deception to anyone who had some knowledge of Europe. However, Mrs. Chou, a traditional Chinese uneducated housewife, has no idea about the secret. As such, author applies *zhe* to the item Hung-chien reads but uses *na* for the same item mentioned by Mrs. Chou. For Hung-chien, the article reveals his duplicity, while for Mrs. Chou it was merely news that she could brag about to her friends.

4.4.1.3 Contrast with a previous description

If a piece of information contradicts a previous piece of knowledge, the speaker will urge the hearer to notice the incongruity. If the hearer does not pay attention to the new information, he may not be able to detect the difference and switch it out with the knowledge that he already knows and accepts. Therefore, it is necessary to use *zhe* to refer to contrasting information, signaling HIGH DEIXIS. In the following example, the speaker, Miss Su, comments on her cousin T'ang Hsiao-fu, with whom Hung-chien has fallen in love. Miss Su does not like T'ang Hsiao-fu, even though they are related, because Miss Su has been continuously trying to seduce Hung-chien.

 4.17) zhe haizi sui xiao, benling da de hen, ta zhua yi ba nanpengyou zai shou li
   wannongzhe ne! (Qian, 1954, p.53)
   'That [*zhe*] girl is very capable for her age. She has slew of boyfriends
   that she fools around with. ' (Qian, 1979, p.58)

In this sentence, Miss Su comments on her cousin T'ang Hsiao-fu, who has been chatting with Hung-chien at supper, with whom T'ang Hsian-fu appeared to share a secret, although neither would reveal it to Miss Su. Miss Su is irritated and angered by their "intimacy" and fears that Hung-chien will fall in love with T'ang instead of with her. Later, when speaking to Hung-chien, she does not want to waste an opportunity to vilify her rival: she lies to Hung-chien, telling him that T'ang juggles many boyfriends at the same time, thereby hoping to trick Hung-chien into thinking poorly of T'ang. To impress these words into his consciousness, she begins her comment with *zhe*, drawing his attention; she then overwhelms him with slander about T'ang.

In the next example, the author discusses the Western philosophers to whom the "philosopher" Ch'u Shen-ming has had correspondence. In his letters, Ch'u praised each of them for their outstanding academic achievements and their contributions to humanity. When receiving Ch'u's letter, each Western philosopher is surprised, because none of them has expected to receive anything from China, a far away and unfamiliar country.

  4.18) tamen lixiang zhongguo shi ge buzhi zenyang bise luowu de yuanshi guojia, er zhe ge zhongguoren xin li shuo ji ju hua, dao you fencun, bian huixin zan Ch'u Shen-ming shi zhongguo xin zhexue de chuangshiren, haiyou song shu gei ta de. (Qian, 1954, p. 81)

  'China, as they saw it, was a primitive country, heaven knows how mean andbackward, and yet here was a [*zhe*] Chinese who wrote with sense. In their replies to Ch'u Shen-ming, they praised him as the founder of a new philosophy of China, and even sent him books.' (Qian, 1979, p. 84)

Closed and backward as China was seen to be, the Western philosophers did not expect any Chinese person to know about their accomplishments in philosophy. Thus it was unusual for them to receive laudatory letters from a Chinese person. In order to mark Ch'u Shen-ming's "heroic undertaking," *zhe* is used to encourage the reader's attention. If *na* were used instead of *zhe*, the sentence would not have such a contrasting meaning. Rather than being surprised, the Western philosophers would seem either to have predicted that they would receive letters from China, or had already received many such letters. According to the author, neither was the case.

4.4.1.4 Co-occurrence with a superlative

A noun phrase with a superlative expression is already eye-attracting by itself. If it co-occurs with *na*, signaling LOW DEIXIS, the grammatical meaning will contradict the lexical meaning: a superlative expression requires more attention from the hearer, since it is to the greatest degree of its kind and definitely processes more features that may be of interest. Moreover, an association with the meaning LOW DEIXIS will automatically diminish the superlative's exceptionality and decrease the urge for the hearer to seek it out.

> 4.19) chuan you guo le Xilan he Xinjiapo, buri dao Xigong, zhe shi faguo chuan yilu zou lai diyige ke kua'ao de benguo zhimindi. (Qian, 1954, p. 14)
> 'The ship passed Ceylon and Singapore and in a few days reached Saigon. This [*zhe*] was the first colony since the start of the voyage that the French could boast of astheir own.' (Qian, 1979, p. 18)

Here, it is hard to argue that *zhe* signals NEAR because Saigon has yet to be reached and is thus beyond the characters' sight. Passengers on this ship did not have a chance to disembark to rest until they reached Saigon because Saigon was the first French colony. "The first" is a superlative expression and, by itself, already alerts the reader to pay attention. Therefore, it is natural to use *zhe* in this sentence, as *na*, would create confusion because it does not signal high attention and contradicts the imperative after it.

4.4.1.5 Ego-centricity

Ego-centricity is a basic feature of the human mind which causes people to want to be the center of attention. Typically, it is difficult for an individual to accept the fact that he/she is not the focus of others' attention. It is even more difficult for humans to refer to themselves as unimportant or to refrain from urging others to pay attention to them. When referring to himself/herself (or a related entity) with first-person pronouns or possessive pronouns, it is likely that the speaker will use *zhe* instead of *na*.

 4.20) women zhe wei laobo guangxu chunian zai zuo jingguan de shihou, youren waiguo huilai song gei ta yi guan kafei, ta yiwei shi biyan, ba bikong li de pi dou ca po le. (Qian, 1954, p.86)

  'That [*zhe*] [Our this old family friend①] old family friend of ours, while serving as aofficial in Peking during the early years of the Kuang-hsü reign [about 1875], received a can of coffee from someone who had just returned from abroad. He thought it was snuff and rubbed off the skin of his nostrils with it.' (Qian, 1979, p.89)

As ego-centricity is fundamental to human beings, everyone wants to be the focus and to receive more recognition from others. This old uncle is preceded by *women* 'we,' which means 'our' in this case. If *na* is applied to replace *zhe*, its meaning of low *deixis* will contradict with the plural form of 'I': 'we' and LOW DEIXIS would correspondently cause confusion to readers as they would receive two signs pointing in opposite directions. However, there are other explanations that may validate the use of the demonstrative *zhe* in this passage. Within the first part of this example, both temporally and spatially, "the old family friend" is FAR. In this example, though, he is preceded by *zhe* because he was typical within that time period, when China first came into contact with foreign products and made a lot of humorous mistakes in their attempts to figure out the probable uses of these items. In some ways it is funny to make jokes, but in others, it is sad: through this individual, we are shown just how late Western culture was introduced

---

 ① "*Women zhe wei laobo*" is an appositive phrase, meaning 'our this old family friend,' literally.

Chapter 4 The Chinese Demonstratives 189

into China. In addition, *zhe* is used here is because all the names mentioned by Ch'u Shen-ming are significant in both Chinese and Western history, and it makes a lot of sense to use *zhe* to refer to celebrities as this signifies their importance.

4.4.1.6 Reiteration of the main focus

Within the flow of actual discourse, a speaker may mention an entity first and then talk about related entities or facts for a while. In order to remind the hearer of the main focus and clarify the topic of the discourse, the speaker may repeat the main focus and redirect the hearer's attention to it, so that the hearer remains on track. Therefore, only by using *zhe* is the speaker able to signal the meaning HIGH DEIXIS and pull the hearer back from other information he/she may have been overwhelmed with.

> 4.21) shishishang, yi ge ren de quedian zheng xiang houzi de weiba, houzi dun zai dimian de shihou, weiba shi kan bu jian de, zhidao ta xiang shushang pa, jiu ba houbu gong dazhong zhanyang, keshi zhe hong tun chang weiba benlai jiu you, bingfei diwei pa gao le de xin biaoshi. (Qian, 1954, p. 208)
> 'He didn't realize that a person's shortcomings are just a monkey's tail. When it's squatting on the ground, its tail is hidden from view, but as soon as it climbs a tree, it exposes its backside to everyone. Nevertheless, the [*zhe*] long tail and red bottom were there all the time. They aren't just a mark of having climbed a higher position.' (Qian, 1979, p. 221)

This is the most penetrating metaphor in the book. The author compares one's faults to a monkey's tail and then describes the tail's appearance, though its significance is not manifested in the first part of the sentence. Therefore, the author reiterates his point by preceding it with *zhe* to focus the reader's attention on the tail, not on tree-climbing. If *zhe* were replaced with *na*, the tail would not be the focus of the sentence, which may cause the hearer to be diverted away from his main point by the tree-climbing example. If the hearer does not re-grasp the tail as the main point, he will have less of a chance to comprehend the analogy the speaker: short-comings are not magically created when one attains a higher position, but rather exist from the very beginning and simply become obvious when one moves up in society.

4.4.1.7　Followed by more information

After initially mentioning an entity, a speaker has two options to deal with it, depending on the role of the entity. If the entity is important to the discourse, it will recur several times and with more information and accuracy than an entity that is merely peripheral. If an entity is mentioned several times and elaborated upon, it will be referred to by *zhe*, which signals HIGH DEIXIS, so that the hearer will be encouraged to seek out new information. Otherwise the hearer will not know to pay attention to the newly introduced information.

The following example is a description of Miss Su, who tries all means to capture Hung-chien's heart from the moment they meet on their voyage back to China. Miss Su, a false and vain character, acts as if she is a well-behaved lady who would never pursue men but rather waits for them to pursue her. Nonetheless, she is so jealous when she sees Hung-chien flirting with Miss Pao that she spreads gossip about Miss Pao in an attempt to undermine her rival and shame Hung-chien into leaving her.

> 4.22) tade pingdan, geng shi Hung-chien yiju, juede zhe shi aiqing chao relie de anwen, fangfu jufeng hou de haiyang bopinglangjing, er dixia suishi qianfu zhe xiongyong fanteng de liliang. (Qian, 1954, p. 24)
> 'Her nonchalance made him apprehensive, giving him the feeling it [*zhe*] was a demonstration of confidence secured by love, just as the sea stays calm after a storm while underneath its tranquil surface lies the power to rise up in a rushing torrent.' (Qian, 1979, p. 27)

In this example, *zhe* refers to "her nonchalance," which makes Hung-chien apprehensive. After *zhe*, the author explains the reason why Hung-chien feels apprehensive, which also provides a more concrete description of Miss Su's nonchalance. It is later shown that Miss Su's indifference is an act. She is, in fact, very nervous and fears that she will not be able to capture Hung-chien and later makes an effort to force Hung-chien to stay with her. When all her efforts turn out to be in vain, she no longer puts on airs or even dares to expose her broken heart to the public. She soon marries a puffy and self-absorbed man, about whom she knows very little. Based on the story, her nonchalance was meant to allow Hung-chien's freedom so that she could have a better understanding of how to capture him later. In the following description the demonstrative anticipates the plot and the final status of the two characters.

4.23) <u>zhe</u> ben lüzi yiwei zou qian yi bu, luobo jiu neng daozui, yushi yi bu zai yi bu jixu xiang qian, zui yu yao yao, jiao yu hui gan, buzhibujue zhong you zou le yi bu. (Qian, 1954, p. 261)

'The [*zhe*] stupid mule thinks that, if it takes a step forward, it can get a bite out of the carrot, so it keeps going forward step by step. The more it hankers for a bite, the faster it goes, and before the mule realizes it, it will have reached the next station.' (Qian, 1979, p. 278)

4.24) shuimian <u>zhe</u> dongxi piqi guai de hen, bu yao ta, ta pian hui lai, qing ta, hong ta, qianfangbaiji gongyin ta, ta na shenfen duo de yingzi dou bu jian.' (Qian, 1954, pp. 288—289)

'[*Zhe*] [Sleep this thing①] Sleep is such a fickle thing. When not wanted, it comes; and when it is invited, coaxed, and enticed along by every available trick, it puts on airs and conceals itself.' (Qian, 1979, p. 309)

---

① "*Shuimian zhe dongxi*" is an appositive phrase, meaning 'sleep this thing,' literally.

Both "the stupid mule" and "sleep" are described in detail. If they were preceded by *na*, both sentences could terminate at the end of the first clause, as there would be no need to provide further information. However, both "the stupid mule" and "sleep" are preceded by *zhe*. As a result, both sentences must continue and, having been alerted, the hearer will wait for further information; he does not feel the sentence is complete. This is also consistent with the hypothesis in that *zhe* requires more of the hearer's attention and more information from the speaker, while *na* requires less attention and does not necessarily need further explanation. In example 4.24, sleep is described in detail. If it is preceded by *na*, the sentence can end with the first part; the statement "Sleep is such a fickle thing" stands on its own and requires no elaboration. But as *zhe* precedes "sleep," the sentence cannot simply stop with the first clause because *zhe* signals that the thought is not yet done.

4.4.1.8 Important information

An entity that is important to the speaker or the discourse should stand out more and therefore should be preceded by *zhe*. If preceded by *na*, the speaker would not be indicating that hearer should direct more attention to the entity, which contradicts the fact that the speaker considers the entity important.

An entity can be considered important for many reasons, including its value, its influence on the speaker, or its role in the discourse.

  4.25) zhe liang wei nainai xianzai de shenti xiang liang ge chi bao cangying de da zhizhu, dou dao le xianran jianshao wuzi rongliang de zhuangtai, mang de Fang Laotaitai yingjiebuxia, na liang ge nü yongren ye chengji chao zhe, zhang guo yi ci gongqian. (Qian, 1954, p. 113)

  'The bodies of these [*zhe*] two young wives were by now like two large spiders which have just feasted on flies. Both had reached the state where the capacity of the house had become visibly smaller. Mrs. Fang was left with more work than she could handle, and the [*na*] two maids decided this was a good time to fuss about a raise, which they got.' (Qian, 1979, p. 117)

In traditional Chinese families, the servants and maids were at the bottom of the household hierarchy, and thus had to obey everyone. In contrast, young pregnant wives were of the highest status and were highly protected and spoiled. Here, the author is using *zhe* to refer to people with a higher social ranking and *na* for people with a lower social ranking. This is unsurprising because in most societies the focus tends to be on those who have a wealthier, better, and happier living status, as everyone hopes to achieve those standards at some time in their life. Moreover, that *zhe* signals HIGH DEIXIS can also be indirectly supported by the use of different classifiers. The author applies *wei* 'person' to the two ladies, which is only used to count the number of people with higher social status or with high-paid salary; it indicates the respect that the author accords to the ladies. In contrast, the author employs *ge* 'item' to the two maids, which can be applied to anything, regardless of whether it is a person or an object. The use of *wei* grants more significance to the two women and directs more of the reader's notice to them, which is consistent with the use of *zhe*.

4.26) Hung-chien zhuixiang tade guowen xiansheng dou jiao bu xiang, bu bi Luosu, Ch'en San-yüan <u>zhexie</u> mingzi, xiang yi zhi shang deng Hawana xuejiayan, keyi gua zai koubian mainong. (Qian, 1954, p. 89)

'Hung-chien searched his mind for the names of his Chinese teachers, but couldn't think of a single worthy one, like Bertie or Ch'en San-yüan, [*zhexie*] names which could be rolled around on the tongue and shown off like a quality Havana cigar.' (Qian, 1979, p. 92)

Both Bertie and Ch'en San-yüan are major names in their respective professional fields during that century. Consequently, they are of greater importance to Hung-chien than his own Chinese teachers. Spatially and temporally, those names are farther from Hung-chien than his own teachers. If preceded by *naxie* 'those,' the names Bertie and Ch'en San-yüan would not be recognized as significant, but rather would be considered as a normal mention and would not be followed by the analogy of the Havana cigar. Also, if *naxie* was added before "guowen xiansheng" 'Chinese teachers,' this would direct even less attention to Hung-chien's Chinese teachers. Due to their unimportance, Hung-chien does not even want to mention or list their names and is also unwilling to direct the hearer to pay more attention to them. By contrast, Hung-chien not only lists Bertie and Ch'en San-yüan's names, but also values them highly in their professional fields: they are analogous to Havana cigars among tobacco products.

The last example in this section is Hung-chien's thoughts on Miss Pao, with whom he both flirted and slept with on the French ship. At that time, Hung-chien was obsessed with her and obsessively thought of her all the time. Because of their relationship, he does not mind that Miss Pao's skin tone is too dark to be considered beautiful according to traditional Chinese standards. Miss Pao hates it whenever anyone mentions the color of her skin, but Hung-chien is very slow-witted and does not know how to please girls; thus, in the following example he compares Miss Pao's skin tone to chocolate, which irritates Miss Pao and ultimately leads to their break-up.

 4.27) you xiang dao Pao Xiaojie pifu an, xiao qilai tiantiande, denghui jianmian keyi jiao ta "heitian", you lianxiang dao hei er tian de zhugulitang, zhi kexi faguo chupin de zhugulitang bu hao, tianqi you re, buyi chi zhe ge dongxi, fouze mai yi xia qing ta. (Qian, 1954, p. 15)

 'He then thought of Miss Pao's dark skin and sweet smile; later when he saw her he'd call her "Dark Sweetness", making him think of dark, sweet chocolate. Too bad that French chocolate wasn't any good and that the weather was too hot for eating it [*zhe*], for otherwise he would treat her to a box.' (Qian, 1979, p. 19)

This whole passage deals with the color of Miss Pao's skin, which makes Hung-chien think of French chocolate. His comment that Miss Pao's skin tone resembles chocolate ultimately results in their first fight and, later, in the antipathy that arises between them. Ignoring Hung-chien's reference to her sweetness and his attempt to flatter her with this nickname, Miss Pao considers this statement insulting. The author wants to make readers pay attention to this detail, which causes a surprising change in the development of the story.

4.4.2 Demonstrating LOW DEIXIS

In addition to situations and aspects that co-occur with HIGH DEIXIS, there are some situations in which *na* 'that,' signaling LOW DEIXIS, is required. These situations include a negative attitude toward an entity, vague identification of an entity, background information, lack of familiarity with the referent, indifference, initial mention of a new item, and information considered unimportant.

4.4.2.1 Speaker's negative attitude

If a speaker does not favor an entity, he will not focus on that entity; that is, if a speaker himself does not want to pay more attention something, he will not urge the hearer to pay more attention to it. Moreover, the speaker will not bring up an unpleasant topic, nor will he want he to talk about it. By using *na*, the speaker tries to direct the hearer's attention to another topic or to another conversation altogether.

In the following example, Hung-chien and Hsin-mei visit another faculty member at the university where they both teach. At first, both Hung-chien and Hsin-mei greet the host and praise his child in the usual way to show appreciation of the invitation and courtesy to their host. But later, when the child misbehaves, their attitude towards him changes.

> 4.28) Hung-chien he Hsin-mei zhaoli shuo zhe xiaohaizi zhang de hao, yang de pang, taolun ta xiang fuqin haishi xiang muqin. (Qian, 1954, p. 241)
> 'Hung-chien and Hsin-mei dutifully remarked on how nice and well-fed the [zhe] baby was and discussed whether he resembled his mother or his father.' (Qian, 1979, p. 257)
>
> na xiaohaizi zhengzai chi ziji de shou, huan le yi ge ren bao, sizhi luan dong, shoushang de ni tuomo, mo le Hung-chien yi bizi ban lian, Hung-chien meng Liu Taitai tuogu, zhihao xinli yanwu. (Qian, 1954, p. 241)
> 'It [na] [That child] had just been sucking its thumb, and when given to another to hold, the jostling caused saliva from its hand to foam all over Hung-chien's nose and the side of his face. Since he'd been entrusted with the child by Mrs. Liu, Hung-chien had to keep his disgust to himself.' (Qian, 1979, p. 257)

The use of different demonstratives cannot be due to the first and second mention of an entity, because when the child is first mentioned in the passage, the demonstrative *zhe*, signaling HIGH DEIXIS, precedes the noun "boy," which contradicts the general rule of first mention: when a noun is mentioned for the first time, *na* is usually used to introduce a new item. In the first sentence, the image of the baby is still adorable: it is puffy, cute, and tempts people to discuss whom the baby resembles. However, in the second sentence, the baby behaves as a naughty and disobedient child who wipes his disgusting saliva on Hung-chien's face. The author shows Hung-chien's change of attitude toward the baby with different demonstratives: *zhe* indicates that the baby is favorable, and *na* that the baby is disagreeable.

> 4.29) pofei haishi xiaoshi, wo jiu meiyou na ge jingshen, ye bu xiang na wei yangtaitai nenggan. (Qian, 1954, p. 238)

'The expense is a trivial matter. I just don't have the [na] energy, and I'm not capable as that [na] foreign woman.' (Qian, 1979, p. 254)

In this example, both Hung-chien and Hsin-mei praise Mr. Han's foreign wife, in front of the Wang couple, for her virtue of being a good wife who takes care of the family. Although she also praised by the group, Mrs. Wang, who prepares dinner for them, is upset and jealous hearing her husband and his colleagues praising another woman in her presence. Also, because of his virtuous wife, Mr. Han becomes famous among students who he occasionally invites to dinner at his home. He is also envied by all the bachelors and husbands, which his foreign wife to become every female's rival. Therefore, in the example, Mrs. Wang uses *na* to show contempt for Mrs. Han and to indicate that she wants to end this vein of the conversation. The sentence still works if one replaces all *na* with *zhe* in the sentence, but it sounds different. With *zhe*, the sentence would merely be stating the fact that Mrs. Wang is not as energetic and enthusiastic as Mr. Han's foreign wife. However the original suggests Mrs. Wang's strong displeasure with and spite toward the foreign wife.

4.4.2.2 Vague identification

If the speaker does not know an entity very well, we can assume that the speaker is not very interested in it, otherwise he likely would have explored it already. Moreover, the speaker will not require the hearer to pay more attention to the entity, if he does not pay much attention to it himself.

4.30) <u>na</u> ji ge yilu tongchuan de xuesheng kan Xiao Fang cai qu le Pao Xiaojie, zao huan shang Su Xiaojie, dui ta daqu ge buting. (Qian, 1954, p. 23)
'When the other [na] students on board saw that Miss Pao had no sooner gone than Little Fang took up with Miss Su, they teased him unmercifully.' (Qian, 1979, p. 26)

This example describes the other students' reaction to both Hung-chien's break-up with Miss Pao and his relationship with Miss Su. The identification of the students who were making fun of Hung-chien's personal issues is rather vague. Hung-chien does not know how many students there are. He does not even know which passengers are students and which are not. The students tease Hung-chien for his ability to change girlfriends so quickly, but they do the same thing, with even more rapidity than he does. They do not tease him because they believe in the moral of loyalty to love, but because they are envious about his luck in love. Here the author uses a less specific demonstrative because it is impossible to single out individual students since there are many who were envious of Hung-chien's love life. Moreover, morality is not the factor in the students' decision to mock Hung-chien. Obviously, the author does not favor these students, hence the *na* that precedes their mention, thereby withdrawing attention from them (Kirsner, 1993).

    4.31) congqian ta yixin yao liuxue, xian <u>na</u> ji ge zhuiqiu ziji de ren meiyou qiancheng, dabuliao shi daxue biyesheng. (Qian, 1954, p. 12)

    'Before, she had had her heart set on studying abroad and despised those [*na*] suitors for their lack of prospects, since they were merely college graduates.' (Qian, 1979, p. 15)

Similar to the previous example, the suitors here are not clearly identified. Because Miss Su despises them for their lack of a higher postgraduate degree from a foreign university, she does not care who her suitors are and doesn't want to get acquainted with them. She does not know how many suitors there are, nor does she know their names. Therefore, "suitors" is a vague identification and is preceded by the LOW DEIXIS signaling demonstrative *na*.

4.4.2.3 Background information

Similar to section 4.4.1.6, in which use of *zhe* is discussed to reiterate the main point of discourse in the flow, this section discusses the use of *na*, the signal of the meaning LOW DEIXIS, for background information that is not main parts of the discourse in order to make the main point more prominent.

> 4.32) yushi Hsin-mei xiache xiang Sun Xiaojie yao le shoudian, jiao Hung-chien ye xiache, liangren yi zuo yi you cenci zhao zhe, <u>na</u> ba liang che song chubin shide gen le tian'an shang de dianguang zou. (Qian, 1954, p.142)
> 'Hsin-mei then got out of his rickshaw, took the flashlight from Miss Sun and asked Hung-chien to get out also. With one person on either side unevenly illuminating the way, the [*na*] eight rickshaws followed the light along the ridges between the fields as though it were a funeral procession.' (Qian, 1979, p.148)

This passage depicts a scene, in which Hung-chien, Hsin-mei, Miss Sun, and two others are pressing on in darkness while it is raining. It is so dark that it is too hard for the rickshaws to move forward. In order to be able to continue on and arrive at the university on time, Hung-chien and Hsin-mei get out of the rickshaws and illuminate the way with flashlights. Spatially, the eight rickshaws are NEAR, because they are between Hsin-mei and Hung-chien and have Li, Ku, and Miss Sun in them. Yet the main idea of this sentence is not about the rickshaws, but rather about Hsin-mei and Hung-chien, who get out of the rickshaw to light the way in the rain. In order to make readers pay more attention to characters, the author applies *na* to the rickshaws to draw attention from them and, thus, put relatively more attention on Hsin-mei and Hung-chien.

4.4.2.4 Low familiarity with the referent

A referent that is unfamiliar to the speaker will not be in the speaker's focus. Otherwise, the speaker likely would have already explored it and would be familiar with it. A referent can be unfamiliar to a speaker for two reasons. First, the referent is too difficult for the speaker to seek out and learn more about. Or second, the referent is within reach of the speaker but is not interesting to the speaker. In any case, the speaker does not focus on the referent and, hence, will not direct the hearer to pay more attention to it.

In the next example, Miss Fan shows a book with the signatures of fictional playwrights to Hsin-mei, who does not intend to pursue her. Miss Fan, however, considers herself attractive among the few available female faculty and staff at the university, and believes that Hsin-mei is determined to pursue her and ask her to be his girlfriend. Yet after a long time, there is no sign that Hsin-mei will ever express his love to her. At that point, Miss Fan comes up with the idea of making herself popular among male faculty and staff in order to compel Hsin-mei to express his love to her; thus, she fakes several signatures of different non-existing playwrights on the cover page of books, which she then forces Hsin-mei to borrow from her. Upon returning the books, Miss Fan says:

> 4.33) tamen naxie juzuojia wuliao de hen, zao song gei wode shu shang hu xie le dongxi, bu neng gei ni kan, dangran, gei ni kan ye meiguanxi. (Qian, 1954, p. 229)
>
> 'But [*naxie*] playwrights are so silly. They write all kinds of nonsense on the books they give me. I couldn't let you see them. Of course, it wouldn't really matter if I did.' (Qian, 1979, p. 245)

Miss Fan claims that the playwrights are pursuing her by writing silly things on the cover pages of the books they gifted her. However, the so-called playwrights did not exist, and therefore there is no way that Miss Fan would be familiar with them. Consequently, she uses *na* to refer to her non-existent pursuers, as it is impossible for anyone to know much about non-existent characters.

A similar example of a non-existent character is demonstrated below:

4.34) "benlai zhi you liang zhang dacaijian, Li Xiansheng zaisan kenqiu ta <u>na</u> wei pengyou, zongsuan nong dao di san zhang." (Qian, 1954, p. 128)

'Ku cut in, "At first only two first-class tickets were available, but Mr. Li asked his [*na*] friend over and over and finally was able to get three."' (Qian, 1979, p. 133)

In this example, Li Mei-ting is referred to by Mr. Ku, who appreciates his effort in getting tickets for all members of the group. In fact, it was a trick Li Mei-ting used when purchasing tickets for all members of the group: he wanted to save money on tickets but he did not want others to have any reason to gossip about him as a stingy guy. So he took over the job to purchase tickets and only bought three first-class tickets for the others, explaining to them that his helpful (but in fact non-existent) friend was not able to get first-class for everyone and that he would be happy to sacrifice himself to stay in a third-class cabinet. The non-existent friend who made the purchase could by no means be a specific person and thus is referred to with *na* instead of *zhe*.

4.4.2.5 Indifference

The speaker can refer to an entity with indifference, either intentionally or unintentionally. He/she either does not care about the entity to which he/she refers, or shows indifference to an entity on purpose. In either case, the speaker will direct less attention to it as the speaker will not want others to pay extra attention to the entity in which he himself is not interested.

In the following example, Miss Su displays a poem written on a paper fan. In an affected manner, she asks Hung-chien and Yüan-lang for their opinions.

4.35) Su Xiaojie shi you niuni zhi se, dao: "Ts'ao Xiansheng de yan'guang zhen lihai, ni laoshi shuo, <u>na</u> shi hai guodequ ma?" (Qian, 1954, p. 71)

'Seemingly bashful, Miss Su said, "How sharp you are, Mr. Ts'ao! Tell the truth. Is the [*na*] poem any good?"' (Qian, 1979, p. 74)

When Miss Su asks Hung-chien and Yüan-lang for their comments on the poem, she wants praise, because the poem was actually composed by her. However, she does not want to reveal that it is her poem and thus receive dishonest flattery from them. In fact, she wants to let them know that the poem is actually hers after getting positive comments. In order to avoid inadvertently suggesting that she has written the poem, she uses *na* to refer to it. Signaling LOW DEIXIS, *na* indicates that one does not care much about the referent, which could also be true because no one puts much emphasis on things about which they does not care. By affecting indifference, Miss Su displays perfect Chinese morals: being modest and discreet about your own work.

4.4.2.6　Introduction of new information

Whenever a new entity is introduced in discourse, the author or speaker by default, will use *na* to refer to it, since there is generally unlikely that an item can be of great importance at the first mention. Even if it is really an indispensable and important part, it still needs to be first introduced to the hearer, so that he/she can get a basic idea of what it is. It is hard to imagine that any speaker would require the hearer to pay much attention to an entity whose importance is as yet unknown in the discourse. But once the entity has been introduced to the audience, it can either be referred to with *zhe* or *na*, depending on its relation to the context. If the entity will be referred to several times and developed throughout the discourse, it will be described in detail and the hearer will be provided with more information. In this case, it will be referred to with *zhe*. If it will not be frequently mentioned in the context, it will be referred to with *na*.

4.36) na nian chuntian, qihou tebie hao. zhe chunqi gudong de renxin xiang yinghai chuchi shi de yayinrou, shoudao yi zhong shengjitouya de tongyang. (Qian, 1954, p. 44)

'The weather that [na] spring was especially beautiful. Stirred by the [zhe] invigorating spring, men, like infants cutting their teeth, somehow itched painfully from the budding of new life.' (Qian, 1979, p. 48)

In this example, the author uses both demonstratives one after the other. In the first sentence, the noun "spring" is mentioned for the first time. No information is given about the spring, so it is only a pure time indicator and is not indicated by the speaker either as worth or not worth more of the hearer's attention. In the following sentence, the author references the aforementioned spring and uses a metaphor to provide a more concrete feeling. Before he began, he used *zhe* to alert the reader, in order to prepare them for an abundant amount of information about that specific spring.

The next example is about a girl that is just introduced. At first mention, the girl is referred to with *na*. Afterward, she is referred to with *zhe*.

4.37) na nühaizi buguo shiliuqi sui, lian huazhuang de jiu xiang cuoyou zhaifen tiao yanzhi nie chulai de jia mianju. (Qian, 1954, p. 54)

'Though [na] she was no more than sixteen or seventeen, her face was made up like a mask kneaded out of gobs of rouge and powder.' (Qian, 1979, p. 59)

keshi zhe nühaizi de lian jia de laoshi, yinwei jue mei ren xiangxin tie zai ta lian shang de na zhang zhifen bobing hui shi tade benlai mianmu. (Qian, 1954, p. 55)

'But this [zhe] girl's face was so obviously faked, for no one would possibly believe that [na] powdered wafer cake pasted on her face could be her own.' (Qian, 1979, p. 59)

In the first sentence, the girl is newly introduced. The author uses *na* to give her a hand onto the stage and let the reader know that there is such a character in the discourse. In the second sentence, the girl is no longer a newly introduced character, but a character that has just been mentioned. When describing a repeated character specifically, he uses *zhe* to attract others' attention and then provides them with more information about the girl. Finally, it might be useful to explain the usage of *na* in the last part of the second sentence: *na* refers to the wafer, which represents the exaggerated make-up on the young girl's face, and signals the author's dislike for and criticism of it.

4.4.2.7 Less importance

In section 4.4.1.8, I argued that *zhe* is used to refer to entities with great importance, either to themselves, to the speaker, or to the society. This section, however, will examine how *na* can be used to refer to entities that are not very important. In that section, I provided several examples that use both *zhe* and *na* to demonstrate the opposition between them and to support the point that *zhe* is used to refer to important entities, while *na* refers to less important entities. One further example is presented here:

> 4.38) Hung-chien xiang tongchuan na pi faguo jingcha, dou shi xiangxiaren chu chumen, mei yi ge bu hanjiong kelian. (Qian, 1954, p.127)
>
> 'Hung-chien thought to himself that those [*na*] policemen on the boat were all from the French countryside and were leaving home for the first time, and every one of them was pitifully poor.' (Qian, 1979, p.132)

In this example, Hung-chien refers to the French policemen with *na*, because they all look like poor, pitiful people from the French countryside who lack a good educational background. Though having faked his Ph.D., Hung-chien considers himself a scholar, who would be held in high esteem in Chinese society. Therefore, there is enough reason for Hung-chien to look down to the French policemen and use the LOW DEIXIS signaling *na* to refer to them.

4.5 Quantitative Validation

In my section on quantitative analysis, I did a counting test for the whole book and then ran a statistical analysis of the 1671 examples of *zhe* and 691 examples of *na*. In this test, the whole sample was computed. Although demonstratives do correlate significantly with MOOD, CHARACTER, and GRAMMATICAL ROLE, the effects sizes, which are measured by the Phi statistic, are very small: .075 for THIS/THAT—MOOD, .106 for THIS/THAT—CHARACTER, and .150 for THIS/THAT—GRAMMATICAL ROLE. Also, there is correlation of GRAMMATICAL ROLE with CHARACTER.

Therefore, it is necessary to examine another text, in which 691 examples of *zhe* and 691 examples of *na* are tested, in order to keep the amount of both demonstratives equal, because examples of *zhe* are more than 70% of the whole sample. Therefore, extracting 980 examples and keeping a 50-50 split should enable a more accurate prediction of the demonstratives, i.e. where some certain demonstrative, either *zhe* or *na*, is used more often.

4.5.1 Demonstratives versus GRAMMATICAL ROLE

I will begin with the correlation of the demonstratives with GRAMMATICAL ROLE. It makes sense to expect that *zhe* is used more frequently and *na* is used less frequently preceding a subject. A sentence usually begins with the subject and it is the action of the subject, which forms the sentence. Thus, it is the subject that requires more attention from the hearer and should be preceded by *zhe*. Similarly, it is the non-subject that does not need as much emphasis as the subject does and follows *na*.

The following table illustrates the correlation between the demonstratives and their grammatical roles:

Crosstab

			GRAM ROLE		
			SUBJECT	NONSUBJ	Total
ZHE/NA	ZHE	Count	369	322	691
		% within ZHE/NA	53.4%	46.6%	100.0%
		% within GRAM ROLE	59.8%	42.1%	50.0%
	NA	Count	248	443	691
		% within ZHE/NA	35.9%	64.1%	100.0%
		% within GRAM ROLE	40.2%	57.9%	50.0%
	Total	Count	617	765	1382
		% within ZHE/NA	44.6%	55.4%	100.0%
		% within GRAM ROLE	100.0%	100.0%	100.0%

Table 4.1

This table can be illustrated by the following chart.

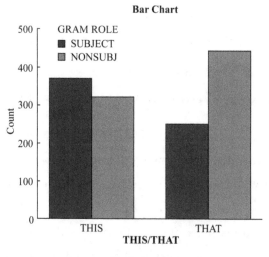

Chart 4.1

According to the chart, it is clear that demonstratives are predictors of GRAMMATICAL ROLE: it is the Subject that favors *zhe*, and it is the Non-Subject that favors *na*. This means that a speaker tends to use *zhe* to refer to the subject of a sentence and *na* to a non-subject. So far, the correlation between the two demonstratives and GRAMMATICAL ROLE can be illustrated extra-linguistically.

4.5.2 Demonstratives versus NUMBER

There is a disagreement between Reid and Diver regarding the relationship of FOCUS and NUMBER. Reid (1977) states:

> People cannot be genuinely interested in everything equally. One is suspicious of the person who says he loves *all* music, or the student who declares himself fascinated by language in general, but no particular aspect more than any other. Similarly, attention is selective; we are all familiar with the difficulty of listening to two conversations at once. Both interest and attention are a function of discrimination and selectivity: the greater the selectivity and individualization, the greater the interest and attention. Consequently one would predict that HIGH FOCUS will favor singular subjects—singularity being an instance of greater individualization—and LOW FOCUS will favor plural subjects—plurality being an instance of lesser individualization. (p. 66)

In the above statement, Reid claims that HIGH FOCUS will favor singular subjects, while LOW FOCUS favors plural subjects. However Diver's argument (1995) contradicts Reid's:

> The prediction to be made is that a lower concentration of attention will usually be employed for referring to a concrete object and a higher for referring to an abstract idea, that a lower concentration will be preferred for a single object, or idea, a higher where what is to be recalled consists of a number of different entities. (pp. 106—107)

Both ideas are logical and convincing. And both linguists support their idea with data. Since the two theories contradict each other, but both are well stated, it is therefore hard to predict anything before examining the data. The following table and chart are based on my data collected from Qian's novel (1954).

Crosstab

			NPNUMBNER		
			SING	PLURAL	Total
ZHE/NA	ZHE	Count	620	70	690
		% within ZHE/NA	89.9%	10.1%	100.0%
		% within NPNUMBER	50.2%	47.6%	50.0%
	NA	Count	614	77	691
		% within ZHE/NA	88.9%	11.1%	100.0%
		% within NPNUMBER	49.8%	52.4%	50.0%
	Total	Count	1234	147	1381
		% within ZHE/NA	89.4%	10.6%	100.0%
		% within NPNUMBER	100.0%	100.0%	100.0%

Table 4.2

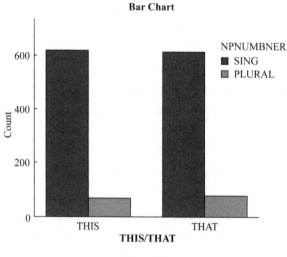

Chart 4.2

Based on the table and the chart, the correlation between the demonstratives and NUMBER is not significant. The probability of using either *zhe* or *na* is almost 50%, which means it is not possible to predict which demonstrative will be used in different NUMBER cases.

However, this result is an adequate way to explain the logical, but contradicting ideas of Reid and Diver: the hearer can either put HIGH FOCUS on singular items because they are more individualized, or the speaker can urge the hearer to pay more attention to plural items because they are greater in quantity and require greater focus from the hearer to understand information provided.

4.5.3 Demonstratives versus MOOD

It is reasonable to assert that most people place more significance on affirmative sentences, which are mostly statements or facts that contain newly confirmed information. In contrast, speakers will also place less emphasis on negative sentences, which need additional correct information and with which one does not want to confuse or mislead the hearer.

Crosstab

			MOOD		
			POS	NEG	Total
ZHE/NA	ZHE	Count	572	119	691
		% within ZHE/NA	82.8%	17.2%	100.0%
		% within MOOD	52.0%	42.2%	50.0%
	NA	Count	528	163	691
		% within ZHE/NA	76.4%	23.6%	100.0%
		% within MOOD	48.0%	57.8%	50.0%
	Total	Count	1100	282	1382
		% within ZHE/NA	79.6%	20.4%	100.0%
		% within MOOD	100.0%	100.0%	100.0%

Table 4.3

The following table and chart illustrate the correlation of the demonstratives and different types of MOOD.

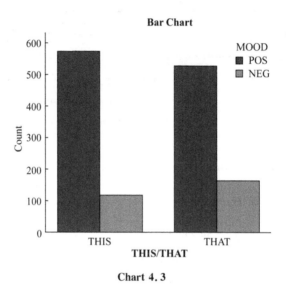

Chart 4.3

From the above table and chart, it can be concluded that, statistically, *zhe* is used more frequently in affirmative sentences while *na* occurs more frequently in negative sentences. Therefore, the correlation between the demonstratives and MOOD is significant.

4.5.4 Demonstratives versus CHARACTER

Central characters are, according to Reid (1977), a particular point of view from which the storyteller tells the story. Some characters are central and some are less so. Therefore, more attention is expected be paid to central characters.

The book *Weicheng* is the story of Fang Hung-chien's development, and the author does not devote much space to the other characters, including Hung-chien's wife Sun Rou-chia, his beloved T'ang Hsiao-fu, and his best friend Chao Hsin-mei. Those characters are like passersby in Fang Hung-chien's life, appearing only for a short period of time. It is expected that HIGH DEIXIS should co-occur with Fang Hung-chien, the main character of the book.

The following table and chart serve as statistical proof of the above hypothesis.

Crosstab

			CHARACTER		Total
			CENTRAL	PERIPHERAL	
ZHE/NA	ZHE	Count	36	655	691
		% within ZHE/NA	5.2%	94.8%	100.0%
		% within CHARACTER	97.3%	48.7%	50.0%
	NA	Count	1	690	691
		% within ZHE/NA	0.1%	99.9%	100.0%
		% within CHARACTER	2.7%	51.3%	50.0%
	Total	Count	37	1345	1382
		% within ZHE/NA	2.7%	97.3%	100.0%
		% within CHARACTER	100.0%	100.0%	100.0%

Table 4.4

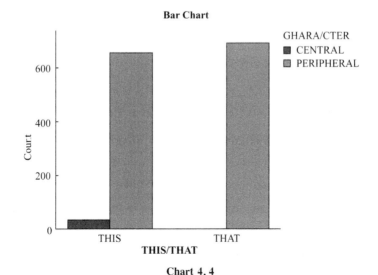

Chart 4.4

The correlation between demonstratives and CHARACTER is extremely significant and supports my hypothesis: in all 691 examples, *na* only precedes the central character once. In contrast, in thirty-six examples *zhe* appears before the central character. The significance is also shown in the Chi square test, which is illustrated in the following table.

	Value	Df	Asymp. Sig. (2-sided)	Exact Sig. (2-sided)	Exact Sig. (1-sided)
Pearson Chi-Square	34.019ª	1	.000		
Continuity Correction[b]	32.103	1	.000		
Likelihood Ratio	43.009	1	.000		
Fisher's Exact Test				.000	.000
Linear-by-Linear Association	33.994	1	.000		
N of Valid Cases	1382				

a. 0 cells (.0%) have expected count less than 5. The minimum expected count is 18.50.

b. Computed only for a 2×2 table.

Table 4.5

In the above table, we find that the two-sided asymmetric significance of the variable CHARACTER is 0, which is less than the usual significance level 0.05 or 0.01. This means that the variable Character and the choice of *zhe* and *na* are highly significantly correlated, which supports the hypothesis that the speaker tends to use *zhe* to refer to main characters and *na* to refer to peripheral characters. [①]

4.5.5 Conclusion

To conclude this section on quantitative validation, I will first

---

① Statistical analysis should be credited to Ruixue Fan, a statistician at Columbia University.

provide a table of variables in the equation in order to isolate all possible variables and show their correlations. Notice that the variable NUMBER is not included in this validation, because, as shown in the previous section, it is not correlated to the use of demonstratives. Therefore, only Grammar Role, Character, and Mood are included.

		B	S. E.	Wald	df	Sig.	Exp(B)
Step 1[a]	Gramrole(1)	−.714	.110	42.050	1	.000	.490
	Constant	.319	.073	18.977	1	.000	1.376
Step 2[b]	Character(1)	−3.528	1.017	12.035	1	.001	.029
	Gramrole(1)	−.682	.111	37.553	1	.000	.505
	Constant	.354	.074	22.942	1	.000	1.425
Step 3[c]	Character(1)	−3.550	1.018	12.170	1	.000	.029
	Gramrole(1)	−.672	.112	36.191	1	.000	.511
	Mood(1)	−.381	.139	7.498	1	.006	.683
	Constant	.654	.133	24.159	1	.000	1.922

a. Variable(s) entered on step 1: Gramrole.
b. Variable(s) entered on step 2: Character.
c. Variable(s) entered on step 3: Mood.

Table 4.6
Variables in the Equation

This table provides some information about the present study. First, all three variables are significantly correlated to demonstratives, because their B values are all very small, much less than the usual significant level 0.01. Second, among these three variables, if we want to rank them based on their effect on the demonstratives, MOOD is the least significant variable, since its significance is 0.006, which is much greater than the significance of either GRAMMATICAL ROLE or CHARACTER. This means that if we need to disregard a variable, of the three, MOOD is the one. Third, among these three variables, GRAMMATICAL ROLE is the most significant. This can be inferred from Step 2 in the table, where the significance of CHARACTER is 0.01, while the significance of GRAMMATICAL ROLE is 0. This shows that if both variables are included in a linear model, GRAMMATICAL ROLE is a more significant variable than CHARACTER. Fourth, these three variables are not significantly correlated. From the table, we can observe that the effect of adding new variables is not significant on the already existing variable. If we take the B value for example, it is −0.714 when only GRAMMATICAL ROLE is included, −0.682 when adding CHARACTER to the model, and −0.672 when all three variables are included. The B value does not show a big difference if more variables are included. If the variables were significantly correlated, the B value would greatly increase. In addition, standard error (SE) also proves that the variables are not correlated. When the model only includes the variable GRAMMATICAL ROLE, SE is 0.110, and it is changed to 0.111 if CHARACTER is added. Furthermore, it is 0.112 if all variables are included. Again, SE does not change much. If the variables are significantly correlated, SE should be extremely unstable and may increase greatly.

Removing more than half the examples of *zhe* and keeping the amount of the examples of every demonstrative the same, the correlation between demonstratives and GRAMMATICAL ROLE, MOOD, and CHARACTER is still significant, but the effect sizes are much larger: 3.55 for THIS/THAT-CHARACTER, .672 for THIS/THAT-GRAMMATICAL ROLE, and .381 for THIS/THAT-MOOD. The second test is more scientific, for the reason that it maintains a 50—50 split and does not let the quantity of the examples affect test results.

4.5.6 Discussion

In addition to my research on the Chinese demonstratives, I also discovered that *zhe* is rarely translated into its English equivalent "this"; neither is *na* translated as "that." In order to validate this observation, I did a statistical analysis by using the data from the qualitative section of this work, removing some examples of *zhe* to keep the amount of examples for both demonstratives equal. The results are shown in the following table:

CHI/ENG	This	That	The	Other	Not transl.	Total
This	11	7	6	6	7	37
That	0	11	14	3	9	37

Table 4.7

What is interesting in this table is that, *zhe* can be translated into the English "that," but *na* is never translated into English "this." This means that in English "this" signals HIGH DEIXIS only to a certain extent, but in Chinese *zhe* is structurally more flexible and semantically designed to occur more often with HIGH DEIXIS. A possible explanation may be that Chinese has more fluidity than English and is more semantically-oriented. This needs further research and exploration.

4.6 Alternative Studies

In the Columbia School perspective, a monosemy can be drawn from the analysis both for "this" and "that": "this" implies HIGH DEIXIS and "that" implies LOW DEIXIS. However, from a Cognitive Linguistics view (Langacker, 1987, 1995), each demonstrative has its polysemy. As described at the beginning of the chapter, "this" refers to things near the speaker and "that" refers to things far from the speaker. Considering the definition of "near" and "far," one can come to the polysemy in several senses: time, location, affirmation, familiarity or certainty, social status, gender, reference and emphasis.

4.6.1 NEAR and FAR in light of time cognition

Taking the terms Trajectory (TJ) and Landmark (LM) as the start and end point (cf. Langacker, 1987, 1995), the human cognition of the temporal distance can be illustrated in the figure below:

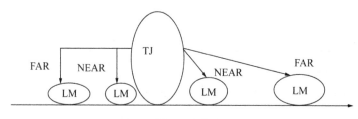

Figure 4.3

As illustrated in the figure, there are two ways for a speaker to process the temporal distance from himself to the referent in question: the first way is, the speaker may consider an event either NEAR or FAR according to his own standards, such as the two projections from the TJ to the two LMs on the TJ's right side. One may refer to either one as NEAR or FAR based on his/her own perceptions. Another way is, the speaker can refer to an already existing entity and decide that the referent in question is either closer to or farther from himself/herself compared to the distance to the already existing entity.

There are examples demonstrating these two ways in Qian's book *Weicheng*.

    4.39) <u>na</u> shihou Su Xiaojie ba ziji de aiqing kan de tai minggui le, bu ken suibian shiyu. (Qian, 1954, p.11)

'In those [na] days she valued her affection too highly to bestow it casually.' (Qian, 1979, p. 15)

In this sentence, Miss Su is regretful that she did not take advantage of the opportunity to find someone while she was in college; then, she considered her love too precious and did not consider her male college classmates qualified to pursue her: she wanted so much to study abroad and get her Ph. D., and those classmates barely had a bachelor's degree. When she finally returned to China with her Ph. D., however, she was disappointed to discover that she was too old and her degree was too sophisticated to encourage any young men to pursue her. Recalling her past, she regrets her decision deeply.

After recalling memories from the past, which the author refers to with *na*, the author then comes back to the narrative present and tries to evaluate Hung-chien's life in the recent years, which, in comparison to the times before studying abroad, are considered NEAR.

4.40) Hung-chien lian shang yansu chenyu, keshi manxin cankui, yinwei zhe si nian li ta congwei xiang qi ta na wei weihunqi. (Qian, 1954, p. 26)

'Fang's face was grave and sorrow-ridden; inwardly he felt ashamed, for during the [zhe] last four years he had never once thought of his fiancée.' (Qian, 1979, p. 29)

Compared to the time before going abroad, which is previously referred to as FAR, the four years studying abroad are closer to the narrative present than the time before studying abroad. Therefore, the time abroad is referred to with *zhe*, meaning NEAR.

4.6.2 NEAR and FAR in light of space cognition

Originally, the function of the demonstratives was to denote entities or places that are either close to the speaker or far from the speaker. There is no standard boundary to separate NEAR from FAR.

218 德语指示词研究

It is the speaker who decides whether an entity or a place is NEAR or FAR.

In the following figure, there is an uncertain boundary set by the speaker which differentiates NEAR from FAR. Anything within the boundary would be referred to as NEAR. And anything outside the boundary would be referred to as FAR.

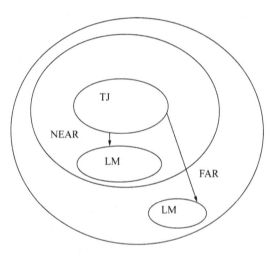

Figure 4.4

The following examples are also from *Weicheng* 'Fortress Besieged.' Both are taken from the same page and clearly demonstrate the mechanism illustrated in the graph.

4.41) chuan shang zhe ji wei, you zai faguo liuxue de, you zai yingguo, deguo, biguo deng dushu, dao bali qu zengzhang yeshenghuo jingyan, yinci ye zuo faguo chuan de. (Qian, 1954, p.2)

'Although some of [zhe] those on board had been students in France, the others, who had been studying in England, Germany, and Belgium, had gone to Paris to gain more experience of nightlife before taking a French ship home.' (Qian, 1979, p.4)

In this example, the speaker sets a boundary at the beginning of the sentence: *chuanshang* 'on board.' The students on the ship are within the boundary, a.k.a. on board, and are recognized as NEAR. In contrast, in the next example, the students not on the ship are recognized as FAR.

    4.42) naxie bu chou meishi de xuesheng, yao dao qiuliang cai manmande ken dongshen huiguo. (Qian, 1954, p. 2)

    '[*Naxie*] Those who had no worries about jobs would wait until the cool autumn before sailing leisurely toward home.' (Qian, 1979, p. 4)

Students who were not worried about finding a job later in China were not on this ship. No one knows exactly where they were. Maybe they are in Paris or Berlin, or anywhere in Europe. These are all possibilities. Wherever they are, they are not on the ship, which means they are outside of the boundary, and thus they are qualified to be referred to by *na*.

4.6.3 NEAR and FAR in light of intimacy cognition

Let us go back to Figure 4.4. If the circles do not mark the relative distance but intimacy *fortis*, the LM near the TJ is considered more favorable than the LM far from the TJ. Thus, *zhe* 'this' can be used for favorable referents within the boundary emotionally positivity and *na* 'that' to less favorable referents that are out of the boundary of likeability.

    4.43) Chou Jingli shoudao xin, juede zhe haizi zhili, bian fenfu yinhang li wenshuke Wang Zhuren zuofu. (Qian, 1954, p. 8)

    'When Mr. Chou received the letter, he felt that the [*zhe*] young man knew etiquette, and so he instructed the bank's chief-secretary Mr. Wang to send a reply.' (Qian, 1979, p. 11)

There is a Chinese saying that the longer the mother-in-law looks at the son-in-law, the more handsome she will find him. This saying describes the love of parents-in-law for children-in-law. In like with this, Mr. Chou was proud of his would-be son-in-law, not only because he was his daughter's fiancé, but also because he wrote a lovely letter to express his love for his daughter (not to mention that Fang Hung-chien had excellent calligraphy). This is why Mr. Chou thought *zhe* 'this' Fang Hung-chien was within his boundary of love, despite the fact that he was not present or even nearby.

  4.44) Pao Xiaojie furan dao: "wo jiu na yang hei me?" (Qian, 1954, p. 16)
   '"Am I so [*na*] dark then?" she [Miss Pao] asked heatedly.' (Qian, 1979, p. 20)

Unlike Fang Hung-chien who finds her dark skin healthy and sexy, Miss Pao does not like her skin tone at all. This is illustrated when she becomes angry at Fang Hung-chien calling her his dark sweetie and attempts to make him understand that she detests the darkness of her skin. Obviously, her awareness of her dark skin tone exceeds the boundary of her comfort zone. Therefore, Miss Pao refers to the degree of darkness of her skin tone with *na*, designating it as FAR.

4.6.4 Alternative studies

I posted a questionnaire on a Chinese social media website similar to Facebook (called xiaonei.com). The situation is this: you and your friends are gossiping about someone, with whom you are in a relationship, but you do not want to let others know about your relationship. How would you describe him/her? Eighty-two people participated and here is the result[①]:

---

  ① [www.xiaonei.com] (March 18, 2009), http://abc.xiaonei.com/knowabc/investigation/Voted.action? invID=3847829.

Sentence	Number
I am not familiar with this girl. (I am male and I like girls.)	14
I am not familiar with that girl. (I am male and I like girls.)	21
I am not familiar with this girl. (I am female and I like girls.)	0
I am not familiar with that girl. (I am female and I like girls.)	0
I am not familiar with this boy. (I am male and I like boys.)	1
I am not familiar with that boy. (I am male and I like boys.)	0
I am not familiar with this boy. (I am female and I like boys.)	13
I am not familiar with that boy. (I am female and I like boys.)	33

Table 4.8

As shown in the table, both males and females favor the use of "that" to refer to someone with whom he or she is not familiar or with whom he or she does not want to show their familiarity and intimacy.

I also designed a questionnaire to explore what kind of role gender plays in the use of demonstratives. In this questionnaire, which was also posted on Xiaonei, I asked my classmates and friends in China to identify the best answer for everyday life. The situation is: if you want to scold someone, what would you say?[1] Seventy-six people replied and the results are displayed in the following table:

Sentence	Number
This woman is fucking shit! (I am male)	14
That woman is fucking shit! (I am male)	14
This man is fucking shit! (I am male)	17
That man is fucking shit! (I am male)	8
This woman is fucking shit! (I am female)	24
That woman is fucking shit! (I am female)	10
This man is fucking shit! (I am female)	23
That man is fucking shit! (I am female)	9

Table 4.9

---

[1] [www.xiaonei.com] (June 12, 2009), http://abc.xiaonei.com/knowabc/investigation/Voted.action? invID=3847505.

The result is very interesting. Males can use either *zhe* or *na* to refer to a female, but tend to use *zhe* more, if referring to the same gender. Females favor *zhe* to refer to both male and female. In my opinion, it reflects the traditional Chinese perception of male superiority and female subjectivity. However, we cannot conclude that either gender favors the use of *zhe* or *na* to refer to the other gender, due to lack to theoretical support and more statistic evidence.

4.7 Conclusion

In summary, in addition to a qualitative study of *zhe* and *na* based on Cognitive Linguistics, thirty-two sentences or sentence sets and six tables as well as four charts were presented in this section. Except THIS/THAT-NUMBER, each of the other three sets supports the hypothesis. The reason why THIS/THAT-NUMBER did not support the hypothesis is that there is more than one possible meaning for each message, which is proven by the statistical analysis. My hypothesis was proven by the qualitative analysis as well as the quantitative validation for the following reasons: first, my claim is that *zhe* means HIGH DEIXIS and *na* means LOW DEIXIS; second, each sentence analysis and correlation, if the correlation of the demonstratives with NUMBER is accepted, shows that the author favors *zhe* to refer to people or things which command people's attention and *na* to point to people or things that require less attention.

Chapter 5 German and Chinese Demonstratives in Discourse

We have established the basic semantic similarities of the demonstratives in both German and Chinese. In both languages, the demonstratives can signal the meanings of HIGH and LOW DEIXIS. Then, the issue that remains to be solved is: but are they used the same way in both languages? To be able to provide an adequate and full-fledged answer to the question, it is necessary to study the behavior of the demonstratives in both languages in discourse and translation.

The focus of this chapter is the similar and different trends in the use of the demonstratives in German and Chinese. The similarities of German and Chinese demonstratives can be traced to the similarities of the semantics of German and Chinese demonstratives; they provide information about the referent, so that the hearer will be able to search it out and locate it. I will provide a detailed analysis of the similarities in the first half of this chapter. In the second half of the chapter, I will discuss the differences in the uses of German and Chinese demonstratives. Different types of mismatching of the demonstratives in German and Chinese will be illustrated. One of the types is that the use of demonstratives in one language may be non-use in the other. This may result from the fact that German and Chinese are typologically distinct.

5.1 The Data

5.1.1 The parallel texts

There are two parallel texts selected for the present study (cf. 1.4; Chapters 3 & 4). The German text is *Der Vorleser* 'The Reader,' a 207-page German novel written by Bernhard Schlink. It is accompanied by its Chinese translation *Langduzhe* translated by Qian Dingping, a famous Chinese scholar who has studied in Germany. The Chinese text is called *Weicheng* 'Fortress Besieged.' It is 335 pages and was written by Qian Zhongshu. Its German translation *Die umzingelte Festung* was completed by Monika Motsch.

While the whole book of *Der Vorleser*, along with its Chinese translation, was studied, only four chapters (Chapter 4 to Chapter 7) of *Weicheng* and its German translation were analyzed in this chapter. It is necessary to use excerpts to balance the lengths of the German and Chinese texts. The four chapters of the Chinese text only have 155 pages and the German translation is about 190 pages, rendering both texts approximately equivalent in length. Another reason of choosing these four chapters in the Chinese text is that they can stand by themselves as a whole story; it starts with Hung-chien and Hsin-mei travelling to Hunan to teach and ends with Hsin-mei's leaving the university.

Der Vorleser and *Weicheng* are very famous and popular novels in Germany and China, respectively. Both books are intimate stories narrated in the third-person and deal with the characters' experiences during World War II. The most important commonality of the two books is that they are equivalently context-related in employing demonstratives to refer to people and objects, both in the past and in the present. Therefore, we may presume that the use and distribution of demonstratives in both languages in both books is proportionally similar and can be studied in comparison to each other.

For all their similarities, however, the books differ in their ideologies; but this difference is not without advantages. Opposing ideologies can bring out various aspects in the choice of demonstratives. In addition, employing a translation simplifies this difference considerably. Since both translators are native speakers of the target languages, they will use the most appropriate word in their own language and ideology.

The translations for both texts are the only versions found in print in both countries. Both are faithful to their original texts and therefore qualify for a comparative study. This does not imply that there are no inadequacies of both translations. One inevitable inadequacy is what Lyons (1979) calls "the impossibility of translation" (p. 235). This means that a translation cannot perfectly convey the original text in another language. The asymmetrical distribution of grammar and lexicon, as well as the translator's style, makes it impossible to have a translation that exactly means the same thing as the original text. However, the number of these abovementioned imperfections of translation is not large and is considered carefully in the present study.

The primary prerequisite of choosing a language sample for examination is that it should both provide instances of the demonstratives in question and cover as wide a usage of the demonstratives in real discourse as possible. For this, novels are better than other genres, such as newspapers, academic writing, and so forth, since novels have narrations, as well as conversations. In both cases, demonstratives may be used to refer to entities or places that are either close or far in time or space and, in addition, do not exclude the possibility that a referent can be emotionally either near or far from the author in narrations, or the speaker in conversations. This is because, in a novel, the author or the speaker of a narrated conversation does not have to have a neutral attitude towards the entity in question. Furthermore, a novel's register is closest to language in real use. A newspaper report is expected to employ a higher and more neutral register. Also, as one needs to avoid inappropriate indications and inferences in an academic article, it is understood that the uses of demonstratives is artificially reduced for the sake of clarity.

In order to validate the texts, we need to have a positive answer to a typical question that may naturally arise. The question is: to what degree does the language in both texts resemble the language in actual use? On one hand, the language in both texts does not depart far from the language in the present. Although there is a slight change in lexicon over the less than half-century of time, grammar has not appreciably changed in both languages. In addition, the employment of new vocabulary cannot lead to an obvious change in the word choice, nor in the sentence structure. Therefore, we may assume that the occurrences of demonstratives in both books are very close to how demonstratives are used in real world speech. On the other hand, due to the lack of convenience of referentiality in a face-to-face conversation, it is expected that more demonstratives will be used in both texts. This, however, is solely a matter of frequency and not a matter of proportion. Thus, using both novels as language sample cannot affect the data and the results either qualitatively or quantitatively (cf. Wu, 2004).

5.1.2 The data

Not all the occurrences of the German and Chinese demonstratives contribute to the overall data in the present study. This is because this study focuses on the discourse and textual uses as well as the locative and temporal uses of the demonstratives. In both languages, the demonstratives have other uses. For example, in German, *dies and jener* 'this and that' is a fixed phrase which does not serve to express referentiality nor differentiality. Similarly, in Chinese, both *zhe* and *na* can be used as gap fillers in discourse. The occurrences of demonstratives of such uses will be excluded in this study (cf. 1.3).

At the same time, as the focus of this comparative study is the entity-referring demonstratives in particular, that specific portion in the data that is concerned with such usages of the demonstratives will be subject to a detailed analysis.

Note that the place-referring demonstratives in German are not part of this study, as they have different forms and sounds. In contrast to the Chinese place-referring demonstratives which also start with *zhe* or *na*, such as *zheli* 'here' and *nar* 'there' (cf. Chapter 2 & 4), the German place-referring demonstratives *hier* 'here,' *da* 'there,' and *dort* 'there,' however, do not share any of the forms or sounds with the German entity-referring demonstratives *dieser* and *jener*. Given that "there is another form, there is another meaning" (cf. Diver, 1995; Garcia, 2009), *hier*, *da* and *dort* are therefore not part of the present study, either.

5.1.3 Stylistic conventions for quoting data

When an utterance is chosen to illustrate the similarities or differences in the use of demonstratives, the original will be given along with its word-for-word gloss and its translation in the other language under examination. For example, if it is necessary to cite an occurrence of a demonstrative from the Chinese text, the original text in Chinese will be written in *pinyin*, the romanization of the Chinese writing system. Also, a word-for-word gloss will be given in English, followed by the German translation of the quoted utterance. Similarly, if an occurrence is cited from the German text, it will be followed by a word-for-word gloss in English and Chinese. Since both German and Chinese are not expected to be known by every potential reader of this study, the use of the demonstrative in translation will be further translated into English in the parentheses with explanations.

5.2　Overview

5.2.1　Overall distribution

"Overall distribution" means that all the tokens of the demonstratives in the corpora will be taken into account. As discussed in the previous section, all the non-referring usages of the demonstratives have already been screened out (cf. 5.1). Thus, the result of this frequency count is not biased. Even though the grammatical roles with which the demonstratives are associated may vary, there is no discrimination in the frequency count.

Therefore, an overview distribution following the above rules can provide a panorama of how frequently the demonstratives are used in both languages in discourse of similar length.

The results are presented in the following tables. The first table shows the frequency of the German demonstratives and the second table represents the Chinese demonstratives.

DM	Number of Occurrences
dies-	45
jen-	2
Total	47

Table 5.1

DM	Number of Occurrences
zhe	934
na	350
Total	1284

Table 5.2

It can be seen from Table 5.1 and Table 5.2 that the total number of occurrences of the German demonstratives is much smaller than the number of occurrences of the Chinese demonstratives. The numerous instances of the Chinese demonstratives may be accounted to the fact that the total occurrences consist of both place-referring and entity-referring demonstratives. In contrast, the German demonstratives are limited to entity-referring ones. If we exclude the instances of the place-referring demonstratives, such as *zheli* 'here' and *nar* 'there,' the result of the frequency count of the Chinese demonstratives is adjusted and shown in Table 5.3:

DM	Number of Occurrences
zhe	902
na	340
Total	1242

Table 5.3

Although the numbers of occurrences of the Chinese demonstratives have been adjusted after sifting out the place-referring demonstratives, they still clearly outweigh the numbers of occurrences of the German demonstratives. Table 5.3 also indicates that in Chinese, the entity-referring demonstratives occur much more frequently than the place-referring demonstratives.

5.2.2 Grammatical roles

As we have already excluded the place-referring demonstratives from the present study, it can be expected that the entity-referring demonstratives will mainly appear in their pronominal or determiner roles. For example, in German the proximal demonstrative *dies* may be used in the following sentences. 5.1a is an example where *dies* is used as a pronominal, whereas in 5.1b, *dies* functions as a determiner.

    5.1a)   Dies   ist   gut.
             DM (this) be.3sg good
             'This is good.'①

    5.1b)   Diese   Idee   ist   gut.
             DM (this) idea be.3sg good
             'This idea is good.'

The same applies to Chinese:

    5.2a)   zhe   hen   hao.
             DM (this) very   good
             'This is good.'②

    5.2b)   zhe   ge   zhuyi   hen   hao.
             DM (this) CL   idea   very   good

---

    ① The use of *dies*- as pronominal is rather rare. There are occurrences, but the frequency is very low (see Chapters 2, 3, & 4).

    ② In Chinese, it is necessary to use the adverb *hen* 'very' to modify a stative verb, such as *hao* 'to be good.' It does not necessarily mean that the subject is being good to a greater extent, but has to precede the stative verb for rhythm (cf. Yao, 2006).

'This idea is good.'

In both 5.1a and 5.2a, the proximal demonstratives *dies* and *zhe* do not refer to a simple entity, but rather represent the whole action that has been mentioned and described before. However, in sentences 5.1b and 5.2b, *diese* and *zhe* function as the determiner and direct the hearer's attention toward the entity in question: the noun immediately following them. In other words, the pronominal function of the demonstratives captures what has been discussed before, while the determiner function links to what follows the demonstratives. We may conclude that demonstratives in pronominal roles contain more information than determiners, because an action conveyed by a demonstrative in pronominal role is complete. However, a demonstrative in a determiner role is not the head of the NP it is in. The head of the NP in question is the noun following the demonstrative (cf. Lyons, 1977; Wu, 2004; Chapter 2).

These brief overviews are the general findings of this study. In the following sections, I will analyze, specifically, the similarity and differences in the use of the German and Chinese demonstratives.

5.3 Similarities in the Use of German and Chinese Demonstratives

In this section, the similarities in the usage of German and Chinese demonstratives will be illustrated. There are three ways in which the uses of German and Chinese demonstratives are similar. First, both German and Chinese demonstratives can be used to refer to concrete entities. Second, both German and Chinese demonstratives can be used to refer to abstract entities that cannot be measured or perceived in physical distance. And third, use of German and Chinese demonstratives depends on how much attraction of the hearer the speaker wants to direct to the referent. This can also be phrased in the Columbia School linguistic terms of HIGH and LOW DEIXIS (cf. Chapters 1, 3, & 4).

Before starting with the similarities, I will provide more tables on how frequently the demonstratives can be translated into their cognates in the other language in the language sample. It is not to be expected that a high percentage of the Chinese demonstratives will be translated into their German cognates. This is because, first, Chinese demonstratives are of broader and more frequent use in the real world than German demonstratives (cf. Chapters 2 & 3). Second, Chinese demonstratives partially take over the function of the articles (cf. Chapters 2 & 4; Li & Thompson, 1981).

Table 5.4 presents the various translations of the German demonstratives and their respective percentages.

Chin. Transl.	*dies-*		*jen-*	
	Number	Percentage	Number	Percentage
zhe	23[①]	51%	0	0%
na	4	9%	2	100%
other	18	40%	0	0%
Total	45	100%	2	100%

Table 5.4

Table 5.5 presents the translations of the Chinese demonstratives and their respective percentages.

[①] The actual count of the frequency of *dies-* translated to *zhe* is smaller than 23 due to the translator's adjustment in consideration of the flow of the translation. In order to minimize the influence of personal perception and preference in the translation on the data, the number here is adjusted according to my translation where the flow of the text is not taken into consideration.

Ger. Transl.	zhe		na	
	Number	Percentage	Number	Percentage
dies-	46	5.1%	12	3.5%
jen-	2	0.2%	4	1.2%
other	854	94.7%	324	95.3%
Total	902	100%	340	100%

Table 5.5

It can be observed in Table 5.4 and 5.5 that the German demonstratives are more frequently translated into their Chinese cognates, but not *vice versa* (51% vs 5.1%). It is also interesting to observe that the number of instances where *zhe* is translated into *dies-* and the number of occurrences of *dies-* are almost the same (46 vs 45). On the one hand, this may provide more support for validating the parallel texts selected for examination and the selection of the four chapters from the Chinese texts; if we assume that the German translation is a perfect, close-to-the-original translation of the Chinese text, and given that the German and Chinese texts are close to each other in the sense of genre and content, we should be able to predict that the distribution and frequency of the demonstratives should be similar in both text at similar length, if demonstratives function as demonstratives. On the other hand, the close numbers of occurrences of *dies-* and of instances where *zhe* is translated to *dies-* indicate that the pronominal *zhe* and the determiner *zhe* along with the NP in which it occurs may be translated into lexical items in German. This does not further suggest that German has a bigger lexicon than Chinese. We will analyze this in the next section.

5.3.1 Referentiality to concrete entities

Demonstratives are able to refer to entities that can be directly pointed to in reality. In both German and Chinese, the demonstratives can refer to entities that are either proximal or non-proximal (cf. Chapters 1 & 2). Although we may suppose that Germans and Chinese have different perceptions of NEAR and FAR in distance, we still have findings that indicate that, to some extent, the Germans and Chinese have a largely overlapping understanding of whether an entity is close to or far from them.

5.3.1.1 *dies-* versus *zhe*

The proximal demonstratives *dies-* and *zhe* are expected to refer to entities in vicinity of the speaker (cf. Chapters 2 & 4). The following example is from the German text where *dies-* is used to refer to the tea tin in front of the speaker.

5.3) "Keine   wie   diese,   obwohl   es   diese   Teedose-n
      nothing like   DM (this)   although   it   DM (these)   tea tin-PM
      damals   auch   schon   gab."
      then   also   already   give.past.3sg

(Schlink, 1995, p. 202)

'Nothing like this, although these sorts of tea tins already existed.'

(Schlink, 1997, p. 214)

5.3C) he   zhe   ge   bu   yiyang,   jinguan   dangshi   yijing
       to   DM (this)   CL   not   the same   although   then   already
       you   zheyang   de   le
       there is/are   such   NOM   PFV

[my translation][1]

---

[1] My own translation is used here, because Qian added the subject to the beginning of the sentence and used *na* to refer to it (Qian, 2008, p. 188). In order to avoid confusion that may be caused by different demonstratives, I translated the sentence without adding any subject to its beginning. It should be noted that Chinese is not a subject-prominent language; as such, a subject is not necessary here.

'It is not the same as this one, although such ones already existed.'

[my word-for-word translation]①

In this example, the first *diese* in the German sentence refers to the tea tin that was standing on the table in front of the speaker. In the Chinese translation, it is translated as *zhe*, followed by a classifier, so that it can function as a noun (see Chapter 2). It is obvious that in this example, when referring to an entity in vision and close to the speaker, both German and Chinese speakers will prefer to use the proximal entity-referring demonstrative in their language.

The next example is from the Chinese text, accompanied by its German translation. With it we will be able to examine whether the same holds true in Chinese.

5.4) xing'er zhe   qiao   ye   you   zou   wan de   shihou
     luckily DM (this) bridge too have walk RC   MM   time

(Qian, 1954, p. 141)

'Fortunately, the bridge soon came to an end.'

(Qian, 1979, p. 147)

5.4G) Zum   Glück   war   auch
      to the   fortune to be. past. 3sg too
      diese   Brücke   einmal   zu   Ende.
      DM (this) bridge   once   to   end

(Qian, 2008, p. 184)

'Fortunately, this bridge was also once to an end.'

[my word-for-word translation]

In this example, *zhe* is used in the original to refer to the bridge in front of the travel group. Its cognate *diese* is used in the German translation. This shows that both German and Chinese demonstratives can be used to refer to concrete entities in vision of the speaker.

---

① A word-for-word translation will be provided along with the translation in the language other than the original, so that the reader can better understand the translation.

5.3.1.2 *jen-* versus *na*

Similarly, the non-proximal demonstratives *jen-* and *na* refer to entities that are not close to the speaker according to the speaker's perception. Typically, an entity out of one's sight is usually referred to with a non-proximal demonstrative. The next examples represent this usage. The first example repeats example 1.2) and is not cited from the German text. This is because there are only two instances of *jen-* in the German text and none of them refers to a concrete entity.

5.5) Vom   Westen   sah   man   eine   Kirche.
      from the west   see.past.3sg   one   ART (one)   church
      'From the west one saw a church.'

      Jene   Kirche   stand   auf   einer   Anhöhe.
      DM (that) church   stand.past.3sg   on   ART (one)   hill
      'That church stood on a hill.'

                              (Hopkins & Jones, 1972; as cited in Vater, 1963)

5.5C) xibian   you   yi   ge   jiaotang.
      west   there is/are   QN (one)   CL   church
      'In the west there is a church.'

      na   ge   jiaotang   zai   shan   shang.
      DM (that)   CL   church   be at   hill   on
      'That church is on a hill.'[①]

                                                             [my translation]

As discussed earlier in the first chapter, the describer/speaker, when conveying the image, starts from the west side of the picture and then introduces a church that stands on a hill. The hearer, possibly not seeing the picture, can then imagine and reconstruct the image. As such, the church is most possibly not the topic of the picture and is, thus, not in focus of the speaker. Therefore, in the original text, *jene*

---

① There is no tense shown in verb conjugation in Chinese (see Chapter 4).

was employed. As in the translation, *na* is the closest translation. If *zhe* precedes "church," then the speaker would be focusing more attention on the church and it would be in the center of the picture. In addition, if "church" is left unpreceded, the speaker is then describing a church in general, not the specific one in the picture. Note that there is no article in the Chinese transcription. Therefore, there is no other option for this situation.

Na is used in the next example from the Chinese text. It modifies *qinqi* 'relative' and refers to Lu's relative who works in the Department of Foreign Affairs. The relative is not present in the scene where he is mentioned. And it is the second and the last time that he is mentioned in the text. This means, that the relative is a peripheral character in the book and is not of any importance.

5.6) na   wei   qinqi   guo   er   wang   jia
      DM (that) CL   relative   serve country   lead to   forget family
      mei   lai   guo   di'erci   xin.
      not   send   EXP   second time   letter

                                                      (Qian, 1954, p. 193)

'Preoccupied with the nation, the relative forgot about his family and never sent a single reply.'

                                                      (Qian, 1979, p. 205)

5.6G) Jener   Verwandte   hielt   treu   zum   Staat,
      DM (that)   relative   hold. past. 3sg loyal   to the state
      aber   nicht   zur   Familie,
      but   not   to the   family
      und   schrieb   kein   zweites   Mal.
      and   write. past. 3sg no   second   time

                                                      (Qian, 2008, p. 250)

'That relative stayed loyal to the state, not the family, and didn't write a second time.'

                                                  [my word-for-word translation]

The relative was mentioned for the first time in this paragraph, but there are several lines before he is re-mentioned here. This relative is referred to by *na* in the original and *jener* in the translation for three reasons. First, the relative works at the Department of Foreign Affairs and is not present in the scene; second, he will not be mentioned thereafter and cannot be preceded by *zhe* or *dies-* (cf. Chapter 3 & 4); third, if the relative is preceded by a definite article in the German text, the reader would be confused as this relative was mentioned several lines before, and would be very difficult for the reader to determine which relative is being referred to. All things considered, *na* and *jener* are the best option.

5.3.2 Referentiality to abstract entities

In addition to the ability to refer to concrete entities, German and Chinese demonstratives are able to refer to abstract entities. Abstract entities are defined as entities that are disassociated from any specific instances (*Webster's*, 1972). Expressed more simply, an abstract entity is something that can never be physically found, seen, or touched. Examples of abstract entities are "thought," "concept," "time," and so forth.

This section exists specifically because German demonstratives *dies-* and *jen-* are replaceable by a combination of article and locative when referring to concrete entities (1.2). However, these combinations cannot refer to abstract entities, such as "idea," as I discussed in the first chapter. For the same reason, they also cannot be applied to "week" which is shown in the next example. In this section, I will not provide any examples from the Chinese text. The Chinese demonstratives, unlike the German ones, do not have any alternatives that have similar meanings. Therefore, I will use the application of *zhe* and *na* in the Chinese translation of the German text to show that they are able to refer to abstract entities.

5.7) Wir war-en　　nie　glücklicher als　in jenen　　　Aprilwochen.
　　 we　be.past-1pl　never happier　　than in DM (those) April weeks

(Schlink, 1995, p. 51)

'We were never happier than in those weeks of April.'

(Schlink, 1997, p. 51)

5.7C) siyue de　　　　　na　　　　 ji① 　ge　 libai　 li, women
　　　April GEN　　　　DM (that)　several CL　week　 in　 we
　　　hai　 conglaimeiyou zheyang　　shen　gan xingfu guo.
　　　still　never　　　　 so　　　　deeply feel happy EXP

(Schlink, 2009, p. 46)

'In those April weeks, we both have never felt happier.'

[my word-for-word translation]

In the original, the author refers to the weeks he spent with Hanna in an April in his early years. The weeks are differentiated from other April weeks of his life. The author did not provide a more detailed description of what he and Hanna did in those weeks, but rather only mentioned those weeks in passing. In the Chinese translation, *na* is the only option possible, because there is no article in the Chinese language and there is no further description of the weeks in the rest of the book.

Dies-, rather than a combination of article and *hier* 'here,' is used to refer to abstract entities.

---

① In Chinese, the noun *xingqi* 'week' requires a classifier when in the plural form. Therefore, the plural form of *na*, *naxie* 'those,' was not used in this example. And *ji* 'several' is to indicate that the number of weeks is either not specified or it is not necessary to specify it. That is also the case for *yue* 'month,' *shichen* 'hour,' and so forth. Unlike these, other units of time such as *tian* 'day' and *nian* 'year' do not require a classifier when in the plural form (cf. Yao, 2006).

5.8) Mit dieser geträumten Erinnerung bin ich beruhigt.
　　　with DM (this) dreamed recognition be.1sg I calmed

(Schlink, 1995, p.9)

'This dream recognition comforts me.'

(Schlink, 1997, p.8)

5.8C) zhe　　　zhong meng de jiyi rang wo pingjing.
　　　DM (this) CL dream MM memory make I calm

[my translation]①

'This kind of dream recognition calms me.'

[my word-for-word translation]

The word *Erinnerung* 'memory; recognition' is abstract, because it is very conceptual and physically not sizable. Because of this, it cannot be preceded by a combination of article and *hier* 'here,' which would suggest a purely physical location. And this sentence regarding the "dream recognition," in the German text, there is an immediate comment on the description of what the author has dreamed of in his childhood. If *jener* is used, the reader will be confused by its instruction of search for a referent that is not right in the previous sentence. And the definite article *der* does not semantically qualify for preceding the "dream recognition," because it does not provide any information of the location of the referent and cannot relate "dream recognition" to the description right before. Other options such as leaving the "dream recognition" unpreceded and modifying it with an indefinite article do not signal the meaning DIFFERENTIATION MADE (cf. Chapter 3), and therefore cannot differentiate this "dream recognition" from others. For the same reasons, *zhe* is used in the Chinese translation.

---

① My own translation is used instead of Qian's here, because Qian's translation of this sentence is stylistically too poetic and is not appropriate. However, Qian used *zhe* in his translation as well (Qian, 2008, p.7).

5.3.3 HIGH and LOW DEIXIS

As discussed in Chapters 3 and 4, both German demonstratives and Chinese demonstratives signal meanings of HIGH and LOW DEIXIS. The proximal demonstratives, *dies-* and *zhe*, urge the hearer to pay more attention to the referent. The non-proximal demonstratives, *jen-* and *na*, do not urge the hearer to focus much attention on the referent (cf. Chapter 3 & 4). When signaling these meanings, the demonstratives may violate the definitions that proximal demonstratives refer to entities that are close to the speaker and non-proximal demonstratives are used to locate entities that are not in the vicinity of the speaker. In this section, I will provide more examples to show that the German and Chinese demonstratives can signal such meanings in a similar way.

5.3.3.1 *dies-* and *zhe* signaling HIGH DEIXIS

In the following example, the "woman" mentioned in the sentence is Hanna, who was accused for misbehaving at the concentration camp and caused many victims to lose their lives due to a bomb explosion. The speaker of the sentence is one of the survivors and was furious when the narrator brought Hanna's savings and regrets to her after Hanna committed suicide. Overwhelmed by her madness, she comments on Hanna and uses *diese* to refer to her.

5.9) "Was   ist   diese   Frau   brutal   gewesen!"
   what   be.3sg   DM (this)   woman   brutal   be.pp

(Schlink, 1995, p. 202)

  'That woman was truly brutal!'

(Schlink, 1997, p. 213)

5.9C) "zhe   ge   nüren   ke   zhen   hen   na!"
   DM (this)   CL   woman   indeed   truly   brutal   RF

(Schlink, 2009, p. 187)

'This woman is indeed brutal!'

[my word-for-word translation]

In this sentence, Hanna is referred to by *diese* in the original text and *zhe* in the Chinese translation. However, Hanna is neither spatially nor temporally close to the survivor who is the speaker of the sentence; the survivor lives in the United States and had not seen Hanna again after the trial in Germany. Furthermore, she was not familiar with Hanna, because she failed to identify Hanna at court and was not sure about what Hanna did when the bomb exploded. Therefore, there is no reason to assume the use of *diese* and *zhe* in the sense of NEAR.

When the survivor meets the narrator in New York and receives Hanna's savings and regrets, she is not comforted by Hanna's gift. Rather, she is irritated because she thinks what she has experienced in the camp cannot not ameliorated by a tiny amount of money and Hanna's apologies. Therefore, she uses *diese* to make the narrator pay more attention to her comment about Hanna. In her comment, she clearly indicates her attitude towards Hanna and then refuses to accept Hanna's amends.

My German informants claim that if *jene* is used instead of *diese*, the degree to which the survivor hated Hanna is much lower than if *diese* is used. Also, as indicated by the syntax "*was ist...*", the sentence renders a very strong claim about the speaker's attitude towards Hanna. If *diese* is replaced by *jene*, this sentence will send out two contradicting messages. One is that the speaker does not hate Hanna too much, signaled by the use of *jene*. The other is that the speaker could not hate her more, signaled by the sentence structure "*was ist...*". Therefore, *jene* cannot be used in this sentence.

In addition, the definite article *die* is not an inappropriate option. It does not correctly indicate how much attention the speaker wanted the hearer to pay to her opinion of Hanna. *Diese* is a more precise option, as there is no reason to choose a less appropriate word to express one's feeling if the most appropriate one is available (cf. Diver, 1995; Garcia, 2009).

In the Chinese translation, *zhe* is used for the same reasons. First, *na* does not convey as strong an attitude of the speaker as *zhe* does; and second, the words *ke* 'indeed' and *zhen* 'truly' contribute to a strong subjunctive feeling in the sentence. If *na* were employed, the sentence would contain two conflicting messages which would confuse the hearer/reader. A similar use of *zhe* can be found in the reports of recent crime committed by Yao Jiaxin, who killed a woman with a knife after hitting her while driving under the influence. When Yao Jiaxin's family later went to the victim's famlily and brought them money to apologize, the victim's family refused the money and continuously used *zhe* to refer to Yao Jiaxin. [①]

In the next example, Fang Hung-chien is referred to by *zhe*. Similarly, *diesen* is used in the German translation. Hung-chien is not present at the conversation between Miss Liu and her sister-in-law. They mention Hung-chien because he is, according to them, one of the prospective husband candidates to Miss Liu. Although Miss Liu has never met Hung-chien in person, her sister-in-law recommends him to her without reservation.

5.10) zhe   ge   xing   fang   de   ni   jian   guo   meiyou?
       DM (this)   CL   last name   Fang   NOM   you   see   EXP   not

(Qian, 1954, p. 225)

[①] Videos of the victim's family commenting on Yao Jiaxin can be found at: http://video.baidu.com/v? ct=301989888&rn=20&pn=0&db=0&s=25&word=药家鑫%20张妙&ie=utf-8

'Have you ever met this Fang fellow?'

(Qian, 1979, p. 240)

5.10G) Kenn-st du diesen Fang?
know-2sg you DM (this) Fang
'Do you know this Fang person?'

[my word-for-word translation]

Similar to example 5.9, it is not a good choice to replace *zhe* and *diesen* with other options such as *na* and *jenen*. If *zhe* and *diesen* are replaced by *na* and *jenen*, the speaker no longer sounds eager to recommend Fang Hung-chien to the hearer. The speaker would sound very indifferent. At the very least, Fang Hung-chien would not be taken seriously by the speaker. Nor would he be a prospective husband to the hearer in the speaker's mind.

5.3.3.2 *jen-* and *na* signaling LOW DEIXIS

As discussed in Chapter 3 and 4, *jen-* and *na* signal the meaning of LOW DEIXIS. In this section, examples will be provided in both languages. In the examples, *jen-* and *na* are used in a similar way. If *jen-* is used in the original text, *na* is applied in the Chinese translation, and vice versa. It is seen from the examples that they can be used in the same situations to refer to the same referent.

In the German example, the narrator remembers the weeks in which he did not see Hanna at all, while he concentrated on studying. It was not at his wish to sacrifice Hanna for school, but Hanna stated that he was not allowed to see her until he passed his class. Those weeks without Hanna were not a pleasant experience to the narrator, nor were they part of the main plot of his story with Hanna.

5.11) Wenn ich mich an das Arbeiten in jenen Woche-n
when I myself of ART working in DM (those) week-pl

erinner-e,	ist	mir,	als	hätt-e	ich
remind-1sg	be.3sg	me	as if	have.subj-1sg	I
mich	an	den	Schreibtisch	gesetzt	und
myself	at	ART	desk	sit.pp	and
wär-e	an	ihm	sitzengeblieben,		
be.subj-1sg	at	it	remain seated.pp		
bis	alles	aufgeholt	war...		
until	everything	catch up.pp	be.past.3sg		

(Schlink, 1995, p. 42)

'When I think about the work I did in those weeks, it's as if I had sat down at my desk and stayed there until I had caught up everything...'

(Schlink, 1997, p. 41)

5.11C)	meidang	wo	huiyi	qi	<u>na</u>	ji	ge	libai
	whenever	I	remember	RC	DM (that)	several	CL	week
	jiu	juede	haoxiang	you	zuo	dao	shuzhuo	pang
	just	feel	as if	again	sit	to	desk	at
	zuo	dao	bu	shang	quanbu	gongke	weizhi	
	sit	to	catch up	RC	all	study	until	

[my translation]①

'Whenever I remind myself of those weeks, I feel as if I sat back to the desk again and remained seated until I have caught up all the school work.'

[my word-for-word translation]

If *jenen* is replaced by the definite article *den*, the sentence will still remain grammatically correct, but will lack follow-up information on the

---

① In this example, I will use my own translation for the reason that Qian put his own understanding of the text in his translation and did not translate the word *jene*. He rather put *mei* 'each' to refer to the hard work in each of the four weeks. In order to have a translation that is closest to the original text and focus on the use of the non-proximal demonstratives, I have used my translation instead of Qian's. It should be noted that Qian's translation *mei* is a stylistic issue and is not related to the use of *na*.

"weeks," according to the language informants. The article *den* would make the "weeks" unclear, in the sense that the reader would search for follow-up sentences for more information about "the weeks." However, preceded by *jenen* and already mentioned previously, the reader is able to locate which weeks the narrator refers to and thus will not have the feeling that the sentence is incomplete. It should be noted that the remainder of the example does not provide more information about the "weeks," but describes the narrator's emotions when reminded of them.

If *jenen* is replaced by *diesen*, on the other hand, the reader will be confused by contradicting messages which are signaled by different components of this sentence. *Diesen*, signaling HIGH DEIXIS and urging the reader to pay more attention to the "weeks," conflicts with the clauses following it. The clauses do not deal with "the weeks" at all and switch the topic to the feelings of the narrator. It is, therefore, a bad communication strategy if the reader is first instructed to pay attention to a referent and then immediately told that the rest of the communication has nothing to do with it. The reader will be at his wits end and lose track of the communication. *Na* is the only and the best option in the Chinese translation for that very reason.

In the Chinese example, Miss Liu strongly disagrees to go to the blind date set up by Mrs. Wang. She refuses to eat for an entire day to demonstrate her rejection of the invitation. Her brother and sister-in-law do not dare remind her of the date, as they are afraid that she will commit suicide. Thus, they wait until the day of the date and observe Miss Liu's behavior and decide to turn to Mrs. Wang for help, if Miss Liu still refuses to go. To their surprise, Miss Liu prepares herself for the date in the morning prior to the date by getting her dress ready.

5.12) na   tian   zaochen,   Liu   xiaojie   jiao   laomazi
       DM (that)   day   morning   Liu   Miss   ask   nanny
       zhunbei   tangyundou,   shuo   yao   yun   yifu.
       prepare   iron   say   want   iron   clothes

(Qian, 1954, p. 226)

'That morning, Miss Liu told the maid to get the iron ready so she could press some clothes.'

(Qian, 1979, p. 241)

5.12G) An   jenem   Morgen   befahl   Fräulein Liu
       on   DM (that)   morning command. past. 3sg Miss   Liu
       dem   Dienstmädchen,   das   Bügeleisen   zu   erhitzen,
       ART   maid   ART   iron   to   heat
       um   ein   Kleid   zu   bügeln.
       for   QN (one)   dress   to   iron

(Qian, 2008, p. 289)

'In that morning, Miss Liu commanded the maid to get the iron heated, because she wanted to iron a dress.'

[my word-for-word translation]

In this example, *na* is the only option to refer to the morning of the date day. There are two reasons for this. First, if *na* were replaced with *zhe*, the author would imply that the morning is the topic of the following passage. This means that there are many more sentences regarding what else Miss Liu did to get ready. However, there is only one more sentence about the situation of the morning in question, but there is a very long paragraph following the sentence that switches the topic from the Lius to illustrating how Miss Fan, another girl invited to the blind date, prepares for the date. Therefore, *na* used in the sentence is to signal the meaning LOW DEIXIS and prepares the reader for the change of topic. Second, if "morning" were not preceded, it would be undifferentiated and could be any morning. Since it is a special day on which Miss Liu surprises her family with her unusual behavior, it would be very confusing for the reader to try to figure out whether this day is a special day or Miss Liu's behavior is her daily routine. The first reason is also why *diesem* cannot be employed in the German translation.

Similar to the reasons why *jenen* cannot be replaced by the definite article in example 5.10, *dem* would not be a suitable choice in the German translation. If *dem* is used, "morning" should be directly preceded or followed by a modifying phrase, such as "of the date" or "before Miss Liu's blind date." Otherwise, it is not clearly indicated that "the morning" is "the morning of the date day."

5.4 Differences Between the Use of the German and Chinese Demonstratives

In the overview of this chapter, I indicated that there are differences between the use of the German and Chinese demonstratives. There were three types of mismatching found in this comparative study after examining the data from the German and Chinese texts and their translations in the other language. First, demonstratives appearing in the text in one language are not necessarily demonstratives or referring phrases in the parallel text in the other language. Second, when they are, they are not necessarily equally represented by the comparable demonstratives or referring phrases in the other language. And third, due to differences in language typology, a great proportion of the discourse reference which is indicated by the use of the demonstratives in Chinese is signaled by the third person neuter pronoun *es* 'it' or NPs preceded by the definite articles. These types of mismatching served as clues to explore the differences in the use of the German and Chinese demonstratives.

In reference to the first type of mismatching, Faerch (1980) suggests that the use of the demonstratives in one language and the non-use in the other are expected to occur in even generically very close languages. In the previous sections, we found out that the use of the demonstratives is not the same in the German text and its English translation. Given that German and Chinese are typologically distinctive, it is expected that this mismatching will be found throughout the corpora.

In this section, I will identify the dissimilarities between the use of the German and Chinese demonstratives in three steps. First, I will examine which differences between the use of demonstratives in the original text and in the translation may be attributed to the linguistic factors, including both differences in the structure of the demonstrative systems themselves and differences in language typology. Second, I will explore which differences in usage can be attributed to differences in linguistic pragmatics, to the extent that these can be related to the structure of the linguistic system. Third, I will take extra-linguistic factors into consideration and see which incongruities in usage must be attributed to other factors such as those which result from the differences between the cultures where the languages are spoken.

5.4.1 Linguistic factors

5.4.1.1 The structure of the demonstrative system

As discussed in Chapters 3 and 4, the German and Chinese demonstratives function differently from each other. The German demonstratives, along with the articles, build up a system of DIFFERENTIATION. In this system, there are seven options for the German speakers to choose from based on the meaning they want the messages to convey, consciously or unconsciously. As a repetition of the table from Chapter 3, the system of DIFFERENTIATION is illustrated by the following table and figures:

			NUMBER	
			ONE	OTHER
DIFFEREN-TIATION	Not Required		Ø+___-Ø	N/A
	Required	Not Made	ein-①+___-Ø	Ø+___-PM
		Made	d-②+___-Ø	d-+___-PM

Table 5.1

$$\text{DIFFEREN-TIATION MADE} \begin{cases} \text{NOT LOCATED: d-+\_\_\_+Ø/PM} \\ \text{LOCATED} \begin{cases} \text{PROXIMAL: dies-+\_\_\_+Ø/PM} \\ \text{NON-PROXIMAL: jen-+\_\_\_+Ø/PM} \end{cases} \end{cases}$$

Figure 5.1

However, there is no article in Chinese (cf. Chapters 2 & 4). Since differentiation still needs to be made in Chinese, the Chinese demonstratives partially take over the function of article (cf. Chapters 2 & 4; Li & Thompson, 1981). Most of the time, the non-proximal demonstrative *na* is used to differentiate an entity from other prospective entities, functioning as an indefinite article. However, *na* is not always used for the sake of differentiation. As discussed in Chapter 4, the use of the Chinese demonstratives can be illustrated as follows:

$$\text{Demonstratives:} \begin{cases} \text{NEAR} \begin{cases} \text{SINGULAR: } zhe, zhege \text{ 'this'} \\ \text{PLURAL: } zhexie \text{ 'these'} \end{cases} \\ \text{FAR} \begin{cases} \text{SINGULAR: } na, nage \text{ 'that'} \\ \text{PLURAL: } naxie \text{ 'those'} \end{cases} \end{cases}$$

Figure 5.2

---

① *ein-* refers to indefinite article *ein* and its inflected forms, see Chapter 2.
② *d-* refers to definite articles such as *der*, *die*, *das* and their inflected forms, see Chapter 2.

$$\text{DEIXIS} \begin{cases} \text{zhe} = \text{HIGH DEIXIS} \\ \quad \text{(requires more attention of the hearer to the referent)} \\ \text{na} = \text{LOW DEIXIS} \\ \quad \text{(requires less attention of the hearer to the referent)} \end{cases}$$

Figure 5.3

Based on the above table and figures, we can assume that the Chinese demonstratives, compared to the German ones, will be used much more frequently. The German demonstratives are limited to signal the meanings of DIFFERENTIATION REQUIRED AND MADE and LOCATED, which only encompass two categories of the system of DIFFERENTIATION. In contrast, the Chinese demonstratives may be used in four of the seven categories. The ones they do not qualify for are to signal the meanings of DIFFERNTIATION NOT REQUIRED and DIFFRENTIATION REQUIRED AND NOT MADE.

We have analyzed the similarities of the use of the German and Chinese demonstratives in the previous section, which include the categories shown in Figure 5.1. And now I will show how the Chinese demonstratives are used to signal DIFFERNTIATION REQUIRED AND MADE.

First, I will show that both *zhe* and *na* can be used to refer to singular entities and signal DIFFERNTIATION REQUIRED AND MADE. This, in German, is signaled by d-+___+Ø.

5.13) zhe   xuexiao   caocao   chuangban,   guimo   bu   da.
       DM (this) school   in a hurry   build up   size   not   big

(Qian, 1954, p. 190)

'Small in size, the school had been put together haphazardly.'

(Qian, 1979, p. 202)

5.13G) Die   Universität   war   hastig   gegründet
        ART   university   be. past. 3sg in a hurry   build. pp
        und   war   noch   klein.
        and   be. past. 3sg still   small

(Qian, 2008, p. 246)

'The university was built up in a hurry and was still small.'

[my word-for-word translation]

In this example, *zhe* is used in the Chinese original, but the definite article *die* is used to refer to the university in the German translation. The referent, the university, is an entity that is differentiated from others, because it is the university at which Hung-chien and Hsin-mei were teaching. Followed by a short description instead of a long paragraph about the university, it is not appropriate to use *diese* here due to a change of topics. Also, it is not necessary to use *jene*, for the reason that the paragraph this example is in is a brief introduction of the university and the town where the university is located. It is not necessary to urge the reader to pay less attention to the university when the narrator is simply listing buildings in the town. Otherwise, *jene* will signal a meaning that is not in the original. This is, however, does not follow the rule of "choosing the least inappropriate" (cf. Diver, 1995; Garcia, 2009).

5.14)   na   xiaohaizi   zhengzai   chi   ziji   de   shou...
        DM (that)   child   right now   eat   self   GEN   hand

(Qian, 1954, p. 241)

'It [the child] has just been sucking its thumb...'

(Qian, 1979, p. 257)

5.14G) Das   Kind   lutsch-t-e   gerade   am   Daumen...
        ART (the)   child   suck-past-3sg   just   on the thumb

(Qian, 2008, p. 307)

'The child was just sucking on the thumb...'

[my word-for-word translation]

In this example, *na* is used to refer to the child which is already introduced. If *jenes* instead of *das* is used in the German translation, the sentence should end here and cannot be followed by a more detailed description of the child. This is because if an entity is already differentiated and located, it does not need to be provided with more information about itself. If *dieses* is applied in this sentence, the reader will be informed by the meaning of *dieses* that he/she should pay more attention to the child. This is not the case, because the main focus of this paragraph is on Miss Liu, who was introduced to Hung-chien as his prospective girlfriend, rather than being on the child.

Second, I will provide examples where *zhe* and *na* are used to refer to plural entities that are DIFFERENTIATED AND NOT LOCATED. This is signaled by d-+___+PM in German.

5.15)   zhexie   kapian   zhao   sijiao   haoma   pailie...
        DM (these)   card   according to   four-corner   code   arrange

(Qian, 1954, p. 152)

'The cards were arranged to the four-corner system.'

(Qian, 1979, p. 159)

5.15G) Die   Karte-n   war-en   entsprechend
        ART (the)   card-PM   be. past-pl   accordingly
        dem   Vier-Ecken-System   geordnet.
        ART (the)   four-corner system   arrange. pp

(Qian, 2008, p. 197)

'The cards were arranged according to the four-corner system.'

[my word-for-word translation]

In this example, *zhexie* 'these' is employed to refer to the cards of Li Mei-t'ing. It must be translated into the definite article *die* and cannot be replaced by *diese* or *jene* for the same reasons discussed in example

5.13.

As for *naxie*, it is used to refer to "students" in the next example and is translated as the definite article *die* in the next example. Similar to *na* in example 5.14, *naxie* cannot be translated to either *diese* or *jene* in the following example. The reasons here stayed the same as the ones discussed in example 5.14.

5.16) ...da xiakeling qian <u>na</u> ji fenzhong de nanguo!
ring bell before DM (that) some minute MM torture

(Qian, 1954, p. 201)

'...the few moments of misery before the bell!'

(Qian, 1979, p. 214)

5.16G) ...die quälenden Minute-n vor der Klingel...
ART (the) torturing minute-PM before ART (the) bell

(Qian, 2008, p. 260)

'...the torturing minutes before the bell...'

[my word-for-word translation]

Note that in all four examples provided in this section, whenever an entity is or needs to be differentiated and specified, *zhe* or *na* will perform this function, for lack of an article system. It is also suggested by Lü (1985) and Li & Thompson (1981) that Chinese has a tendency to use the non-proximal demonstrative *na* in particular in the way the German definite articles are used.

So far, we can make the interim conclusion that the Chinese demonstratives *zhe* and *na* possess combined features of the German demonstratives and definite articles.

5.4.1.2 Tense

In addition to the lack of articles, Chinese does not possess a verb conjugation system to show subject-verb agreement (cf. Chapters 2 & 4). Because of this, the time when the activity takes place needs to be shown by other means. An NP with *zhe* or *na* as the determiner can be used in sentences to indicate time. In German, such combinations can either be translated to *jetzt* 'now' and *damals* 'then,' or be left out if the time is already indicated by means of verb conjugations or temporal conjunctions.

The following examples illustrate that *zhe* and *na* can indicate time in some NPs, which results in their non-use of the German demonstratives. In example 5.17, the NP *zhe shihou* 'this time' literally, is translated to *jetzt* 'now' in the German translation. And in example 5.18, similarly, the NP *na shihou* 'that time' is translated as *damals* 'then.'

5.17) <u>zhe</u>   shihou damen,   you   shei hui   lai?
       DM (this) time   knock   EXT   who   POS   come

(Qian, 1954, p. 233)

'Just then there was a knock at the door, "who would that be?"'

(Qian, 1979, p. 249)

5.17G) Wer   komm-t   denn   jetzt zu   Besuch?
       who   come-3sg   actually   now   to   visit

(Qian, 2008, p. 298)

'Who comes to visit right now?'

[my word-for-word translation]

5.18) shei jiao   nimen   <u>na</u>   shihou   bu   lai   a?
       who   tell   you guys   DM (that)   time   not   come   RF

(Qian, 1954, p. 230)

'Who told you not to come over then?'

(Qian, 1979, p. 246)

5.18G) Sie   hätt-en   uns   eben   damals   besuchen   sollen!
       you. formal   have. subj-pl   us   even   then   visit   should

(Qian, 2008, p. 294)

'You should have visited us even then.'

[my word-for-word translation]

It may also be the case that *zhe* and *na* in temporal NPs are left out in the German translation, if the tense is already indicated by the sentence structure, verb conjugation or temporal conjunction. In example 5.19, 5.20 and 5.21, the use of *zhe* and *na* is expressed by a non-use of *dies-* and *jen-* in the translation, because the tense of each example is indicated by the sentence structure, verb conjugation and temporal conjunction respectively.

5.19) zhe   shihou, shen   shang fa   re, lian shang fa   hong,
      DM (this) time   body   on   start hot face on   start red
      jianghua kaishi   kouchi.
      talk   start   stutter

(Qian, 1954, p. 201)

'At that point he turned hot all over, his face flushed slightly, and he began to stutter.'

(Qian, 1979, p. 213)

5.19G) Heiß   und   errötend fing   er   an   zu   stottern.
       hot   and   flushed   start.past.3sg   he   at   to   stutter

(Qian, 2008, p. 259)

'Hot and flushed, he started to stutter.'

[my word-for-word translation]

In this example, the structure "*fing… an… zu…*" indicates that a new activity starts at that moment. Therefore, there is no need to have *damals* 'then' in the German translation.

5.20) dou shi ni   na   tian guan   zui le   wo.
      all be   you DM (that) day   force drink RC   PFV I

(Qian, 1954, p. 119)

'It's all from getting sick that day you made me drunk.'

(Qian, 1979, p. 124)

5.20G) "Das   komm-t   alles von   dem   Alkohol,
        ART   come-3sg all   from   ART   alcohol
        den   du   mir   eingeflößt   ha-st."
        which   you   me   pour in-pp   have-2sg

(Qian, 2008, p. 157)

'It all comes from the alcohol that you have poured in me.'

[my word-for-word translation]

In the German translation of this example, the perfect tense is used to indicate that the pouring-in of alcohol event has taken place before. Therefore, *na tian* 'that day' was left out in the German translation, because the perfect tense signals the meaning of FINISHED (cf. Kirsner, 1972; Reid, 1977; Diver, 1987).

In the translation of the next example, the temporal conjunction *als* 'as' is used in a subordinate clause to indicate the relative time of the event. Since the time of the event is already clear, it is understandable to leave out *na shihou* 'then' and not have it translated as *damals* 'then' in the translation.

5.21)   wo   na   shihou qiao fang   xiansheng gen Li   xiansheng
        I   DM (that) time   see   Fang   Mr.   and Li   Mr.
        liangren zheng le   yan, wo   kan   zhe ni,
        both   open   PVF   eye   I   stare   DUR you
        ni   kan   zhe   wo,   qihuhu   de,   zhen haowanr!
        you   stare DUR   I   mad   CSC   truly funny

(Qian, 1954, p. 169)

'It was so funny to see Mr. Fang and Mr. Li glaring at each other and panting.'

(Qian, 1979, p. 179)

5.21G) "Wirklich amüsant", bemerk-t-e   Fräulein Sun lächelnd,
        really   funny   comment-past-3sg   Miss   Sun smiling

"als	Herr	Fang	und	Herr	Li	sich	anstarr-t-en	und
as	Mr.	Fang	and	Mr.	Li	themselves	stare-past-3pl	and
vor	Wut	fauch-t-en."						
of	anger	hiss-past-pl						

(Qian, 2008, p. 220)

'"Really funny," commented Miss Sun, "as Mr. Fang and Mr. Li stared at each other and were angry."'

[my word-for-word translation]

5.4.1.3 Zero-anaphora and NP as subject

In the second chapter, I discussed the zero-anaphora phenomenon in Chinese (cf. Chapter 2; Li & Thompson, 1979, 1981). The frequent absence of third person pronouns for reference can rather be accounted for by the phenomenon of the homophonous third person pronouns (cf. Lü, op cit.; Li & Thompson, 1981). This means that in Chinese, there are no phonemic distinctions between the male, female, and the inanimate third person pronouns. These pronouns can only be differentiated from each other in writing by means of radicals (cf. Wu, 2004).

The identical phonological encoding in the Chinese third-person pronouns results in a practical problem: if a third person pronoun is used, it causes confusion as to which referent the pronoun is referring. This autonomous problem has naturally reduced the frequency of use of third person pronouns.

As Lü indicates (1985), there used to be no third person pronouns in ancient Chinese for the subject position to begin with. If the subject position had to be filled, an NP was used. This also resulted in the even more infrequent use of third person pronouns for the subject position.

Therefore, in this section, I will show examples where the Chinese demonstratives *zhe* and *na* function as pronominal and as determiner of an NP to start a sentence. In such cases, a neuter inanimate third person pronoun is used in the Germanic languages, of which German is one.

The first two examples in this section show that the Chinese demonstratives can function as pronominals to start a sentence, as they are translated to the German neuter third person pronoun *es* 'it' (cf. 5.1 & 5.2).

5.22) zhe   shi   dajia   de   shi.
       DM (this)   be   everyone   GEN   stuff

(Qian, 1954, p. 122)

'... this is a matter concerning everyone.'

(Qian, 1979, p. 127)

5.22G) Es   war   Gemeinschaftsmahl.
       It   be.past.3sg   everyone's matter

(Qian, 2008, p. 160)①

'It is everyone's matter.'

[my word-for-word translation]

5.23) na   zui   hao.
       DM (that)   most   good

(Qian, 1954, p. 197)

'That's good, then.'

(Qian 1979, p. 209)

5.23G) Dann   ist   es   gut.
       then   be.3sg   it   good

(Qian, 2008, p. 255)

'It is good, then.'

[my word-for-word translation]

The next two examples demonstrate that when an NP with a

---

① This translation is slightly adjusted due to a stylistic issue. *Es* 'it' was translated for *zhe* (Qian, 2008, p. 160).

Chinese demonstratives as determiner is needed to fill in the subject position, it can also be translated as the neuter third person pronoun in German.

5.24) zhe   fangfa   queshi hen   lingyan.
       DM (this) method indeed very effective

(Qian, 1954, p.107)

'The method is very effective, though.'

(Qian, 1979, p.110)

5.24G) Aber es   war   tatsächlich ein   Wundermittel.
       but   it   be. past. 3sg   really   QN (one) panacea

(Qian, 2008, p.141)

'But it was really a panacea.'

[my word-for-word translation]

Notice that the German neuter definite article *das* can to some extent be interchangeable with *es* in the subject position (Lovik et al, 2009; Di Donato et al, 2010).

In examples 5.21 and 5.22, pronominal *zhe* and *na* appear in the subject position and are translated as *es* in German. The fact that, as discussed at the beginning of this section, it is not favored in Chinese to employ the inanimate third person pronoun *ta* 'it' for reference and as subject of a sentence, is seen to indirectly promote the use of *zhe* and *na* to fulfill the referential need. After trying several times to replace *zhe* and *na* with *ta* 'it,' it sounds impossible to avoid the awkwardness entailed in the use of *ta*. This, as posited by Lü (1985), suggests that the Chinese demonstratives *zhe* and *na* and the German neuter third person pronoun *es* share certain discourse referential roles. It also indicates that *ta* 'it' in Chinese does not have as much power of referentiality as *zhe* and *na* have. This may result in *zhe* and *na* taking over this reference-tracking function in discourse and appearing as pronominal in the subject position.

In examples 5.23 and 5.24, when referring to the same referent, an NP modified by *zhe* and *na* is used in Chinese, whereas in German, *es* is employed. This indicates that for signaling the same entity, there are cases when *es* itself will do in German, but a *zhe-* or *na-* introduced NP is required in Chinese. In such NPs, *zhe* and *na* serve as determiners and specify "the speaker's categorical, or ontological, assumptions about the entity in question" (Lyons, 1995, p.308). This fact can also be the result of the infrequent use of the third person pronouns in Chinese.

Based on the four examples in this section, we can add the reference-tracking function to the already existing functions of the Chinese demonstratives *zhe* and *na*. The German demonstratives, with the frequent use of the neuter third person pronoun *es* 'it,' are not expected to have as great a reference-tracking function as *zhe* and *na* do.

5.4.2 Pragmatic factors

As the word itself implies, pragmatics is concerned with how language is actually used. Therefore, the semantics of demonstratives cannot be separated from pragmatics. Both pragmatics and demonstratives do not have any absolutely correct or incorrect expressions, because both need to take the speaker into consideration. This means that the actual choice of the word or structure changes if the speaker's aspect changes.

If we define pragmatics as the way in which self-expression is encoded, we can perceive it through certain grammatical and lexical mechanisms (Lyons, 1995; Traugott, 1988; Sweetser, 1988). Note that a specific mechanism in one language may not exist in the other, such as the German tense system, which is absent in Chinese. Thus, Chinese cannot use the tense system to encode the expressive function of language (cf. Crystal, 1979).

Demonstratives, as discussed in previous chapters, are dependent on the speaker's perception, because spatial, temporal, or emotional distance must be interpreted in terms of individual involvement. In particular, the Chinese demonstratives carry the meaning of the speaker's attitude towards the referent, in addition to the more objective spatial and temporal distance evaluated by the speaker.

In the following sections, I will examine three pragmatic factors that result in the differences between the use of German and Chinese demonstratives. The first is the use of appositive phrases in Chinese. The second is the co-occurrence of the demonstratives with a personal pronoun in an NP in Chinese. And the third factor is the use of a combination of definite article and locative as an alternative to the German demonstratives.

5.4.2.1 Appositive phrases with *zhe* or *na*

Appositive phrases are defined as having two NPs or one pronoun and an NP to refer to the same entity. The use of appositive phrases, however, is not found in the German text.

5.25) women   <u>zhe</u>   zhong haowu   lüxing jingyan   de   ren
      we   DM (this)   kind   without   travel experience   MM   people
      zhaoguan   ziji   dou   zhaoguan   bu   lai.
      take care of oneself   even   take care of   not   PC

(Qian, 1954, p. 130)

'People like us with no traveling experience can barely look after ourselves.'

(Qian, 1979, p. 135)

5.25G) Bei   unserer   Unerfahrenheit komm-en   wir
        with   our   inexperience   come-1pl we
        kaum   selbst   zurecht.
        barely   self   right

(Qian, 2008, p.169)
'We can barely do ourselves right with our inexperience.'
[my word-for-word translation]

In this example, *women* 'we' and *zhe zhong hao wu lüxing jingyan de ren* 'this kind of people without traveling experience' enter into an appositive relation. Both refer to Hung-chien and Hsin-mei. The use of appositive phrases as in this example is observed to have a pragmatic effect. Both *women* 'we' and *zhe zhong hao wu lüxing jingyan de ren* 'this kind of people without traveling experience' are there to strengthen the speaker's point of view that both are incapable of traveling by themselves due to inexperience. This scene describes Hung-chien's extreme dissatisfaction with travelling to Hunan to teach at a new university. When informed that Hsin-mei would take Miss Sun with them, Hung-chien felt it was even more unacceptable, as this meant that he had to take care of Miss Sun on the long and difficult journey. However, the sentence does not sound harsh with the application of appositive phrases.

In order to illustrate the pragmatic strengthening effect of the use of appositive phrases, I will provide variations of the utterance from the last example in the following:

5.25b) women zhaoguan   ziji   dou   zhaoguan   bu   lai.
        we   take care of   oneself   even take care of   not   PC
        'We cannot even take care of ourselves.'

5.25c) women zhe   zhong ren
        we   DM (zhe)   kind   people
        zhaoguan   ziji   dou   zhaoguan   bu   lai.
        take care of   oneself   even take care of   not   PC

'People like us cannot even take care of themselves.'

5.25d)	women	zhe	zhong	haowu	lüxing	jingyan	de	ren
	we	DM (this)	kind	without	travel	experience	MM	people
	zhaoguan	ziji		dou	zhaoguan	bu	lai.	
	take care of	oneself		even	take care of	not	PC	

'People like us with no traveling experience can barely look after ourselves.'

Compare the above three variations of the utterance from the last example. While their basic propositions are similar, the assertiveness is reduced from 5.25b to 5.25d. In sentence 5.25b, it is a direct negation that "we," Hung-chien and Hsin-mei, are more than able to take care of themselves. With *zhe zhong ren* 'this kind of people,' the assertiveness of sentence 5.25c is mellowed. Hung-chien and Hsin-mei's ability to take care of themselves is not being directly negated; the utterance rather suggests a general category of people of which Hung-chien and Hsin-mei are members, and rejects the idea that the two are alone in their lack of ability. And in sentence 5.25d, the assertiveness is mellowed even more by providing additional information on the category of poor travelers. This sentence sounds much softer because the inability to travel well is attributed to inexperience.

5.4.2.2 Co-occurrence of *zhe* or *na* with a personal pronoun in an NP

In Chinese, pragmatic strengthening can be seen when the demonstratives co-appear with a personal pronoun in an NP (cf. Wu, 2004). In co-occurrence, a demonstrative functions as an intensifier of the statement indicated in the sentence. Such co-occurrence takes place throughout the Chinese text. However, it is not detected in the German text or in the German translation of the Chinese text.

In the next example, the stationmaster used such a combination to address to the bus station he was in charge of.

5.26) women zhe   chezhan guanli   you   weishan   zhi   chu.
      we   DM (this)   station manage EXT incomplete MM   place
                                                          (Qian, 1954, p. 145)

'There's much room for improvement in the way our station here is run.'
                                                          (Qian, 1979, p. 151)

5.26G) Unsere Busstation   ha-t   gewiß   noch   administrative Mängel.
       our   bus station   have-3sg   indeed   still   administrative lack
                                                          (Qian, 2008, p. 188)

'Our bus station indeed still has administrative imperfection.'

[my word-for-word translation]

In this example, the NP *women zhe chezhan* 'our this station' would signal the same referent as *women chechan* 'our station.' This means that *zhe* is suppressed. Also, *zhe* is seen to add emphasis and agreement of the speaker to the statement that the bus station is still not good enough, with the undertone that he, the speaker and the bus stationmaster, is very modest and is open to criticism. In this particular context, the use of *zhe* is pragmatically motivated. With the pragmatic motivation of *zhe*, the imperfection of the administration of the bus station and the virtue of being modest, through the undertone of the utterance, are both strengthened. *Zhe*, therefore, is used in this example to help articulate the attitude of the speaker.

5.4.2.3 Definite article and locative as alternative of demonstratives in German

As analyzed in Chapters 1 and 3, a combination of definite articles and locatives can be used as alternative for the German demonstratives and has replaced the demonstratives in the majority of cases, unless abstract entities are referred to. This is generally the case in the German text.

Exceptions of using such combinations to refer to abstract entities may take place with specific meanings. In the next example, *weixian* 'danger' is referred to by *zheyang* 'this kind' in Chinese, but by a combination of definite article and locative in the German translation.

5.27) tamen zhu zai shanghai de   ren   zhenshi zuishengmengsi,
      they live in Shanghai MM people truly   live in luxury

      zen zhidao chumen you   zheyang   de weixian.
      how know   go out EXT   DM (this kind) MM danger

                                                    (Qian, 1954, p. 138)

'People living in Shanghai go around in a dream world. How could they know there are such dangers on the road?'

                                                    (Qian, 1979, p. 143)

5.27G) Die Shanghaier   leb-en in   einer   Traumwelt,
       ART Shanghai local live-3pl in   ART (a)   dream world

       von den   Gefahren hier hab-en   sie   keine Ahnung.
       of   ART (the)   danger   here have-3pl they no   idea

                                                    (Qian, 2008, p. 178)

'The Shanghai locals are living in a dream world and have no idea of the danger here.'

                              [my word-for-word translation]

The definite article *den* and locative *hier* 'here' is used because *diesen* would confuse the reader, as they would not know whether the danger is meant "such danger" or "the danger here." When taking the first clause of this sentence into consideration, the speaker clearly makes a claim that people living in Shanghai would have no idea of the danger he experienced right in this town. In order to communicate his exact meaning and also to avoid misunderstanding and ambiguity, the speaker used the combination of the definite article *den* and locative *hier* 'here' in this example, despite the fact that the referent "danger" is an abstract entity.

5.4.3 Extra-linguistic factors

Language is undeniably affected by the culture in which it is spoken. Although we should not completely rely on Whorf's theory (1956) of linguistic determinism, we still need to take culture into consideration. Culture is not limited to the geographical environment one lives in, but instead is the language community. This does not mean that Whorf's claim about culture determining language and one's view of world is entirely correct; however, his theory is, to some extent, on the right track in its positing that culture plays an indispensable role in one's conceptualization of the world. This can be illustrated by the differences in the grammatical and lexical categories between languages (cf. Lakoff, 1987).

5.4.3.1 Implicitness and higher referentiality

According to Lin (1935, 1938), Chinese people are more implicit. In "*Lunyu*" 'The Analects,' Confucius teaches that people should neither *shiyan* 'lose words' nor *shiren* 'lose people.' By *shiyan*, Confucius means that if one knows that the hearer is too stubborn to accept others' advice, one should not waste one's words attempting to persuade him. Otherwise one cannot reach the life-time goal of becoming a *junzi* 'man of nobility.' Also, Confucius encourages people to talk less and do more. Last but not least, he postulates the concept of *zhiren* 'to know people.' He further explains that one should get to know people before talking to them, for the reason that this is the most efficient way to communicate. These doctrines may be the reasons why Chinese people try to use minimal words and be implicit.

This cultural characteristic is related to the use of demonstratives in the Chinese language. In the corpora, one interesting finding is that

Chinese does not prefer to use possessive pronouns to relate entities to each other. As shown in the data, there are times when *zhe* and *na* are used to refer to an entity, whereas German employs possessive pronouns to refer to the entity in question. Admittedly, it is more explicit if one uses possessives to refer to an entity than if one uses demonstratives, especially when pointing is not involved. However, we cannot judge that the more frequent use of possessives makes German a better or more efficient language. Just as the Germans are comfortable with using possessives to refer to entities, the Chinese find their ways to correctly and effortlessly locate the referent referred to by the demonstratives. This is shown in the example below:

5.28)   <u>zhe</u>   wei   fang   xiansheng   zui   ai   sahuang.
        DM (this) CL   Fang   Mr.   most   like   lie

(Qian, 1954, p. 135)

'Mr. Fang here likes to tell lies.'

(Qian, 1979, p. s 140)

5.28G) Unser   Herr   Fang   hier   erzähl-t   Ihnen   bloß   Märchen.
        our   Mr.   Fang   here   tell-3sg   you. formal   merely   fairy tales

(Qian, 2008, p. 175)

'Our Mr. Fang here only talks about fairy tales.'

[my word-for-word translation]

As discussed in Chapter 4, the Chinese demonstratives can indicate the speaker's attitude towards the referent. Though we cannot claim that *zhe* only refers to favorable entities and *na* to unfavorable ones, because the speaker's preference is not the only ruler used to choose the best word choice[①], *zhe*, as discussed in 5.3, can be viewed as an intensifier of the speaker's statement. This is also a culture-related issue, as is

---

① See Xu (1987, p. 146) "… in Chinese, th[e] distinction [in proximity] is made on both psychological and factual grounds."

shown in the following example:

5.29)　wo　　zhe　　　　ge　　ren　　　ting　　hao　　de.
　　　　　I　　DM (this)　CL　person　pretty　good　AP
　　　'I am a pretty good guy.'

As discussed in 5.3, *zhe* can be viewed as an intensifier of the statement. If one does not use the NP *zhe ge ren* 'this+CL+person' in the sentence, it does not necessarily mean that the speaker himself agrees to the claim that he/she is a good person. By strengthening the referent, the speaker indirectly encodes an undertone of agreement in the sentence. This is a way of complimenting oneself in the Chinese culture. Directly praising oneself, such as the common statement "I am very good at..." is not viewed favorably in the Chinese culture, as one must be modest to be a *junzi* 'man of nobility.'

5.4.3.2　Explicitness and relatedness

In contrast to the implicitness in the Chinese culture, the Germans are much more direct and explicit (Russ, 1994). Even beyond the obvious example of the implicit Chinese, some Westerners will, at times, feel offended by the German directness and explicitness. It is perhaps an overstatement, though not by much: Germans are used to speaking truth without reservation.

The German language, too, is very direct, and both reveals and conveys more information than many other languages, such as Chinese and English. As discussed in Chapter 2 and 3, when a German speaks of having visited his/her neighbor yesterday, he/she reveals the gender of the neighbor: *ich habe gestern meinen Nachbarn besucht* 'I have visited my (male) neighbor yesterday' versus *ich habe gestern meine Nachbarin besucht* 'I have visited my (female) neighbor yesterday.' In contrast, both in English 'I have visited my neighbor yesterday' and in Chinese *wo zuotian baifang le linju* 'I have visited (my) neighbor yesterday,' the gender of the neighbor remains unspecified.

From the Chinese sentence *wo zuotian baifang le linju* 'I have visited (my) neighbor yesterday,' we can see that the neighbor is not even specified as "my" neighbor. Similarly, a Chinese will hardly ever say "I called my mom yesterday," but say *wo zuotian gei mama da le dianhua* 'I called mom yesterday.' In contrast, a German would say *ich habe meine Mutter angerufen* 'I have called my mom' very frequently. This can indicate that Germans are more explicit about personal relationships than Chinese are. In addition to example 5.28, there are also examples in the German text. In those examples, a German demonstrative is used in the original, but is not used in the Chinese translation.

5.30) Sie konn-t-e kaum wissen, daß ich diesen Besuch
 she can-past-3sg never know that I DM(this) visit
 nicht nur hinausschob,
 not only postpone.past.3sg
 sondern mich vor ihm drück-t-e.
 but myself from it press-past-1sg

(Schlink, 1995, p.183)

'She had no way to know that I was not only putting off this visit, but avoiding it.'

(Schlink, 1997, pp.193—194)

5.30C) ta nali hui xiaode, wo budan ba Ø tanjian
 she no way POS know wo not only BA jail visit
 tuoyan xiaqu, hai genben shi xiang taotuo.
 postpone DC also at all be want run away

(Schlink, 2009, p.169)

'She has no way to know that I not only postpone the visit, but also want to run away from it totally.'

[my word-for-word translation]

In Chinese it is not necessary to specify which visit it is. Any participant who is familiar with the speaker would know immediately to which visit this refers.

5.5 Conclusion

The following chart serves as a summary of the similarities and differences in the use of the German and Chinese demonstratives:

Category	German DMs	Chinese DMs
Similarities		
Function as pronominal	Yes	Yes
Function as determiner	Yes	Yes
Reference to concrete entities	Yes	Yes
Reference to abstract entities	Yes	Yes
Signal DEIXIS	Yes	Yes
Differences		
Linguistic Factors		
Function as definite article	No	Yes
Grammar and temporal NP	Yes	No
As subject in an NP	If necessary	Frequent
Pragmatic Factors		
In Appositive Phrases	No	Yes
As attitude indicator	No	Yes
Alternatives	Yes	No
Extra-linguistic Factors		
Preference of pronoun over DM	Yes	No

Chart 5.1

In this chart we can see that, at the basic level, the German and Chinese demonstratives have similar functions. However, German and Chinese are two typologically distinctive languages. Their demonstratives differ from each other linguistically, pragmatically, and extra-linguistically. German, a subject-prominent language, is structurally not as flexible as Chinese, a topic-prominent language.

5.6 Discussion

As discussed in the comparison of the German and Chinese demonstratives, Chinese is a language that is more flexible in structure and includes, to a greater extent, the involvement of the speaker.

If we want to make a distinction between what is in the linguistic system and what is not, we need to consider what the pragmatic and extra-linguistic factors in both languages are. As German articles and demonstratives can be employed based on the meaning needed, the Chinese demonstratives do not have a one-to-one match to meanings. Other aspects, such as pragmatic factors and cultural factors play an important role in the Chinese language. Therefore, although the Columbia School approach is considered to post relatively sparse meanings for signals, it is adequate in constructing a system of DIFFERENTIATION for the German demonstratives. In contrast, the Chinese demonstratives, though signaling HIGH and LOW DEIXIS, do not have semantic exhaustive oppositions in the system of DEIXIS and thus cannot benefit as much from a Columbia School analysis. In this case, we should adopt another theoretical approach and build more of the pragmatic and cultural factors into the language. Cognitive Linguistics, for example, may be a better choice, as it focuses on how conceptualization plays a role in the language and does not try to assign a sparse meaning to each word, but rather analyzes each word within the processes of the human mind.

When applying the Columbia School analysis and Cognitive Linguistics in language teaching, one should limit each to the different stages of the learners. At the beginning, the learner does not possess a fundamental understanding of how the grammar and lexicon work in the target language. If introducing each word with a rather sparse meaning, as posited by the Columbia School analysis, the beginning language learner will still have no idea of which structure and vocabulary are adequate to use. A Cognitive Linguistics analysis will better help a language learner, as it can provide more specific conditions on how the decisions are made for choosing the correct structure and lexicon. When the learner progresses to an advanced level and needs to know more about the most intrinsic differences between words with similar meanings and usages, the Columbia School analysis may be of greater assistance, because it provides the meaning from a native speaker's perspective: if there is another form, there is another meaning. A native speaker does not process the language as a language learner does. The language is merely a combination of sound waves with meanings to a native speaker (Diver, 1995). Without knowing the boundary of words, a native speaker can communicate perfectly using the language, that is, use the "sparse meanings" proposed by the Columbia School approach.

References

16-jähriger Schwarzfahrer muss fast drei Jahre in haft. (2013, January 29). *Web*. Retrieved from http://web. de/magazine/nachrichten/panorama/17075876-16-jaehriger schwarzfahrer-jahre-haft. html

Adamson, S. (1994a). Subjectivity in narration: Empathy and echo. In M. Yaguello (Ed.), *Subjecthood and subjectivity* (pp. 193—208). Paris: Ophrys.

Adamson, S. (1994b/1995a). From empathetic deixis to empathetic narrative: stylisation and (de-)subjectivisationas processes of language change. In S. Wright & D. Stein (Eds.), *Subjectivity and subjectivisation* (pp. 195—224). Cambridge: Cambridge University Press.

Adamson, S. (1995b). Empathetic narrative-a literary and linguistic problem. In W. Ayres-Bennett & P. O'Donovan (Eds.), *Syntax and the literary system* (pp. 17—42). Cambridge: Cambridge French Colloquia.

Bates, J. (1976). Review article on David C. Bennett's spatial and temporal uses of English prepositions: An essay in stratificational semantics. *Lingua*, *39*, 353—365.

Biber, D., Conrad, S. & Reppen, R. (2002). *Corpus linguistics: Investigating language structure and use*. Cambridge: Cambridge University Press.

Bierwisch, M. (1967). Syntactic features in morphology: General problems of so-called pronominal inflection in German. *To honor Roman Jakobson: Essays on the occasion of his seventieth birthday*, *11 October 1966*. The Hague: Mouton.

Biq, Y. (2007). Lexicalization and phrasalization of na collocates in spoken Taiwan Mandarin. *Contemporary linguistics*, *2*, 128—139. Retrieved from http://www. ddyyx. com/en/qkjs. asp

Bolinger, D. (1987). Echoes reechoed. *American speech*, *62*, 261—279. doi: 10.

2307/454810

Brown, G. (1995). *Speakers, listeners, and communication: Explorations in discourse analysis*. Cambridge: Cambridge University Press.

Brown, G. & Yule, G. (1983). *Discourse analysis*. Cambridge: Cambridge University Press.

Buddihistische Philosophie. (n. d.). In *Wikipedia*. Retrieved February, 21, 2013 from http://de.wikipedia.org/wiki/Buddhistische_Philosophie#Vergleich_mit_anderen Philosophien.

Bühler, K. (1990). *Theory of language: The representational function of language*. D. F. Goodwin (Trans.). Amsterdam: John Benjamins. (Original work published in 1934).

Chafe, W. (1976). Givenness, contrativeness, definiteness, subjects and topics. In C. Li (Ed.) *Subject and topic* (pp. 27—55). New York: Academic Press.

Chafe, W. (1979). The flow of thought and the flow of language. In T. Givón (Ed.), *Syntax and semantics: 12. Discourse and syntax* (pp. 159—181). New York: Academic Press.

Chafe, W. (1980). *The pear stories: Cognitive, cultural, and linguistic aspects of narrative production*. Norwood, NJ: Ablex.

Chafe, W. & Danielewicz, J. (1987). Properties of spoken and written language. In R. Horowitz & S. J. Samuels (Eds.), *Comprehending oral and written language* (pp. 83—113). New York, NY: Academic Press.

Chao, Y. (1968). *Language and symbolic systems*. Cambridge: Cambridge University Press.

Chen, P. (1986). *Referent introducing and tracking in Chinese narratives*. (Unpublished doctoral dissertation). University of California, Los Angeles.

Chomsky, N. (1957). *Syntactic structures*. The Hague: Mouton.

Chomsky, N. (1965). *Aspects of the theory of syntax*. Cambridge, MA: MIT Press.

Chomsky, N. (1969). *Topics in the theory of generative grammar*. Hague: Mouton.

Christensen, M. (1994). *Variation in spoken and written Mandarin narrative discourse*. (Doctoral dissertation). Retrieved from Ohio State University Dissertation Database.

Christensen, M. (2000). Anaphoric reference in spoken and written Chinese narrative discourse. *Journal of Chinese linguistics*, 28(2), 303—336. Retrieved from http://www.cuhk.edu.hk/journal/jcl/.

Clancy, P. (1980). Referential choice in English and Japanese narrative discourse. In W. Chafe (Ed.), *The pear stories: Cognitive, cultural, and linguistic aspects of narrative production* (pp. 127—198). Norwood, NJ: Ablex.

Comrie, B. (1985). *Tense*. Cambridge: Cambridge University Press.

Comrie, B. (1989). *Language universals and linguistic typology*. (2nd ed.). Oxford: Basil Blackwell.

Confucius. (2005). Lunyu. *The analects of Confucius*. A. Waley (Trans.). New York, NY: Routledge.

Contini-Morava, E. (1976). Statistical demonstration of a meaning: the Swahili locatives in existential assertions. *Studies in African linguistics*, 7, 165—173. Retrieved from http://sal.research.pdx.edu/.

Crystal, D. (1979). Neglected grammatical factors in conversational English. In R. Quirk, S. Greenbaum, G. Leech, & J. Svartvik (Eds.), *Studies in English linguistics* (pp. 153—166). London: Longman.

Danchev, A. (1969). The parallel use of the synthetic dative instrumental and periphrastic prepositional constructions in Old English. *Annuaire de l'université de Sofia, Faculté des letters*, LXII, 40—100.

Davis, J. (2000, February). *On abstinence and abdication: Italian si*. Paper presented at The 6th International Conference on Columbia School of Linguistics in Rutgers University, New Brunswick.

Dehan cidian [The German-Chinese dictionary]. (1982). Shanghai: Shanghai Yiwen Chubanshe.

Denny, J. P. (1978). Locating the universals in lexical systems for spatial deixis. In D. M. Farkas, W. J. Tacobson, & K. W. Todrys (Eds.), *Papers from the parasession on the lexicon* (pp. 70—84). Chicago, IL: Chicago Linguistics Society.

Deutscher, Guy. (2011). *Through the language glass: Why the world looks different in other languages*. London: Arrow Books.

Diessel, H. (1999). *Demonstratives: Forum, function, and grammaticalization*. Amsterdam: John Benjamins.

Diessel, H. (2006). Demonstratives, joint attention, and the emergence of grammar. *Cognitive linguistics, 17*(4), 463—489. doi: 10.1515/COG.2006.015.

Di Donato, D. R., Clyde, M., Vansant, J., Briggs, J., Busges, M., Schneider, K. H., & Daves Schneider, L. (2012). *Deutsch: Na klar!: An introductory German course* (6th ed.). New York, NY: McGraw-Hill.

Diver, W. (1969). The system of relevance of the Homeric verb. *Acta linguistica hafniensia, 12*, 45—48. Retrieved from http://www.tandfonline.com/toc/salh20/current.

Diver, W. (1984). The grammars of homeric Greek and classical Latin. (Unpublished textook for Linguistics G6803). Columbia University, New York, NY.

Diver, W. (1987). The dual. *Columbia university working papers in linguistics, 8*, 100—114. Retrieved from http://journals.tc-library.org/index.php/tesol.

Diver, W. (1995). Theory. In E. Contini-Morava, B. Sussman Goldberg, & R. Kisner (Eds.), *Meaning as explanation: Advances in linguistic sign theory* (pp.43—114). Berlin: Mouton de Gruyter.

Diver, W. and Davis J. (2012). Latin voice and case. In Huffman A. and Davis J. (Eds.) *Language: Communication and human behavior: The linguistic essays of William Diver* (pp.129—154). Leiden/Boston: Brill.

Duden: Die deutsche Rechtschreibung. (2002). Berlin: Dudenverlag.

Ehrlich, V. (1982). *Da* and the system of spatial deixis in German. In J. Weissenborn & W. Klein (Eds.), *Here and there: Cross-linguistic studies on deixis and demonstration* (pp.43—64). Amsterdam: John Benjamins.

Erbaugh, M. S. (2001). The Chinese pear stories: Narratives across seven Chinese dialects. Retrieved from http://www.pearstories.org/

Faerch, C. (1980). A contrastive description of deixis in Danish and English. In J. Fisiak (Ed.), *Theoretical issues in contrastive linguistics* (pp.365—376).

Amsterdam: John Benjamins.

Fang, M. (2002). The grammaticalization of the demonstratives zhe and na in spoken Beijing. *Zhongguo yuwen*, 4, 343—356. Retrieved from http://www.zgyw.org.cn/EN/article/showDownloadTopList.do.

Fillmore, C. (1982). Frame semantics. The Linguistic Society of Korea (Ed.) *Linguistics in the morning calm* (pp. 111—137). Seoul: Hanshin Publishing Co.

Garcia, E. C. (1975). *The role of theory in linguistic analysis: the Spanish pronoun system*. Amsterdam: North-Holland.

Garcia E. C. (1979). Discourse without syntax. In T. Givón & C. Li (Eds.) *Discourse and syntax* (pp. 23—49). New York, NY: Academic Press.

Garcia, E. C. (2009). *The motivated syntax of arbitrary signs: Cognitive constraints on Spanish clitic clustering*. Amsterdam: John Benjamins.

Geschichte Pommerns. (n. d.). In *Wikipedia*. Retrieved January 1, 2012 from www.de.wikipedia.org/wiki/Geschichte_Pommerns.

Gildin, B. (1979). Subject inversion in French: natural word order or *l'arbitraire du signe*. In F. Neussel (Ed.), *Essays in contemporary Romance linguistics*. Rowley, MA: Newbury House.

Givón, T. (1979). Discourse and syntax. In T. Givón (Ed.), *Syntax and semantics* (Vol. 12) (pp. 105—108). New York, NY: Academic Press.

Givón, T. (1983). *Topic continuity in discourse: A quantitative cross-language study*. Amsterdam, Philadelphia: J. Benjamins Publishing Company.

Gorup, R. (2002). Serbo-Croatian deixis: Balancing attention with difficulty in processing. In W. Reid, R. Otheguy, & N. Stern (Eds.), *Signal, meaning and message: perspectives in sign-based linguistics* (pp. 137—155). Amsterdam: John Benjamins.

Gorup, R. (2006). Se without deixis. In J. Davis, R. J. Gorup, & N. Stern (Eds.), *Advances in functional linguistics: Columbia School beyond its origins* (pp. 195—210). Amsterdam: John Benjamins.

Greenberg, J. H. (1963). Some universals of grammar with particular reference to the order of meaningful elements. In J. H. Greenberg (Ed.), *Universals of languages* (pp. 58—90). Cambridge, MA: MIT Press.

Greenfield, P. M. & Smith, J. H. (1976). *The structure of communication in early language development*. New York, NY: Academic Press.

Halliday, M. & Hasan, R. (1976). *Cohesion in English*. London: Longman.

Hartmann, D. (1982). Deixis and anaphora in German dialects: The semantics andpragmatics of two definite articles in dialectical varieties. In J. Weissenborn & W. Klein (Eds.), *Here and there: cross-linguistic studies on deixis and demonstration* (pp. 187—208). Amsterdam: John Benjamins.

Hayashi, M. & Yoon K. (2006). A cross-linguistic exploration of demonstratives in interaction with particular reference to the context of word-formulation trouble. *Studies in language*, *30*(3), 480—540. doi: 10.1075/sl.30.3.02hay.

Heim, M. (2011, December 20). Translation: a cure to Globish. L. Lin (Trans.) *China social sciences daily*. Retrived from http://www.csstoday.net/Index.html.

Hockett, C. F. (1960). The origin of speech. *Scientific American*, *203*(3), 89.

Hopkins, E. & Jones, R. (1972). Jener in modern standard German. *Die Unterrichtspraxis*, *5*(1), 15—27. Retrieved from http://onlinelibrary.wiley.com/journal/10.1111/(ISSN)1756—1221.

Hopper, P. J. (1979). Aspect and foregrounding in discourse. In T. Givon (Ed.), *Syntax and semantics* (Vol. 12) (pp. 213—241). New York, NY: Academic Press.

Hopper, P. (1998). Emergent grammar. *The new psychology of language: Vol. 2: Cognitive and functional approaches to language structure* (pp. 155—175). Mahwah, N.J.: Psychology press.

Huffman, A. (1997). *The categories of grammar: French lui and le*. Amsterdam: John Benjamins.

Huffman, A. (2006). Diver's theory. In J. Davis, R. Gorup, & N. Stern (Eds.), *Advances in functional linguistics: Columbia School beyond its origins* (pp. 31—62). Amsterdam: John Benjamins.

Jackendoff, R. (1983). *Semantics and cognition*. Cambridge, MA: MIT Press.

James, W. (1950). *The principles of psychology* (Vol. I). New York, NY: Dover.

Janssen, T. A. J. M. (1976). *Hebben-Konstrukties en Indirekt-Objektskonstrukties*. Utrecht: H & S Publishers.

Janssen, T. A. J. M. (1995a). Deixis from a cognitive point of view. In Contini-Morava & B. S. Goldberg (Eds.), (pp. 245—270). Berlin: Mouton de Gruyter.

Janssen, T. A. J. M. (1995b). Heterosemy or polyfunctionality? The Case of *maar* 'but, only, just'. In T. F. Shannon & J. P. Snapper (Eds.), (pp. 71—85). Lanham, Md. : University Press of America.

Janssen, T. A. J. M. (1996). *Reported speech*. Amsterdam/Philadelphia: John Benjamins Publishing Company.

Jing-Schmidt, Z. (2005). *Dramatized discourse: The Mandarin Chinese ba-construction*. Amsterdam: John Benjamins.

Kirsner, R. S. (1972). On deixis and degree of differentiation in modern standard Dutch. (Doctoral dissertation). Retrieved from Xerox University Microfilms.

Kirsner, R. S. (1977). On the passive of sensory verb complement sentences. *Linguistic Inquiry*, 8(1), 173—179.

Kirsner, R. S. (1979). Deixis in discourse: An exploratory quantitative study of the modern Dutch demonstrative adjectives in discourse and syntax. In T. Givón (Ed.), *Syntax and semantics* (Vol. 12) (pp. 355—375). New York, NY: Academic Press.

Kirsner, R. S. (1993). From meaning to message in two theories: Cognitive and Saussurean views of the modern Dutch demonstratives. In R. A. Geiger & B. Rudzuke-Ostyn (Eds.), *Conceptualizations and mental processing in language* (pp. 80—114). Berlin: Mouton de Gruyter.

Kirsner, R. S. (2011). Instructional meanings, iconicity, and l'arbitraire du signe in the analysis of the Afrikaans demonstratives. In B. de Jonge & Y. Tobin (Eds.), *Linguistic theory and empirical evidence* (pp. 97—137). Amsterdam: John Benjamins.

Kirsner, R. S. (2014). *Qualitative-quantitative analyses of Dutch and Afrikaans grammar and lexicon*. Amsterdam/Philadelphia: John Benjamins.

Köpcke, K. M. (1988). Schemas in German plural formation. *Lingua*, 74(4), 303—335. Retrieved from http://www.journals.elsevier.com/lingua/.

Köpcke, K. M. (1998). The acquisition of plural marking in English and German revisited: schemata versus rules. *Journal of child language*, *25*(2), 293—319. doi: 10.1017/S0305000998003407.

Köpcke, K. M., Panther, K. U., & Zubin, D. (2010). Motivating grammatical and conceptual gender agreement in German. *Cognitive foundations of linguistic usage patterns* (pp. 171—194). doi: 10.1515/9783110216035.171.

Köpcke, K. M., & Zubin, D. A. (2009). Gender control-lexical or conceptual? Trends in linguistics. *On inflection* (pp. 237—262). doi: 10.1515/9783110198973.237.

Lakoff, G. (1987). *Women, fire and dangerous things: What categories reveal about the mind*. Chicago: University of Chicago Press.

Langacker, R. (1985). Observations and speculations on subjectivity. In J. Haiman (Ed.), *Iconicity in syntax* (pp. 109—150). Amsterdam: John Benjamins.

Langacker, R. W. (1987). *The foundations of cognitive grammar, vol. 1: Theoretical prerequisites*. Stanford: Stanford University Press.

Langacker, R. (1994). Cognitive semantics. In R. E. Asher & J. M. Y. Simpson (Eds.), *The encyclopedia of language and linguistics II* (pp. 591—593). Oxford: Pergamon.

Langacker, R. W. (1995). Raising and transparency. *Language*, *71*(1), 1.

Langacker, R. W. (1997). A dynamic account of grammatical function. In J. L. Bybee, J. Haiman, & S. A. Thompson (Eds.), *Essays on language function and language type: Dedicated to T. Givon* (pp. 249—273). Amsterdam: John Benjamins.

LaPolla, R. J. (1990). *Grammatical relations in Chinese: Synchronic and diachronic considerations*. University Microfilms International.

Lehrer, A. (1986). English classifier constructions. *Lingua*, *68*, 109—148.

Levy, D. (1979). Communicative goals and strategies: Between discourse and syntax. In T. Givon (Ed.), *Syntax and semantics* (Vol. 12) (pp. 183—210). New York, NY: Academic Press.

Li, P. & Lu, S. (1980). Tan ci de xushi: Fuci shi shici haishi xuci? [On sybstantiality and functionality of words: Are verbs substantive or function words?]. *Yuyan jiaoxue yu yanjiu*, *3*, 30—35. Retrieved from http://www. blcu. edu. cn/yys/3_mag_1/3_1_magazine1. asp.

Li, C. N. , Thompson, S. A. , & Li, C. N. (1976). Subject and topic: A new typology of language. In C. N. Li (Ed.), *Subject and topic* (pp. 457—489). New York, NY: Academic Press.

Li, C. & Thompson, S. (1976). Subject and topic: A new typology of language. In C. Li (Ed.) *Subject and topic* (pp. 457—89). New York: Academic Press.

Li, C. & Thompson, S. (1979). Third-person pronoun and zero anaphora in Chinese discourse. In T. Givon (Ed.), *Syntax and semantics* (Vol. 12) (pp. 311—335). New York, NY: Academic Press.

Li, C. & Thompson, S. (1981). *Mandarin Chinese: A functional reference grammar*. London: University of California Press.

Li, C. N. , & Thompson, S. A. (1987). Mandarin Chinese: a functional reference grammar. *Journal of Asian studies*, *42*(3).

Lin, Y. (1935). *My country and my people*. New York, NY: Reynal & Hitchcock.

Lin, Y. (1938). *The wisdom of Confucius*. New York, NY: Random House.

Linde, C. (1979). Focus of attention and the choice of pronouns in discourse. In T. Givon (Ed.), *Syntax and semantics* (Vol. 12) (pp. 337—354). New York, NY: Academic Press.

Liu, B. (1920, September 16). Jiao wo ruhe bu xiang ta [How can I not miss her?]. *Beijing Morning Post*.

Liu, Y. , Pan, W. , & Gu, W. (1983). *Shiyong xiandai hanyu yufa* [A practical grammar of modern Chinese]. Beijing: Foreign Language Teaching & Research Press.

Liu, Y. (1994). Yingyu xinghe chuantong guanzhao xia de Hanyu yihe chuantong. [The paratactic tradition in Chinese as seen from the point of view of the hypotactic tradition in English]. In Z. Lin & L. Xiao (Eds.), *Yingyu-Hanyu bijiao yanjiu* [Comparative Chinese-English studies] (pp. 163—177). Changsha: Hunan Science & Technology Press.

Lovik, T. A. , Guy, J. D. , & Chavez, M. (2012). *Vorsprung: A communicative introduction to German language and culture*. Boston: Heinle.

Lu, X. (1956). Qiu ye [Autumn Nights]. *Yecao*, 6. (X. Y. Yang & N. D. Dai, Trans.). Beijing: Foreign Languages Press.

Lu, X. (1991). *Lu Xun sanwen quanbian* [Selection of Lu Xun's prose]. L. Qian & D. Wang (Eds.). Hangzhou: Zhejiang Wenyi Chubanshe.

Lu, J. (1988). Xiandai hanyu zhong shuliang ci de zuoyong [On the functions of quantifiers and classifiers in modern Chinese]. *Yufa yanjiu he tansuo*, 4, 172—186.

Lu, J. (2003). *Xiandai hanyu yufa yanjiu jiaocheng* [A course of studies of contemporary Chinese grammar]. Beijing: Peking University Press.

Lü, S. (1980). *Xiandai hanyu babai ci* [A dictionary of 800 words in modern Chinese]. Beijing: Shangwu Yinshuguan.

Lü, S. (1985). *Xiandai hanyu zhidai ci* [Demonstratives and pronouns in modern Chinese]. Beijing: Xuelin Chubanshe.

Lü, S. (1990). *Lü Shuxiang wenji I: Zhongguo wenfa yaolue* [Collected works of Lü Shuxiang I: Essentials of Chinese grammar]. Beijing: Shangwu Yinshuguan. (Original work published in 1942).

Lyons, J. (1977). *Semantics I & II*. Cambridge: Cambridge University Press.

Lyons, J. (1979). Deixis and anaphora. In T. Myers (Ed.) *The development of conversation and discourse* (pp. 88—103). Edinburgh: Edinburgh University Press.

Lyons, J. (1991). *Natural language and universal grammar*. Cambridge: Cambridge University Press.

Lyons, J. (1995). *Linguistics semantics*. Cambridge: Cambridge University Press.

Maslow, A. H. (1943). Dynamics of personality organization. ii. *Psychological review*, 50(1), 541—558.

Mediziner entdecken Ursache für nervenleiden ALS. (2011, August 22). *Zeit online*. Retrieved from http://www.zeit.de/wissen/gesundheit/2011—08/ursache-amyotrophe-lateralskleroe.

Nunberg, G. (1993). Indexicality and deixis. *Linguistics and philosophy*, 16(1), 1—44. doi: 10.1007/BF00984721.

Ochs, E. (1979). Planned and unplanned discourse. In T. Givon (Ed.), *Syntax and semantics* (Vol. 12) (pp. 51—80). New York, NY: Academic Press.

Pasierbsky, F. (1982). Zur historischen Entwicklung der persondeixis im Chinesischen. In J. Weissenborn & W. Klein (Eds.), *Here and there: Cross-linguistic studies on deixis and demonstration* (pp. 253—271). Amsterdam: John Benjamins.

Pinker, S. (1994). *The language instinct: How the mind creates language*. New York: W. Morrow and Co.

Preece, D. & Schulze, M. (1999). *Linking elements in German compounds: Courpus study and computational implementation*. Ann Arbor, MI: University of Michigan Press.

Prisca, A. & Euba, N. (2007). *Stationen: ein kursbuch für die mittelstufe*. Heinle.

Qian, Z. S. (1954). *Weicheng*. Shanghai: Chenguang Chuban Gongsi.

Qian, Z. S. (1979). *Fortress besieged*. J. Kelly. & N. Mao (Trans.). Taipei: Bookman Books.

Qian, Z. (2008). *Die umzingelte festung*. M. Motsch (Trans.). Munich: Schirmer Graf Verlag.

Quirk, R., Greenbaum, S., Leech, G., & Svartvik, J. (1985). *A comprehensive grammar of the English language*. London: Longman.

Reid, W. (1977). The quantitative validation of a grammatical hypothesis. *Columbia university working papers in linguistics*, 4, 59—77. Retrieved from http://journals.tc-library.org/index.php/tesol

Reid, W. (2006). Columbia School and Saussure's langue. In J. Davis, R. Gorop, & N. Stern (Eds.), *Advances in functional linguistics: Columbia School beyond its origins* (pp. 17—39). Amsterdam: John Benjamins.

Rijpma, E. & Schuringa, F. (1962). *Nederlandsespraakkunst*. J. Naarding (Ed.). Groningen: J. B. Wolters.

Russ, C. (1994). *The German language today: A linguistic introduction*. New York, NY: Routledge.

Schlink, B. (1995). *Der vorleser*. Zürich: Diogenes Verlag.

Schlink, B. (1997). *The reader*. C. Janeway (Trans.). New York, NY: Vintage

Books.

Schlink, B. (2009). *Langduzhe*. D. Qian (Trans.). Nanjing: Yilin Chubanshe.

Sima, Q. (1982). *Shiji* [Records of history]. Beijing: Zhonghua Shuju.

Smith, M. B. (1987). *The semantics of dative and accusative in German: an investigation in cognitive grammar*. University Microfilms International.

Sweester, E. (1988). Grammaticalization and semantic bleaching. In S. Axmaker, A. Jaisser, & H. Singmaster (Eds.), *Proceedings of the fourteenth annual meeting of the Berkeley Linguistic Society* (pp. 389—405). Berkeley, CA: Berkeley Linguistic Society.

Talmy, L. (1983). How language structures space. *Spatial Orientation: Theory, research and application* (Vol. 1, pp. 225—282). New York: Springer Publishing Company.

Tao, H. (1999). The grammar of demonstratives in Mandarin conversational discourse: A case study. *Journal of chinese linguistics*, 27 (1), 69—103. Retrieved from http://www.cuhk.edu.hk/journal/jcl/.

Teng, S. H. (1981). Deixis, anaphora, and demonstratives in Chinese. *Cahiers de Linguistique-Asi orientale*, 10 (1), 5—18. Retrieved from http://www.brill.com/publications/journals/cahiers-de-linguistique-asie-orientale

Traugott, E. (1988). Pragmatic strengthening and grammaticalization. In S. Axmaker, A. Jaisser, & H. Singmaster (Eds.), *Proceedings of the fourteenth annual meeting of the Berkeley Linguistic Society* (pp. 406—416). Berkeley, CA: Berkeley Linguistics Society.

Über zwei tonnen metall gestohlen. (2013, February 7). *Solinger-Tageblatt*. Retrieved from http://www.solinger-tageblatt.de/Home/Solingen/Ueber-zwei-Tonnen-Metall gestohlen32fafe87—4d94—4865—aa32—efd5806aec2e-ds

Vater, H. (1963). *Das system der artikelformen im gegenwärtigen Deutsch*. Tübingen: Niemeyer.

Visser, F. T. (1969). *An historical syntax of the English language. An Historical syntax of the English language*. E. J. Brill.

Wang, L. (1954). *Zhongguo yufa lilun* [Chinese grammar theory]. Shanghai: Zhonghua Shuju.

Wang, L. (1959). *Zhongguo xiandai yufa* [Contemporary Chinese grammar] (Vol. 1—2). Hong Kong: Zhonghua Shuju.

Wang, L. (1987). *Zhongguo xiandai yufa II* [A grammar of modern Chinese II]. Taizhong: Landeng Wenhua Shiye Gongsi. (Original work published in 1943)

Webster's new world college dictionary. (1972). New York, NY: The World Publishing Co.

Wegener, H. (1985). *Der dativ im heutigen Deutsch*. Tübingen: Gunther Narr Verlag.

Weissenborn, J. & Klein, W. (1982). *Here and there: Cross-linguistic studies on deixis and demonstration*. Amsterdam: John Benjamins.

Whorf, B. L. (1956). A linguistic consideration of thinking in primitive communities. In J. B. Carroll (Ed.), *Language, thought, and reality: Selected writings of Benjamin Lee Whorf* (pp. 65—86). Cambridge, MA: MIT Press.

Wierzbicka, A. (1980). *Lingua mentalis: The semantics of natural language*. New York: Academic Press.

Wu, H. (1991). Jushou 'name' de cixing [On the part of speech of clause initial 'name']. *Zhongguo yuwen, 224*, 360—362. Retrieved from http://www.zgyw.org.cn/EN/article/showDownloadTopList.do

Wu, Y. (1994). Lun Yingyu yu Hanyu de xinghe he yihe de chayi [On the differences between English and Chinese in paratax and hypotax]. In Z. Liu & L. Xiao (Eds.), *Yingyu-Hanyu bijiao yanjiu* [Comparative English-Chinese Studies] (pp. 152—162). Changsha: Hunan Science & Technology Press.

Wu, Y. (2004). *Spatial demonstratives in English and Chinese: Text and cognition*. Amsterdam: John Benjamins.

Xiandai hanyu cidian. (2004). Beijing: The Commercial Press.

Xiandai hanyu cidian. (2012). Beijing: The Commercial Press.

Xu, Y. (1987). A study of referential functions of demonstratives in Chinese discourse. *Journal of Chinese linguistics, 15*(1), 132—151.

Xu, J. (2008). Hanyu ziran huihua zhong huayu biaoji 'na(ge)' de gongneng fenxi [A functional analysis of the discourse marker na(ge) in natural talk]. *Yuyan Kexue, 1*, 49—57.

Yang, Y. (2007). 'Zheme' he 'name' pianzhang bu duichen kaocha [A study of the textual asymmetry of 'zheme' and 'name']. *Yuyan wenzi yingyong*, 4, 53—60.

Yao, J. (2006). Xiandai hanyu juedui chengdu fuci yanjiu [A Study of the degree adverbs in modern Chinese]. Yanbian: Yanbian University (unpublished master's thesis).

Zubin, D. A. (1977). Egocentrism: its effect on the form and use of grammar. *Case*, 9.

Zubin, D. A. (1978). *Semantic substance and value relations: A grammatical analysis of case morphology in modern standard German*. Ph. D. dissertation. Columbia University.

Zubin, D. A. (1979). Discourse function of morphology: The focus system in German. In T. Givon (Ed.), *Syntax and semantics* (Vol. 12) (pp. 469—504). New York, NY: Academic Press

Zubin, D. A. & Hewitt, L. E. (1995). The deictic center: a theory of deixis in narrative. In J. Dushan, G. Bruder & L. Hewitt (Eds.) *Deixis in narrative: A cognitive science perspective* (pp. 129—154). Mahwah, New Jersey: Laurence Erlbaum Associates, Inc.

Zubin, D. A., & Köpcke, K. M. (1985). Cognitive constraints on the order of subject and object in German. *Studies in language, volume 9*(9), 77—107.

Zubin, D. A. & Li, N. (1986). Topic, contrast, definiteness, and word order in Mandarin. *BLS* 12. 292—304.

Acknowledgements

I could not have finished my Ph.D. study nor completed any academic work without the help, tolerance and support of many people. First, I would like to thank my Ph.D. advisor, Professor Robert S. Kirsner. I should admit that I was struggling with English and graduate school, and it was great luck to have Professor Kirsner come to me, "forcing" me to read papers written by Columbia School linguists and to talk about my thoughts and problems. The first time I felt that I was really interested in a specific linguistic field and might be able to do research later was the Winter Quarter of 2008 when I first took Professor Kirsner's linguistic course. Then I was able to have him as my advisor and mentor, feeling well-protected until I left the US. Without his patience, encouragement, understanding, inspiration and help, any progress would have never been made. He has been supporting me intellectually and spiritually throughout my years at UCLA, and has been extremely flexible to accommodate my schedule. I used to call him "Professor" to show my admiration and respect – he prefers "Bob", though – I still do and will keep doing so.

I am also grateful to have Professor Christopher M. Stevens as my M.A. advisor. He has been a great mentor, never failing to inspire me with his enlightening discussions of my work. Since I did not have much exposure to linguistics before arriving at UCLA, Professor Stevens' linguistic courses formed the ground of my linguistic knowledge.

I am also indebted to Professor Hongyin Tao. He has opened a brand new horizon to me by introducing me to the world of Corpus Linguistics and providing me with opportunities of teaching Chinese, from which I have gained most of my ideas. They together constitute most valuable interdisciplinary resources.

Many thanks are also to other people who have contributed to this book directly and indirectly. To Professor Michael H. Heim who not only has taught me how to use translation as a research resource, but also has guided me in many research and translation projects. I would like to thank S. Kye Terrasi and Andre Schuetze whose friendship means a great deal to me. They have helped me with analyzing the German data and supported me emotionally at the final stage of my dissertation. I also gratefully acknowledge my debt to David Hull, Patricia Pawiley, Taylor Walle, and Jessica Horvath who have proofread, revised and formatted my manuscript. And of course, to Fangxu Zhu, who edited this book and helped me in the application for the *Kami Yama Kikin* 'Kami Yama Scholarship for Academic Publication'. For her understanding and patience, I cannot thank her enough.

During my years at UCLA, financial support was provided by the Dean and the Department of Germanic Languages. This book reflects part of my graduate school training there.

Since 2013, my academic work has been financially supported by Peking University and the Chinese Ministry of Education.

I would also like to take the opportunity to express my gratitude to all my teachers at Nanjing Foreign Language School and Peking University.

Finally, my gratitude goes to my family. My grandfather, Lidong

Wang, has first encouraged me to explore the beauty of language. A big thank you to my parents Delong Lin and Haiqin Wang, who have been extremely supportive and understanding. The biggest thank you of all goes to my wonderful husband Xunzhe Li, who has been supporting me for the past 17 years. I cannot be more grateful.

(The following part was added to the book shortly before it goes to press.)

I need to thank Danyang Li and Qiongyu Fan. Without their professional advice, I could not have gone through the time when my mom died of lung cancer.

I miss you, mom. You were a strong fighter.